HAMLET

EDWARD ARNOLD (PUBLISHERS) LTD
41 Maddox Street, London, W.1

Printed in Great Britain by
Butler & Tanner Ltd., Frome and London

General Editors

JOHN RUSSELL BROWN
& BERNARD HARRIS

Contents

List of Plates

Abbreviations

Bradley A. C. Bradley, *Shakespearean Tragedy* (1904).

Draper J. W. Draper, *The 'Hamlet' of Shakespeare's Audience* (1938)

Granville-Barker H. Granville-Barker, *Prefaces to Shakespeare. Third Series: 'Hamlet'* (1937).

Hankins J. E. Hankins, *The Character of Hamlet and Other Essays* (1941)

Kitto H. D. F. Kitto, *Form and Meaning in Drama* (1956).

Knights L. C. Knights, *An Approach to 'Hamlet'* (1960).

Mack Maynard Mack, 'The World of Hamlet', *Tragic Themes in Western Literature*, ed. Cleanth Brooks (1955).

N.C.S. New Cambridge Shakespeare, *Hamlet*, edited by J. Dover Wilson (1934).

Dover Wilson J. Dover Wilson, *What Happens in 'Hamlet'* (1935).

Preface

In adding a new book to the library of *Hamlet* criticism the first intention is to maintain, the second to extend, the discussion of commonly agreed subjects of theatrical and literary vitality in the play. And since '*Hamlet* without the prince' is a proverbial phrase, for irrelevancy it is proper that the most general and sustained concern of this book should be with the relationship of prince and play, human character and dramatic role, role and structure, character and speech.

Peter Ure explores Shakespeare's dramatic creation, from Richard III to Hamlet, of unique characters, defined by traditional rôle and realised in human individuality. David William particularises some difficulties of the role of Hamlet for the actor, among them a modern audience's reception of supernatural events. But the emphasis is not placed upon the problems so much as on their corresponding potentness.

James Walton, in a full and detailed consideration of the play's narrative structure, draws upon recurrent themes, particularly that of self-defeat, to define the 'undefeated constancy' of Hamlet himself. George Hunter, similarly sympathetic to the sustained positive capability of Hamlet, discerns the difficulties and possibilities, for Hamlet and for us, in the concept of the hero and the nature of his heroism. Patrick Cruttwell considers both the contemporary Elizabethan world, its setting and morality, and some prominent criticism of the play, in extending the terms of reference in the debate on Hamlet's moral integrity. These, and other, critical pre-occupations, are given further documentation and critical comment in T. J. B. Spencer's account of English and European evaluations of hero and play over the centuries.

Three chapters deal with different elements of the 'play-world' which is *Hamlet*. E. A. J. Honigmann investigates the politics of Shakespeare's Denmark, and suggests some of the many and complex uses to which the dramatist puts them in his creation of a unique organism. R. A. Foakes analyses the linguistic structure of *Hamlet*, relating character, speech, action and theme, finding a correspondence between their variety and that possessed by Hamlet himself in his great range of roles and many voices. J. R. Brown, taking Gordon Craig's advice on producing Shakespeare's tragedies, studies the setting, movements and tempo, the 'large and sweeping impression' of the play in performance.

Finally, a short chapter by S. W. Wells provides a summary of some major contributions to the literature of *Hamlet* criticism and offers a guide to reading. This makes unnecessary, too, the practice followed in other volumes of the *Stratford-upon-Avon Studies* of printing notes before individual chapters. Critical studies are referred to on many occasions in this book in short form, and a list of abbreviations on p.6 is given for convenience. References to Shakespeare's text have been made to the Globe edition of the works, unless otherwise indicated.

Future volumes of the *Stratford-upon-Avon Studies* at present being prepared include *Restoration Theatre*, *American Poetry* and *Late Shakespeare*.

JOHN RUSSELL BROWN
BERNARD HARRIS

I

Character and Role from Richard III to Hamlet

PETER URE

★

A MAN, it is commonly said, devotes himself to a task, or undertakes a duty, or fulfils himself (or fails to) in a role. The two elements, and the relationship between them, are sometimes determined and prescribed, as, for example, the priest who performs a ritual or the fireman who rescues the old woman from the burning tenement. Priest or fireman have submitted themselves; they are not expected to reinterpret or decide afresh what is to be done. Literature has not on the whole greatly relished such absence of the liberty of interpreting, although perhaps it celebrates more than it used to those who feel themselves to be, in Stephen Crane's phrase, intruders in the land of fine deeds. Even Conrad, who wrote those words for Podmore in *The Nigger of the Narcissus, the* saying of Podmore's life—'Galley! . . . my business! . . . As long as she swims I will cook!'—often cheapened the mystery of heroism by the florid comments which the novelist owed to his art.

Shakespeare's heroes are leaders of men; to move easily in an air of fine deeds seems to them their birthright. The unvarying eloquence, the high assumption that a rainstorm of words will perpetually refresh an occasion and sensibly benefit the inexpressive multitude springs from the tradition in which he worked; it is responsible for those wastes of ingenious verbalising which disfigure much Elizabethan writing and for that contempt for the unlanguaged which sometimes disfigures even Shakespeare himself. But chiefly it is used by him for the sake of that liberty of interpreting which the performance of a ritual or a 'business', in Podmore's sense, normally precludes. A method of the plays is to stress the two elements: to depict the hero's devotion of himself to a role in society, to the burden of an office such as kingship,

9

a relationship such as fatherhood, a 'royal occupation' such as soldiering, and to depict as well the eloquence with which he confronts them. It is often because we are made aware of the gap, not the consonance, between the man and the office that the situation becomes profound and exciting, and permits rich inferences about what the hero's inward self is like. It is the character faced with his role, forced to decide about it, the quality of his response, that Shakespeare shows us, not just his performance in the role. Does he act it out with joy or pain, rightly or wrongly? Is it something which gratifies his imaginative needs, his need for love or glory or power, or is it something which starves and appals? Shakespeare's great characters come alive and appeal to us in their mistakings as well as in their imaginative fulfilments of themselves. He often allows history or tradition to define the nature of the role that is offered, the more sharply to bring out the spectacle of the individual fitting himself (or failing to fit himself) to it. Presumably most persons in the Globe audience in 1599 shared Polonius's knowledge that Brutus killed Julius Caesar in the Capitol; but it seems doubtful if they came to watch him do it in the spirit of those who attend a ritual, even if the lofty scene was, as we are nowadays told, acted over in front of a cosmogonically significant structure that proclaimed orthodoxies about order and disorder from every painted star and marbled pilaster.

What they saw, indeed, was a Brutus in a state of agonised depression finally bringing himself to fulfil the role which everyone around him had cast him for and was busy prescribing as his peculiar duty. Cassius has heard, he says,

> Where many of the best respect in Rome—
> Except immortal Cæsar—speaking of Brutus,
> And groaning underneath this age's yoke,
> Have wish'd that noble Brutus had his eyes. (I.ii.59)

'Brutus, thou sleep'st,' says the urgent voice, 'awake and see thyself . . . Speak, strike, redress!' But Brutus must get his conception of the task laid upon him into a posture satisfying to his imagination and to his idea of himself before he can strike, although it is in part his tragedy that this idea of himself is to some extent a reflection from Cassius's politic mirror. He warms up as this gradually happens. When he has persuaded himself that Caesar must be killed (and his awkward, private reasoning is quite different from the spleenful envy that Cassius had offered as reason enough), we see him wrenching and re-defining the role to make it match his own conception of what is due to him. His voice takes on the urgent note of re-interpretation, of the man who has at length found a way to make his task satisfying to his imagination, as when he persuades the conspirators not to swear:

> Swear priests and cowards and men cautelous,
> Old feeble carrions and such suffering souls
> That welcome wrongs; unto bad causes swear
> Such creatures as men doubt; but do not stain
> The even virtue of our enterprise,
> Nor th'insuppressive mettle of our spirits,
> To think that or our cause or our performance
> Did need an oath. (II.i.129)

He had disliked the role of conspirator, naming it 'a monstrous visage'; it does not fit the self which he loves. They shall not swear in order to make it the less a conspiracy, not a conspiracy at all, some nameless, finer enterprise. The murder, too, must not be a murder— re-define it, instead, as a sacrifice or a purgation ('We shall be called purgers and not murderers'). Another term which he uses is 'actors'— 'with untired spirits and formal constancy'. Elsewhere in the play Caesar, too, acts up to his idea of himself ('I am constant as the northern star . . .'); and Shakespeare is equally careful to make us understand the effort that this costs him: there is the scene where he twice changes his mind about going forth on the Ides of March; there are the many places where he wilfully and consciously assumes the 'Caesar' voice as an actor assumes his formal constancy. Brutus and Caesar are both so intent on adjusting the situation to their imaginative needs, to the figures which they wish to cut before themselves and the world, that they overlook its practical perils; Cassius and Antony do not seem to have the same needs as they, and in death alone is Brutus released from the distorting pressures of the single-minded. The same release is afforded to Dryden's Mark Antony from similar pressures. Brutus might well have said, with that later Antony:

> For death, for aught I know,
> Is but to think no more.

It is his reinterpretation of the fixed role that accounts for much of the liveliness of Brutus. We may look in other plays for a variety of relationships between character and role; possibly what is called *characterisation* in Shakespeare and accounts for our sense (once much emphasised by the commentators) of the extraordinary vitality of the personages and the intimacy of their appeal resides somewhere in the interplay between character and role. The fact that the role—fallen king, famous regicide, Revenger—is often defined by history or tradition need not make the hero's approach to it any less effectual in drawing out, by the sterness of the test it imposes, the unreachability or rigour of its prescription, all that is unique in the character and all that defines his individuality and separates it from anyone else's. This is why it is dismaying to find a recent commentator, who so well understands this conception of the role in Shakespeare, writing of it as though the role in *Hamlet* overrides what used to be called Hamlet's character:

> As for Hamlet's character, the experience [of *Hamlet*] is related less to that than to what overrides it and renders it irrelevant. In this play, as in many other tragedies, the experience of the protagonist is not the deployment of a determinate character, but the assumption, and then the enactment, of a determinate *rôle*. Rôle predominates over character, because once it is assumed by an actor, it will be much the same whatever his nature may be. It overrides that nature: the play is its acting out.[1]

Here it seems fair to extend the analogy between an actor and a character in a play, and to say that a character in a Shakespeare play sometimes resembles an actor because he has to choose or refuse a part, learn it, rehearse it, try to understand it, and finally perform it (or perhaps refuse to perform it) well or ill or with one of the many gradations in between. That is his experience; it is surely one that allows plenty of liberty for the expression of qualities that individuate him as a man and as an actor. Perhaps some such process is meant to be included in the phrase 'assumption and enactment', used by Holloway; but this meaning is not much supported by the reading itself of *Hamlet* which he gives us. It would be a great mistake to try to reinstate 'determinate character' in its old place of honour in Shakespearian criticism; but must 'determinate role' be substituted? It is not, perhaps, too wild an injustice to Holloway's subtle and powerful book to say of it that, like Brutus in the play, it requires all the murders to appear like sacrifices, and all the characters to tend to the condition of ritualists. But Brutus

---

[1] J. Holloway, *The Story of the Night* (1961), p. 26.

had overlooked (as Antony did not) the possibility that a ritual and a sacrifice, however sincerely and fervently performed, can be made to resemble, for the unpersuaded, a common murder after all. 'Ordinary wishes and sympathies', Holloway writes concerning the closing scenes of four great tragedies,

> such as make up the normal fabric of life (or are commonly supposed to do so) are suspended, while the characters engage in the self-conscious completing of a recognisable kind of event, with such a validity of its own as sets it beyond considerations of pleasure or pain. Here is the note of ritual, of ceremony . . .[2]

But what we observe in *Antony* or *Macbeth* are characters who nerve themselves to complete their roles. The ritual is always faltering on the edge of 'ordinary wishes or sympathies':

> No more but e'en a woman, and commanded
> By such poor passion as the maid that milks.

The emblematic chalice is held by a hand that trembles somewhat, and this directs our attention to the man or woman that holds it; we can even think—and Shakespeare's theatrical metaphors often invite us to—about the actor whose name is written down on the programme and of how he is doing. In Shakespeare, mastering the role at all levels, both inside and outside the play, is a process which is constantly being re-enacted and never ceases so long as the character is still alive and the audience is still present. This peculiar quality distinguishes his theatre from most other kinds of ranking classical drama. He does not raise his personages on stilts of Alexandrine rhyme or cover the tawdry human face with a mask. The difference is one that has often aroused amongst cultivated people such as Thomas Rymer the suspicion that some kind of undignified trick is being played upon them, that the priest has departed from the sacred text and is making up the words as he goes along. Hamlet and Lear, Yeats supposed, 'do not break up their lines to weep'; but this is just what Shakespeare directs them to do.

This idea of nerving oneself to a role, of rehearsing, of improvising, is one which bears strongly on *Hamlet*. There are plays earlier than *Hamlet* which might, from this point of view, be regarded as being amongst its predecessors. Of these, *Richard III* and *Richard II* mediate opposite extremes amongst the varieties of interplay between individual and role.

[2] *Ibid.*, p. 147.

It is partly because Richard III proposes so many roles for himself and because his story gives him the freedom to do so that it is permissible to make inferences about his individuality. Richard assumes by turns the parts of the loving brother, the passionate wooer, the pious make-peace, the protector-uncle, the heir reluctantly called to the throne. He assumes them with an alacrity and lack of scruple or preparation which show that they are only means to the end of his own advancement; he sees them as devices and not as burdens which demand any portion of his essential self, as mere happy prologues to the omen coming on. His imperturbability is that of the clown, so content and efficient in making fools of others that he is impervious to their curses. The element of parody in all these performances, just below the borderline of detection by the gulls (although he can afford to go very far indeed in the presence of the exceptionally stupid Lord Mayor and his company), signals to the audience the extent to which they are obliquely related to the real thing—the brother who is truly affectionate, the prince who is genuinely pious—and at the same time expresses Richard's happy confidence, his mastery as an artificer, his understanding of how men are deceived by shows and professions. The parodic rendering is accentuated as his confidence increases. This is Richard's character, the skill and fulfilment of his life. He is defined through this activity. The particular way in which he does it, not simply as a clever hypocrite or an evil Machevil, but as one whose joy is to go outside his being, to give splendid performances of expected and traditional roles, deceiving by means of their recognisability the credulous and conventional, indicates his contempt for the moral and emotional needs which created the roles in the first place and so made them available either to be played sincerely or—if one is like Richard—to be exploited with all his calculating energy.

All this is done, we must infer, so that he may attain supreme power. But he says little or nothing about that ultimate objective, and this is significant. It is not for him to brood over riding in triumph through Persepolis, or to approach the golden rigol with the numinous circumspection shown by Prince Hal. His pleasure, like Iago's, is in the action of the moment. When he does become king, he is, in a sense, trapped, and not only by his enemies gathering outside. He can no longer engage in his characteristic pleasurable activity, and play the part of king with his usual merrily critical detachment, when he *is* the king. The heavily traditional role now has to be really lived, the self and the role must coalesce, and in this kind of living Richard is incompetent. Driven into the centre, towards which he has so long been working, he must build upon the centre; but the self on which he must build, now that he is driven into it by fear and by being deprived of his power to sway men by his peculiar skills as a player of parts, turns out to be an inexpressive chaos:

> Richard loves Richard; that is, I am I.
> Is there a murderer here? No—yes, I am.
> Then fly. What, from myself? Great reason why—
> Lest I revenge. What myself upon myself!
> Alack, I love myself. Wherefore? For any good
> That I myself have done unto myself?
> O, no! Alas, I rather hate myself
> For hateful deeds committed by myself! (V.iii.183)

From this nothing can be fetched except a rigid, despairing bravado. The centre has become a bear-pit's centre, or a boar-hunt's. Richard is a character who enjoys playing parts so long as their effectiveness as tricks keep his audience (within the play) in a daze; out of his pleasure at these continually successful feats he comments to the audience (outside the play) and invites them to admire his skill, and even plays another part for the benefit of that audience alone: the Vice/Iago figure so well expounded by Bernard Spivack,[3] the merry, bunch-backed villain, the dreadfully wicked prince. So always he keeps his inward self concealed, until he mounts the supposedly longed-for throne. This role alone turns back upon him and demands, because it is by the design of the play the last and most important, that he show his inward being: 'Now that you are king, *be* king.' But Richard cannot in reality *be* anything, or cannot in reality submit himself to an audience; he can only astonish it, and keep his counsel.

Richard III, then, is a ready taker-on of roles of a circumscribed and shallowly theatrical kind, the kind that merely deceive, and do not communicate with the mimic's self. Through this, and through the counter-truth that he fails in another kind of role—one which compels such communication—the characterological, and no doubt the moral, point about him is made. His successor, Richard II, more nearly resembles Brutus because we see him adjusting the part for which others cast him to inner imaginative needs before he can play it with any confidence or satisfaction.

[3] See *Shakespeare and the Allegory of Evil* (1958).

In the deposition scene (IV.i), for example, Richard has had his part
set down for him by Bolingbroke and Northumberland, and by the
whole current of events and design of the play. In Act III he has been
stripped of all power and transformed, it seems, into the usurper's
puppet, a condition which he wearily and sardonically acknowledges
to Northumberland:

> What must the King do now? Must he submit?
> The King shall do it. Must he be depos'd?
> The King shall be contented. Must he lose
> The name of king? A God's name, let it go.

and:

> Most mighty prince, my Lord Northumberland,
> What says King Bolingbroke? Will his Majesty
> Give Richard leave to live till Richard die?
> You make a leg, and Bolingbroke says ay. (III.iii.143)

The emphasis on *king* and *must* stresses Richard's awareness, even at
this stage, of the desperate and paradoxical impropriety of what is
happening. He is next expected to perform a public act of abdication.
Bolingbroke requires this of him for political purposes 'or the commons
will not then be satisfied'; he must surrender his right in the 'common
view' so that men may deem that he is 'worthily depos'd'. It is to be a
carefully staged professional spectacle; the text for it will be the articles
of the signed deed of abdication, which Northumberland tries to insist
upon Richard's reading aloud. This is Richard's ordained role. But
Richard, while he accepts the role—as he cannot choose not to do—
radically reinterprets it in ways which bring before the audience's
consciousness, if not Bolingbroke's, its inner dynastic significance and
its personal, tragic meaning, the tragedy of the king who is forced to
deliver up the sacred Name commingled in his anointed person. The
entire episode as conceived by Bolingbroke and his party is by Richard
wrenched awry in order to fulfil Richard's imaginative needs and to
express the exact and individual character of his suffering. The structure
of the scene supports him. It begins in a public and external way with
the noisy quarrel in parliament, deepens with the Bishop of Carlisle's
appeal to dynastic allegiance and national guilt, and culminates in
Richard's Passion. A Passion is the most public and significant kind of
performance on the most exalted scaffold; at the same time it embodies
the completest actualisation of the self, its supreme expressiveness. In

Richard's the mishandled crown becomes an image of grief, the act of abdication his own apostasy, the bystanders not witnesses in the court of parliament but participators in a mysterious crime. When Northumberland tries to divert the current of Richard's reinterpretation and force him back to the prearranged text, Richard passionately maintains his hold on his own reading of the scene:

RICHARD: ... What more remains?
NORTHUMBERLAND: No more; but that you read
   These accusations, and these grievous crimes
   Committed by your person and your followers
   Against the state and profit of this land;
   That, by confessing them, the souls of men
   May deem that you are worthily depos'd.
RICHARD: Must I do so? And must I ravel out
   My weav'd-up follies? Gentle Northumberland,
   If thy offences were upon record,
   Would it not shame thee in so fair a troop
   To read a lecture of them? If thou wouldst,
   There shouldst thou find one heinous article,
   Containing the deposing of a king
   And cracking the strong warrant of an oath,
   Mark'd with a blot, damn'd in the book of heaven.
   Nay, all of you that stand and look upon me
   Whilst that my wretchedness doth bait myself,
   Though some of you, with Pilate, wash your hands,
   Showing an outward pity—yet you Pilates
   Have here deliver'd me to my sour cross,
   And water cannot wash away your sin.
NORTHUMBERLAND: My lord, dispatch; read o'er these articles.
RICHARD: Mine eyes are full of tears; I cannot see.
   And yet salt water blinds them not so much
   But they can see a sort of traitors here.
   Nay, if I turn mine eyes upon myself,
   I find myself a traitor with the rest;
   For I have given here my soul's consent
   T'undeck the pompous body of a king;
   Made glory base, and sovereignty a slave,
   Proud majesty a subject, state a peasant.
NORTHUMBERLAND: My lord—
RICHARD: No lord of thine, thou haught insulting man,
   Nor no man's lord; I have no name, no title—

B

> No, not that name was given me at the font—
> But 'tis usurp'd. Alack the heavy day,
> That I have worn so many winters out,
> And know not now what name to call myself ! (IV.i.222)

Richard II is therefore at the opposite extreme from Richard III. He pours his whole self, all his capacity for imaginative understanding of the moment, into his role, which becomes in this sense entirely his own, prescribed for him though it is. In so doing he exhausts the self. In yielding up the crown he yields up his identity, symbolically destroying himself when he smashes his image in the looking-glass. In the prison-scene he has become, because no longer a king, something less than a man to himself—the Jack in Bolingbroke's timepiece, his beast of burden, *nothing*:

> by and by,
> Think that I am unking'd by Bolingbroke
> And straight am nothing. (V.v.36)

Throughout the play he has so identified himself with his sacred name of king, has employed it so much as a centre of imaginative strength which overrode everything and maintained its significance even when all its armies and followers melt away from him, that his abandonment of it draws upon and expends the last resources of his life. Losing that name, he becomes literally a nameless thing. Meanwhile the name has gone elsewhere—to 'Lancaster', and to 'Henry, fourth of that name'.

In this play, the varied imaginative communion which the protagonist enjoys with his kingly name is, as the crises of the story disclose, at the root of his being, which is annulled when he is forced to resign it. Richard's personal interpretations give us the taste of his individuality; there is plenty in the play to show us how limited, and how disregardful of grim actuality, his interpretations are, and yet how they are related to some historically important practicalities bearing on the sacred name, which later are to prove bitter to Bolingbroke and his son. Richard III, by contrast, with his habit of withdrawing himself from his roles, finds that the role can in the final crisis demand something in himself which it is not in his power to bestow; his detachment conceals not Stoic constancy or apathy, but corrupted self-love which can afford no outgoings. In both characters it is plain that the inward man has miscalculated his relation to his assignment, taking it for too much or for too little: an outgoing that leads to wasteful annulment in the hostile air, an ingoing that mines inward upon inexpressive and uncreative confusion. But if both characters are in this sense morally exemplary, Richard II, unlike his predecessor, is amongst the first of Shakespeare's major tragic characters. The nature of his tragedy suggests that Shakespearian tragic heroes will tend towards the condition of Passion, not of ritual. The two are not the same; there is no Passion in which the self does not suffer. Men have assigned the one function to gods and the godlike, the other to their servitors. Of the young soldier who felt himself to be an intruder in the land of fine deeds Stephen Crane wrote:

> It seemed to him supernaturally strange that he had allowed his mind to manœuvre his body into such a situation. He understood that it might be called dramatically great.[4]

Perhaps it is in this area that Hamlet's tragedy arises. How is he to adjust to what Othello called his 'cause'?

*   *   *

In *Hamlet*, John Holloway says, 'we have a recognisable kind of situation, a man engaged in a known career':

> What is central is the recognisable rôle which has been assumed, the situation (familiar in a general way in the very idea of the revenge play and the malcontent) which is progressing phase by phase before our eyes.[5]

Hamlet does not delay; he deliberately dedicates himself in I.v, to the role of avenger; the rest of the play is the story of how he discharges it. His soliloquies stress not procrastination but preoccupation with the role:

> It is now possible . . . to see the stress on delay in the soliloquies as being not so much for the sake of stressing delay itself, as of showing how the protagonist is preoccupied with his rôle, in order to stress that it *is* a rôle: a recognisable 'part', undertaken by him what might almost be termed a preordained course and end. . . . Hamlet's life is one to be lived under the imposition of a great task, an imperious demand from outside. The speeches show him for a man taken up with the demands made upon him by that fact.[6]

---

[4] 'A Mystery of Heroism' in *Stephen Crane*, ed. R. W. Stallman (1954), pp. 384-5.
[5] Holloway, *op. cit.*, p. 28.
[6] *Ibid.*, pp. 28-9.

This is a Hamlet who seems to require a minimum of adjustment, even less than Brutus, who at least endured a sleepless night accommodating his Genius to his mortal instruments. But Holloway's last sentence is amenable to expansion and qualification. And the predecessors of Hamlet —if we may number Brutus and the two Richards among them— suggest that if Shakespeare was perceptive of the recognition which is accorded to role by audience and *dramatis persona* he was at the same time deeply concerned with agreement and disagreement between character and role, with what happens to the individual when the traditional function makes its demands upon him, or he upon it. There is a wavering frontier where the individual is in communion with his role, re-shaping it or being shaped by it. This element of indistinctness is particularly marked in *Hamlet* and it is impossible to feel that Holloway's account does full justice to it. If *The Spanish Tragedy* is any guide, immediate recognisability indeed is one of the things which is deliberately not built into the revenger's role by its tradition: as soon as he has cut down the dead body of his son, Hieronimo immediately acknowledges the duty of revenge:

> At tamen absistam properato cedere letho,
> Ne mortem vindicta tuam tum nulla sequatur; [7]

but his first conception of it is of legal justice, and it is a long time before circumstances and his own ponderings lead him to reject the *vindicta mihi* principle and become the Revenger that we all know. The first audiences of *Hamlet* had a right to expect some fairly wide variations; a characteristic of the revenger in the hands of Marston, Webster, Middleton, or Tourneur is precisely its fluid and evolutionary deployment, and the expectations attaching to the role might be considered to be much less well defined and more relative than those attaching to, for example, the tyrant or the Machevil. The obstinate sense, also, that there is something in Hamlet's temperament which, when he is confronted with his task, demands that he, like Brutus, must adjust it to a posture satisfying to his imagination, to his idea of himself and of the world, makes it very difficult to ask from the play the answers to two obvious questions: *What* is the nature of the ordained role? and *when* does he assume it? For Holloway the answer to the first is apparently supplied by the putative type-figure of the Revenger/ Malcontent, and to the second by what Hamlet does in I.v. But when

[7] *The Spanish Tragedy*, ed. Philip Edwards (1959), II.v.79–80.

there is a constant intercourse going on between character and role, the one modifying the other—and it is this that would seem to be the story of the play—the Hamlet and the role of I.v may later on each become something so different, as a result of their intercourse, that we can no longer say that the same relation—one of 'assumption'—obtains between them. It is perhaps not begging the question to say that *what* and *when* keep on needing to be answered right through the play to the end. But it is just this that requires some demonstration.

Hamlet begins the play in a state of severe and suicidal depression, of 'unmanly grief' compounded with shock and fear. The Ghost's commands to him are complex, not only 'Revenge his foul and most unnatural murder', but the reminder that the old king was 'Cut off even in the blossoms of my sin . . . If thou hast nature in thee bear it not', and also 'Let not the royal bed of Denmark be/A couch for luxury and damned incest'. It is probably safe to assume that this means 'Kill Claudius', too, because the incest will cease with his death. Finally, 'Taint not thy mind, nor let thy soul contrive/Against thy mother aught. . . .' Hamlet immediately assumes the role, ready to 'sweep' to his revenge:

> Thy commandment all alone shall live
> Within the book and volume of my brain (I.v.102–3)

and writes down in his tablets a memorandum in code, an apophthegm which means 'Claudius!'; and, as Holloway says, the swearing ceremony at the end of the scene constitutes 'a deliberate self-dedication, made as conspicuous as possible, to the rôle of a revenger'.[8] Its discovery has given him a cause. The eagerness with which he embraces it is the response of the undirected, suicidal Hamlet of the first soliloquy welcoming the imposition of a recognisable pattern upon his life.

However, the role has to be lived through as well as formally acceded to, and it is now that its development and variations begin. The next piece of information we have about Hamlet is his farewell to Ophelia as reported by her in II.i. The eager excitement of the soliloquy after the ghost's appearance, when Hamlet looked forward to clearing the decks for action, has disappeared. The experience of casting off the role of lover so that the exclusive role of revenger may be assumed turns out to be extremely painful, doubly 'piteous'. For Hamlet does from the first seem to interpret the one role as though it excluded any

[8] *Op. cit.*, p. 27.

other, and perhaps the ghost would have approved, though he does not enjoin this. Then we have the sad, deprived Hamlet of the 'except my life' speech, the 'heavy disposition' of the speech to Rosencrantz and Guildenstern (II.ii.304 ff.). Divesting himself of all 'pressures past' turns out to be a heavy task which reduces him to a simulacrum of his first condition; the process of stripping for the role gains no comfort from the role itself. It is not easy to accept the view that Hamlet's radical discontent and apparent loss of direction here is merely the malcontentism of the revenger (which in any case became part of the tradition largely through Shakespeare's invention of it for this occasion), because the mood is so clear an echo of the one that prevailed in the first soliloquy, before Hamlet became a revenger at all. What seems uppermost is the personal sense of deprivation, of vacuity; it is as though Hamlet had never taken on the role at all, as though all were to be done again; the process of stripping himself of everything but the exclusive commitment has gone so far that the prospect of *any* commitment seems to have disappeared. This is pointed up in the scene with the players (II.ii), where Hamlet envies the capacity of the First Player to fling himself into the role assigned to him. There could hardly be a clearer demonstration than this scene of the difference, as it seems to Hamlet, between himself and the man who 'forces his soul' into a part, who pours his skill and imagination into his chosen role. The soliloquy ('O what a rogue and peasant slave . . .'), besides asserting his consciousness of what he must do, also asserts, unless we ignore the plain meaning of Hamlet's statements, an equally exacting awareness that he ought to have done it already: 'I/A dull and muddy-mettled rascal, peak/Like John-a-dreams, unpregnant of my cause.' The 'cause' has not yet quickened him; his imagination will not waken. There seems to be a difference between formally undertaking a role, before one quite realises what it is and as a relief from undirectedness, and actually performing it.

   Hamlet offers one explanation for the condition in the next soliloquy, which it is hard not to see, in part at least, as a resigned and puzzled comment on the gap between undertaking and performance. In the scene with Ophelia that follows (III.i) the gap begins to close. The rejection of Ophelia, of the lover's role, which evolves from the 'piteous' to the brutal, and the threat to Claudius ('all but one, shall live') have a community, not an antithesis, of feeling; this community of emotional tone between the stripping off of the one role and the assumption of the other argues that the character is fast approaching the condition of murderous integrity and single-mindedness in which the deed of revenge can properly be done. The play-scene only confirms this; after the play, Hamlet now really is a revenger, according to his own definition of the function in a previous soliloquy, ready to make mad the guilty and appal the free. This is what it is really like to be a revenger, he thinks, and he savours it ('now could I drink hot blood'). This is sincere acting, his imagination has been caught. It is Shakespeare—this seems the only way of putting it—or Shakespeare's conception of the chances that rule mortal life, that intervenes, and not only because there were two more Acts to get through but also out of tenderness for his hero and for the sake of the end, justifying the means, of making him a yet more interesting and far-exploring character.

For matters are so arranged that when Hamlet, full revenger, encounters Claudius he is at prayer. The instructions given to Hamlet by the ghost are fairly explicit on the point ('Thus was I . . ./Cut off even in the blossoms of my sin,/Unhousel'd, disappointed, unanel'd;/No reck'ning made . . .'). It would plainly be wide of the ghost's mark and the revenger's function to kill Claudius at this moment; Hamlet's reasoning, fully consonant with the revenger's role in its most complete aspect, cannot be gainsaid. It is neither his fault nor his excuse that at the one time when he is fulfilled in the revenger's role his interpretation of that role, 'correct' as it is, demands that he should *not* execute the revenge rather than that he should.

The murder of Polonius (III.iv) is in part the groundwork for further plot-making. As the only explicit act of destruction carried out by the embodied revenger it is protected against necessarily sealing a full commitment to the part by the way in which it is performed. It therefore resembles the manner in which Hamlet is prevented, or protected, from sealing revenge by finding Claudius at his prayers and not drunk asleep or in some other condition that would more equitably have corresponded to the old king's. For Hamlet kills Polonius in a blaze of thoughtless fury, his mind empty and unknowing, certainly not with the full lunge of the revenger, his bloody intention enforcing his sword's point against the chosen victim:

> HAMLET: How now! a rat?
> Dead, for a ducat, dead!

POLONIUS: O, I am slain!
QUEEN: O me, what hast thou done?
HAMLET: Nay, I know not:
Is it the King? (III.iv.23)

It is only later that Hamlet says 'I took thee for thy better', an observation that refers not to his state of mind when he attacked the unseen figure behind the arras, but to the thought that came into his mind when he heard the Queen's exclamation of horror. There are other things in the scene that ensues that make it difficult to say whether Hamlet is still as adjusted to his role as revenger as he was in the prayer-scene. The ghost had said 'Let not the bed of royal Denmark be/A couch for luxury and damned incest', and this is the burden of Hamlet's charge to his mother ('go not to my uncle's bed'). But, as we have seen, it is not easy to assume that the ghost was saying 'amongst your other duties as revenger is that of putting a stop to the incest' instead of 'kill Claudius, and a good reason for killing him is that it will end the profanation of the royal bed'. Hamlet had brooded on the incest in the first soliloquy; it is a part of him before ever he assumes the revenger's duty. The re-appearing ghost, with his talk of 'almost blunted purpose', does not much help to resolve the ambiguity, if ambiguity there is; only if we could feel sure that it is an important, and as it were separate clause in the 'dread command' ('At least put an end to the incest'), could we read what Hamlet now says to his mother as a sharpening of vengeful purpose.

More than half aware of what is in store for him, he submits to being sent to England and as he goes meditates once more on his role in the Fortinbras soliloquy. It is close in spirit to the two other major solilquies that preceded it ('O what a rogue' and 'To be or not to be . . .') and goes far towards cancelling out those moments when Hamlet is revenger incarnate. It mediates his sharp awareness that he is under a dread command; but surely by now this awareness constitutes more than just a sign or an acknowledgement; his awareness is that of a man who is more susceptible to being aware than is common, who habitually 'thinks', in the sense in which Dryden's Mark Antony applies the word. The scope and quality of the soliloquies at least would be superfluous and inartistic if Shakespeare were not making a point about Hamlet's individuality: that he is continually looking *at* his role, measuring himself against it, and that it is this more often than the name of action that the role persistently calls forth in him and that he brings to it. Once again he explicitly accuses himself of being unpregnant in his cause, he does not know why:

> How stand I, then,
> That have a father killed, a mother stained,
> Excitements of my reason and my blood,
> And let all sleep? (IV.iv.56)

There seems no reason not to believe Hamlet here. Hamlet searches for a posture in which to grasp his role, and this indicates how he approaches it. The search is itself a sign of Hamlet's constant tendency to move into the shifting borderline between 'assumption' and performance, even though he has once already in his experience crossed the borderline into Revenge itself. When Richard II or Brutus settle into their interpretations we can recognise the fact immediately by their eager demeanour, by their confident and passionate utterance, by their mastery of opposing currents in the scene. We cannot accord this recognition to Hamlet soliloquising apart from the currents of action that run on, like Fortinbras's troops, without him. Hamlet nourishes his imagination on enactment, but much more rarely releases it into the stream of action itself; he differs in this respect from the earlier heroes and unmistakably from Othello, who must immediately live out what his imagination seizes upon, and whose deeds, such as the murder of Desdemona, are shaped by his own creative reading of them; he transcends murder, as Brutus does, or so he thinks. There is direct communication between his unforced 'soul' and his cause. Hamlet is not like this. Even after he has in one impulse assumed his role, in another experienced or enacted it, neither event seems finally to commit him to it. He can withdraw back into the condition where the deed yet to be done, signalling its message of obligation, constantly reminds him that it can only do so *because* it has not yet been done.

Is Hamlet then committed after his return from the sea-voyage? Does he come back marble-constant, settled in his assignment? The count against Claudius has of course lengthened and defined itself:

> Does it not, thinks't thee, stand me now upon—
> He that hath kill'd my king and whor'd my mother;
> Popp'd in between th' election and my hopes;
> Thrown out his angle for my proper life,

> And with such coz'nage—is't not perfect conscience
> To quit him with this arm? And is't not to be damn'd
> To let this canker of our nature come
> In further evil? (V.ii.63)

The 'dread command' of the ghost (nowhere mentioned directly in this part of the play) is here included in and transcended by what amounts to a bill of indictment. The audience, too, have seen Claudius more openly at his evil work for several preceding scenes; he has become something that must be stopped. Hamlet accepts the role of justicer, but there is a great deal in this part of the play that seems designedly to contrast with what has gone before. Whatever Claudius is finally punished for, he is not punished only because he 'kill'd my king and whor'd my mother', and his plots are seen in broad daylight and are no longer filtered primarily through Hamlet and the ghost. Hamlet no longer conceives of his own action as dependent upon his personal state of feeling, upon his emotional temperature of the moment which made him feel that it could not be done at all unless he was in the mood for it. He does not need to sound himself and discover that his thoughts are sufficiently 'bloody', as he does in the soliloquy after the play-scene. On the contrary, in his account to Horatio of his adventures at sea, he describes a kind of action where something is done without the doer's having to work himself up to it:

> Being thus benetted round with villainies—
> Ere I could make a prologue to my brains,
> They had begun the play. (V.ii.29)

For this Hamlet has a metaphysical explanation, the guidance of Providence:

> Our indiscretion sometimes serves us well,
> When our deep plots do pall; and that should teach us
> There's a divinity that shapes our ends,
> Rough-hew them how we will. (V.ii.8)

And when, later in the scene, Horatio warns him how little time he has left before Claudius's messenger arrives with the news from England, he is confident and yet passive ('the interim is mine'):

there is a special providence in the fall of a sparrow. If it be now, 'tis not to come; if it be not to come, it will be now; if it be not now, yet it will come—the readiness is all. (V.ii.230)

'Readiness' is something very different from that worked-up-for-the-occasion state of feeling which characterised Hamlet when he was the full revenger of III.2-4. His dominant note throughout the whole of the last Act supports this. Submission to Providence seems to take precedence over dedication to Revenge. In that broader perspective—Revenge incapsulated, as it were, within a larger movement—the punishment of a king now doubly, trebly advanced in evil is something that will be achieved by Providence with Hamlet as its instrument; all that he need do when the time comes is to let his brains begin the play.

If we say that this represents a Hamlet absolutely, metaphysically committed to the revenger's role, we must also say that he was committed to it before in Act III after the play-scene and during the prayer-scene. But the two commitments are not of the same kind. The measure of the difference between them is that between 'bloody thoughts', with all their accompanying tempest-driven perturbations, and 'readiness', with its note of submissive calm intermingled with natural dread ('thou wouldst not think how ill's all here about my heart'). Here change of character, the development of Hamlet's individuality, is signalised by the different approaches, or varieties of commitment to the role. On the one hand, there is the approach that consists of still nerving himself to the task long after he has formally assumed the responsibility for it and then the discharge of it in a burst of passion which at the same time carefully conforms to the pattern of the 'dread command' laid down by the ghost. On the other hand, Hamlet, 'benetted round with villainies', submits to the course of events in the confidence that Providence will order them. In those final events, the process, which Hamlet is not accomplished in, of forcing his soul to his own conceit is absent. Indeed, 'readiness' implies that Hamlet no longer *needs* to work himself up and pour his imagination and passion into the deed because he no longer labours alone under the imposition of a command that had seemed to him in the beginning to demand an absolute dedication and concentration of his whole self, the stripping off of all his other roles, the abandonment of 'all saws of books, all forms, all pressures past'. These changes are responsible for the feeling at the end of the play that Hamlet does not commit himself to the revenger's role in the ways he once did when he assumed it in I.v and when he enacted it in the prayer-scene, that it is Providence—the way the story turns out—which, in making itself

responsible for the story, commits Hamlet, who freely accepts. (As in
Measure for Measure, it is hard to tell whether Shakespeare is saying that
Providence is a kind of storyteller or a storyteller is a kind of Providence.)
If Hamlet does not commit himself but is committed, however freely
he submits, it can be said that he is less the revenger, that he is able to
achieve the act of revenge without ever really becoming a revenger,
that the larger perspective frees his inward self from the role: because
all does not now depend upon him and because the end can be accomplished without his being 'in the mood' for it, the identification of the
self with the revenger, the coalescence of the two, is no longer en-
joined upon him. The role is no longer seen as something which has to
be created by being quickened with his inward self, his passion and
imagination, as Brutus or Richard II create their roles; it is formed by
Providence not by the character, and is presented to Hamlet in the
shape of a concatenation of events which play into his hand, just as
they did on the voyage to England. Providence, or the storyteller,
has to this extent abolished the role.

In sum, Brutus and Richard II resemble Hamlet in that what they
are constrained to do is reshaped by them in accordance, so far as is
possible, with their needs and values, their ideas of themselves and of
the world. Hamlet's world is in the beginning unshaped to a greater
extent by the first blow of the constraining duty, but the resemblance
holds; if he has a harder struggle than they, he also has a further reach,
a second chance. He does not exhaust himself in the one interpretation
as Richard II exhausts himself in remoulding his deposition into a
Passion; he is saved, as Brutus is not, from committing the final deed
so soon as he has first nerved himself to it. From this limited point of
view, these characters can be seen as preparations for Hamlet, just as
the final condition of Richard III—the inward self unable to find any
way of adjusting itself to the role—seems at times, if we are to believe
the soliloquies, to be a condition that threatens Hamlet. Richard III
stands at the beginning of the line, incompetent. If the nature of
Hamlet's 'second chance' is taken into account, Hamlet, however,
perhaps in the end escapes from the line altogether; he glimpses a freedom which is beyond role. As he liberates himself gradually from
Claudius's dark monarchy, this freedom grows more absolute and
at length is named: Horatio speaks of its angelic music, Hamlet calls
it 'silence'. For *Hamlet* is ambiguous to the last.

II

Hamlet in the Theatre

DAVID WILLIAM

*

THERE is an essay by Lascelles Abercrombie called *A Plea for the Liberty of Interpreting* (1930) in which he tells a story about a scholar whose chief interest outside his work was female emancipation. In the course of an analysis of the 4th Book of the *Aeneid*, this scholar suggested that Virgil's treatment of the story of Dido and Aeneas champions that cause. The Queen of Carthage is to be seen signalling Stygian encouragement to Mrs. Pankhurst. Abercrombie goes on to point out the reason for such well-meaning nonsense. It is simply inattention. As soon as preoccupations extraneous to the text invade its interpretation, subjectivity runs riot. It is not always easy, however, to exclude the extraneous impulse or detect the moment of its irruption. Hence the great variety of Hamlets.

Ideally, of course, there is only one Hamlet—Shakespeare's. The rest are through a glass more or less darkly. It cannot be otherwise. Any great work of art has a region of mystery where the experience communicated is so intense, so complex and so desirable that responses cannot be unanimous. Unfortunately, the moment this is admitted, work begins on the Tower of Babel.

At present, the tendency towards co-operation in understanding Shakespeare is rather strong; stronger, I would say, than it has ever been. Men from the Theatre and men from Academe actually consult each other about their work. Actors and directors give lectures and read books (a few even write them) whilst scholars attend productions of the plays or even produce them themselves. All the same, the contemporary Shakespeare industry is not free from its own brands of inattention and self-deception. Pendulums have swung, and yesterday's sins of omission are today's sins of pride. Textual integrity, for instance, has sometimes reached puritanical proportions. Dr. Dover Wilson is still busy pushing the snowball of recension up the hill of enjoyment, though there is still a long way to go. One should not undervalue the qualities of such work, but its defects blur the image which it is meant to restore. When, for example, it comes to doubting the authenticity of the Duke's great speech in *Measure for Measure* beginning 'He who the sword of heaven would bear'[1] (III.ii.275), then all opportunities to protest should be taken. In such matters the evidence of the stage must be conclusive. Given a good actor in the part in a good production of the play, the speech will emerge not only as dramatically potent but also as stylistically organic.

The theatre too has its own modes of inattention. Misconstruction by directors, visual distractions by designers, inexpressive diction by actors—all these are liable to weaken and distort the meaning of the play. Whereupon the scholars declare that the theatre cannot be relied on and that the true trusteeship of the plays is theirs after all.

The most ambivalent source of inattention, however, is contemporary thought itself. Modern ideas significantly absorbed within the play's total structure cannot but make for an experience of immediacy and vitality; overstressed, however, the balance is destroyed.

Whatever cultural orientation is in vogue is bound to be reflected in all metropolitan productions of *Hamlet*. To-day that vogue is psychological. Culturally speaking, we are in the debt of Freud. That is fine, that is progress, until Shakespeare is hauled in to help settle the account. A few years ago there was a production of *Hamlet* at the Old Vic in which the climax of the closet-scene was a zonking great kiss on the lips between Hamlet and his mother. It was neither a persuasive advertisement for the relevance of the Oedipus complex theory to the play, nor an appropriate expression of the prince's attitude to his mother's dishonour (despite violently grimaced distress-signals at the end of the embrace). All it did tell us was that there had been inattention; neither the director nor the players had understood Shakespeare or Freud in relation to that scene.

The same scene, however, suggested very different possibilities to a Victorian audience. There is a picture of it in an 1861 revival. Phelps is the Hamlet. The prince is shown as a figure of middle-aged respectability (Phelps was fifty-seven at the time) with his right arm raised in a gesture of admonitory rectitude (which seems to have disconcerted the

[1]See New Cambridge Ed., pp. 110 and 141

Athenaeum critic . . . 'the excessive use of his right arm and hand sometimes offends in a remarkable way'). The queen crouches beside him
in an attitude of stricken penitence. It is like a parody of Mr. Gladstone
showing fallen women the Way Back. Yet we should not mock
Phelps. Only a few years earlier Macready had, with difficulty,
successfully concluded a campaign to prevent prostitutes from plying
their trade upstairs at Covent Garden during performances. The
theatre lacked the middle-class image which, for better or worse, it now
reflects. Hence, actors and managers felt obliged, whenever possible,
to assert examples of moral respectability that would satisfy the Victorian domestic conscience.

The Victorian cultural vogue, then, was prophylactically moral,
merging into the romantic piety of Irving's Shakespeare. In what way
are our Hamlets bounded in their contemporary nutshell instead of
achieving the infinite space which the play offers?

Theatrically, we are, comparatively speaking, in a comfortable
position. Poel's Elizabethan Stage Society experiments began that
rediscovery of the skill of Shakespeare's dramaturgy which even yet
we have not sufficiently absorbed. Lip-service is incessant. People are
appointed to advise on something called verse-speaking (as if it were
distinct from acting); dons are summoned to give intellectual ballast to
directors' lucubrations; schools' matinees are sell-outs; Bardville itself
is a boom town. There are even headier auguries: the Government has
at last (if somewhat grudgingly) undertaken to create a National
Theatre with Shakespeare as the keystone of the arch; 1964 looms.

Nor is this all. The general standard of classical acting is potentially
higher now than it has been at any time in the last fifty years. I do not
think directors always make the best use of it, but the material is there.
The picture is very encouraging, but something is missing. I would
call it—to use a word fallen into disuse nowadays—glory. We have
the best Quinces and Macduffs and Snugs and Mistresses Quickly and
Poloniuses in the world. But where to-day can the enlightened playgoer look with confidence for his Lear, his Othello, his Cleopatra?
What leading actor who has come before the public during the last
twenty years has established or consolidated his reputation with performances in the great tragic roles? We appear to have lost touch with
tragedy, and, with it, glory. The record of the best directors is similar.
The most admired Shakespearian productions in the last few years
(admired, that is, in terms of a *tout ensemble* rather than individual

excellence) have been Brook's *Measure for Measure*, Gielgud's *Much Ado About Nothing*, Guthrie's *Henry VIII*, and Zeffirelli's *Romeo and Juliet*. But what of Brook's *Hamlet* or Gielgud's *Macbeth* or Guthrie's *Lear* or Zeffirelli's *Othello*? They have either failed or not been attempted. And *Antony and Cleopatra* has only been given twice in London and once at Stratford during the last fifteen years.

Why is this? There are more productions of Shakespeare to be seen than ever before; the hungry sheep look up and can gormandise to their hearts' content. What has gone wrong? Some may think—nothing. For some, Olivier's Macbeth or Gielgud's Lear may have been definitive performances, unforgettable experiences. I am sorry to have to disagree with such people, especially about two supremely distinguished players. I wish I could say that I thought everyone was entitled to his own opinion of Shakespearian acting; it is only because the possibilities of these plays is so much greater than we are accustomed to experience that I venture to question the validity of responses which are satisfied by modern performances of Shakespearian tragedy.

The reason for this deficiency lies partly with the public and partly with the theatrical profession; ultimately, of course, it unites in that strange reciprocal actor-audience relationship which exists not just on this evening in that theatre, but, over a given period, begins to breed a certain kind of audience and a certain kind of actor. For the moment, however, I would like to try to analyse the audience's part.

Too many people seem to go to the theatre in search of a temporary sensation rather than an abiding experience. The enjoyment focuses on comparing Sutherland's Violetta to Callas', or Guiness' Hamlet to Redgrave's, rather than on recognising Violetta or Hamlet and deriving imaginative excitement from the encounter. It is not simply that there is too much criticism but that the intentions of the critics (amateur or professional) are not high enough; Stravinsky was very illuminating about this in an interview with *The Observer* (17 June, 1962):

the person who practises the vocation of music should not be judged by the person who has no vocation and does not understand musical practice, and to whom music must therefore be of an infinitely less fundamental consequence.

What he says of music is just as true of the theatre. The theatre-going public—abetted by the languid mediocrity of most of the critics—is on the way to emasculating the art of the stage; towards detaching plays from the passionate actuality of their origin—their risk and heat and abundance—and forcing them into limitless critical cold storage where Hamlets are heaped on Hamlets and Othellos overcrowd Othellos until the wrapping is everything and the contents nothing. This is the threat of decadence that hangs over all the representational arts in this country at the moment. They are available and expendable. They are too often the topics of mandarin conversation, the occasions of books, the improvements of careers, and too seldom the illuminations of the possibilities of life and death that the best and bravest imaginations have kindled for us.

Nowhere is this illumination brighter than in tragedy. Not only because it is the most comprehensive definition of tragedy that I have read, but also because its polarisation between life and literature suggests some of the difficulties of acting tragedy, I quote a relevant section from Peter Alexander's *Shakespeare's Life and Art*:

'For it is the paradox at the centre of tragedy, that what we admire most in the man undoes him. He may, like Achilles, be driven to the fatal situation by his own fury and contriving, or be guided there by his duty, like Socrates; but once there, even though the man has a thousand faults, it is what is noble in him that makes him a tragic figure. And though this may be as different in various men as the savage virtue of Achilles and the courageous humanity of Socrates, it is always the expression of man's free will and of a loyalty conscious or unconscious to something beyond the rebuke of the ignorant present . . . . Tragedy is no more than an extreme instance of the exercise of that self-determination which gives men bounded in the nutshell of their material existence the infinite space their souls desire. Here it is unaccompanied by the flattering chances that so often attend on the exertions of the brave and free; a worldly wisdom may now withhold the approval it would in happier circumstances be the first to bestow. Those who still admire it must choose it for its own sake with all its dangers thick upon it. And the tragic poet accepts the challenge of the situation to make clear not merely his preference for what is human and noble 'but the degree of preference; the passionate and pure choice, the inward sense of absolute and unchangeable devotion' . . . . even if the preferences and loyalties which find so universal an expression and acceptance in his drama may not seem to all the surest intimations of immortality, they are certainly among the profoundest of those communings with our internal Being with which, as Wordsworth reminds us, 'revelation coincides, and has through that coincidence alone (for otherwise it could not possess it) a power to affect us.'

(pp. 146–8)

The location of these 'preferences and loyalties' and their eloquent deployment must be the point of departure for any responsible production of *Hamlet*.

I have seen seven productions of the play and have acted in four (twice as Hamlet). None of them achieved more than a partial illumination. The play and the part of Hamlet are of course so rich and varied that even to achieve that is valuable; yet if one is to keep faith with its possibilities and demonstrate the 'intimations of immortality' contained in the tragic experience one must at least concede that a clue to the play's secrets may be suggested by the very inadequacies of performances in the theatre.

As far as I can remember the one thing which *all* the productions I have seen or played in lacked was a sense of the reality of the supernatural. I have never seen the ghost. It now seems to me that the paramount object of any production of *Hamlet* should be to establish the dramatic reality of the ghost as richly as possible. Having secured their leading actor, most directors concentrate for their main *tout ensemble* image on making the atmosphere of the court as convincing as may be; this is of course a most important object, but it does not merit the supreme intentions of the director because, even when achieved, it cannot provide the source of the tragic experience. That source lies, I suggest, in the collision in Hamlet's soul between loyalty to a moral vision which recoils from an unpondered act of retribution and a no less loyal or natural attachment to a supernatural soliciting which he knows at last cannot be ill.

There is nothing original about this, but it is as well to be clear about one's theatrical destination before attempting to chart the route to it. The chief flaw of every modern production of *Hamlet* is a vagueness of response to the implications of Act I.

Most of us no longer acknowledge the supernatural as a central factor in our own experience, still less as something to which we might concede the tremendous moral sanction which the dead king claims. Consequently there is a recurring timidity or even indifference towards any positive imaginative commitment to the expression of that experience on the stage. The scenes, however, have to be given some semblance of life and meaning, so we fall back on a melo-dramatic gallimaufry of phosphorescent make-up, disappearance tricks and vocal bugaboo. All this is unnecessary. If only we could trust and take the opportunities which Shakespeare so explicitly offers then the power and humanity of this section of the play will amply compensate for whatever scepticisms accompany us outside the theatre.

No play opens more wonderfully. Within twenty lines time, place and mood are established; the castle battlements, midnight, dark and cold and a sense of dread immediate as the guards change and speak of the figure they have seen. Then—and it is an incompetent production that cannot communicate some of the awe and mystery of this moment —they break off the excited whispering, as, in full armour, sorrowful and silver-bearded, the majesty of buried Denmark comes slow and stately by. The ghost says nothing in the scene; in that afflicted silence the actor must plant the seed of his supernatural identity. No less eloquent are Shakespeare's indications to the other actors in the scene. Terror, real and invincible terror, is the response of the two soldiers both in and out of the presence of the dreaded sight. Horatio at first presents a firm counterpoint. But three lines after his scepticism is visibly confounded, the consolations of his 'philo-sophy' disintegrate, as he gazes harrowed with fear and wonder at the spectre.

The question 'what?' having been answered, the concernancy now shifts to 'why?' Horatio's two important speeches before the ghost's re-appearance give us first the local habitation of the play and then strike the first notes of dramatic irony ('the like precurse of fierce events'). Then the ghost returns.

Again, I cannot recall any production in which this second appearance differed in mood and movement from the first. Yet there is surely an important difference. This time we are to see nothing of the solemn march; instead: "Tis here—'tis here— 'tis gone.' The stately going by of the earlier appearance is exchanged for an urgent haste for which we cannot yet assign a reason. The episode ends with a sensational *coup de théâtre*. As if in answer to the frantic entreaties of its questioners, the figure lifts its head; suddenly a cock crows; and it is gone. It is one of Shakespeare's unfailingly brilliant dramatic devices; this coincidence of the momentous with the mundane, the familiar context for the unfamiliar experience. (Compare Cleopatra and the clown.)

Up to the moment of the ghost's second disappearance, we know a little about the political background of the play; ethically, however, we are, so to speak, still in the dark. We do not know what kind of society these men inhabit or what beliefs and values they hold. When enlightenment comes, it comes in words so famous and beautiful that their dramatic relevance is apt to be overlooked:

> Some say that ever 'gainst that season comes
> Wherein our Saviour's birth is celebrated,
> The bird of dawning singeth all night long:
> And then, they say, no spirit can walk abroad;
> The nights are wholesome, then no planets strike,
> No fairy takes, nor witch hath power to charm;
> So hallow'd and so gracious is the time. (I.i.158)

Here is the first intimation that we are in a Christian country; the fact that it is an ordinary soldier who speaks the lines (as opposed to any kind of religious specialist) merely enhances their dramatic authority. The play's ethical territory is now charted.

I will pass by the scenes that introduce us to Hamlet himself and to Ophelia; whatever problems they raise for the players, they do not require such a strenuous projection of the imagination as the opening scene of the play or the two scenes that complete Act I.

By the end of this Act Shakespeare will need to have established one set of the 'preferences and loyalties' whose conflict is to form the main action of the play. Act I states the claims of 'resolution' (death); into the scales must now be placed the counterclaim of 'thought' (life). The 'To be or not to be' soliloquy reflects their tragic equipoise. But by the time this is reached, we have encountered a Hamlet whose awareness of the dilemma has reached an intensity both of passion and of irony. Not only that; but also a Hamlet whom, for all his cruelty and violence, we are plainly intended to recognise as:

> The expectancy and rose of the fair state
> The glass of fashion and the mould of form
> The observed of all observers. (III.ii.159)

Everything that blurs this image of Hamlet—both for himself and for everyone else—is suggested in his first soliloquy and then con-

firmed in the scenes with the ghost. As the play develops, therefore, and we move further away from those scenes we shall need to have
as charitable a remembrance as possible of the figure who, himself
beyond the uses of this world, laid so terrible a duty upon the shoulders
of one still involved in them, and laid it there with but the most
cursory acknowledgement of what suffering it might entail. The only
indication the ghost gives of what his mandate may cost Hamlet is just
before he leaves him:

> But howsoever thou pursu'st this act
> Taint not thy mind, nor let thy soul contrive
> Against thy mother aught . . . . (I.v.84)

'Taint not thy mind!' The dramatic irony of that exhortation is apparent as soon as Hamlet is alone.

If, therefore, the ghost is not to lose in the balance of sympathies, he
must be invested with something more than the awe and fear with
which he is introduced. And, indeed, there is a further quality which
Shakespeare throws into the scales to ensure the balance; it is the quality
of pity. We may find it first (before Hamlet himself appears) in that
startled fugitive departure; the majesty of the world on parole from
purgatory. But we are not prepared for it. Not until Shakespeare
makes Hamlet himself the intermediary does it approach real dramatic
effect. The pathos of the son's love for his father dwells in almost every
expression of that love. It is, however, a very varied pathos, nowhere
nobler than in the reticence of his reply to Horatio:

> He was a man; take him for all in all.
> I shall not look upon his like again. (I.ii.187)

or more eager than when he questions them about the apparition.
But for its full impact, we must wait until father and son are face to
face and alone. Then, in three words the awe and frenzy of the preceding scene gives way to an utterance of pity so absolute and involuntary that the depths of Hamlet's generosity of heart are plumbed in one
stroke: 'Alas poor ghost.' That the ghost should instantly reject this
response cannot affect it. The feeling has been declared and cannot be
withdrawn.

And when Hamlet is alone, and in a maelstrom of passion which he

can neither understand nor control, it is this quality of pity which keeps
asserting itself like a light in a storm.

> Remember thee!
> Ay, thou poor ghost. . . .

and though it may flicker and go out in the wild and whirling dialogue
with the soldiers when he staggers closer to the brink of madness than at
any other time, and though in that very mania he may seek to extin-
guish it in gusts of rhetoric and ridicule while he fights to wrest the
oaths of secrecy from the others, as soon as their hands are on his sword,
it shines out again as never before in those poignant words of committal
and release when he knows that the secret is safe: 'Rest, rest, perturbed
spirit.' When the oath has been taken and the cry from the cellarage is
heard no more, Hamlet knows that the cup has passed to his lips and
takes all perturbation on himself. The pity of it has reached its fullest
expression and the play now moves into its next and much more
manageable phase. The counsels of thought begin to prefer their claims
to those of resolution.

The difficulties of these early scenes, both for the actors and the
director, can hardly be exaggerated. In 'O all you host of heaven'
(I.v.92), for instance, I think that Hamlet finds his biggest challenge in
the whole play. Not only is the imaginative exertion required so intense and so extreme, but the violent and abrupt changes of mood
demand—in addition to huge emotional reserves—a technical control
of voice and body well beyond what most actors may be expected to
possess. The speech begins with short, explosive phrases:

> O all you host of heaven! O earth! what else?
> And shall I couple hell? O fie! Hold, hold, my heart;
> And you, my sinews, grow not instant old,
> But bear me stiffly up. (I.v.92)

The breathing—which should always be a prime consideration in
speaking Shakespeare—will need to be rapid both in intake and output
to fit so exclamatory and terse a style. But this staccato phrasing, the
jerky transition from idea to idea, might present no special problems of
delivery if it expressed merely the neurotic ravings of a man who had
lost contact with reality, cast adrift on floods of inorganic and direction-
less feeling. We must feel the very opposite; the turbulence of the diction springs from Hamlet's desperate and tremendous need to retain

contact with the principal realities that he knows—the great assurances
of body and soul. All the most powerful guarantees are invoked—
heaven, earth and his own senses. Thus, even within the first three-and-
a-half lines of the speech the actor must picture not only the waves of
feeling that dash and foam upon the rocks of thought and reason, but
also the deep currents and groundswell of morality and tradition and
the high banks of faith which determine the course of his soul on its
perilous voyage.

Gradually the speech yields a dominating theme—remembrance. The
next nine lines pour out white-hot with a total determination, a total
commitment to the ghost's final injunction. The sense, though losing
nothing in urgency or intensity, spreads out into ampler and more
organic phrasing. The breath-span will need to be longer, and the
explosive word in each line very carefully placed and stressed to point
the development, of thought and decision. Then, with 'O most
pernicious woman', a great cross-torrent of passion surges in, and there
is a return to the disjointed structure of the first part of the speech. As
ever, with Shakespeare's mature writing, the manipulation of vowel
and consonant is masterly, and a valuable echo of the sense throughout.
The sustained 'm' sound in the three 'remembers', for instance, if
properly heard and then uttered by the actor, vividly supports that
pressure of pity and irony which reaches its extreme moments whenever
the word recurs.

I have attempted to show some of the technical aspects of this speech
chiefly to suggest that Shakespeare's style is his supreme stage-direction,
and that the richness of his mature writing is never more marvellously
shown than in the stylistic adaptation he can always make to suit
theatrical requirement. For Hamlet, I think that all actors who have
played the part would agree that I.iv and v are the most exhausting
scenes in the play.

There is a further difficulty; one which is connected to that question of
intensity which, as I have tried to suggest, is the principal source of
privation in our experience of tragedy. Most of the acting they are
required to do ought ultimately to be enjoyable for actors, and, given
appropriate talent, not too difficult. There is much in the part of Hamlet
that is accommodating to any talented young actor. The scenes with
Polonius, and with Rosencrantz and Guildenstern, for example, which
exhibit an acute if mordant mind coping so wittily and so perceptively
with its inferiors, impose no strain on the imagination which a suit-

able actor cannot face with happy artistic address; the scene with the players invites a display of humanity and princely ease which provides a welcome relaxation from the adjacent intensities. Again, in the more meditative passages of the play, in the graveyard, before the duel and in 'To be or not to be', the actor can find opportunities of warmth and gravity and spirituality which, if he goes about them with the right tact and discipline, will stretch his range of thought and feeling without leaving an accusing sense of distance between the objective and its achievement.

Actors' temperaments vary a lot, of course; and they are not always likely to agree about the scenes they find most comfortable to play. Those with Ophelia and the Queen present emotional challenges with no important conceptual difficulties and thus rely for their dramatic truth on areas of feeling well within the 'negative capabilities' of most actors likely to be playing the part. The second scene with the ghost (in the Queen's closet) is, I think, easier than the first. Its placing is largely ironic: the ghost re-appears at the very moment when Hamlet is most violently disobeying the third of his commandments—'nor let thy soul contrive against thy mother aught.' Hamlet perceives the irony at once:

> Do you not come your tardy son to chide,
> That, laps'd in time and passion, lets go by
> The important acting of your dread command?
>
> (III.iv.106)

The placing of the scene is significant for another reason. Having spared the king at his prayers, Hamlet has gone beyond the point where his actions are determined or influenced by anyone but himself. Once more, to redress the balance of claim and counterclaim, Shakespeare must remind us of the appeal from the grave. Such chiding as there is is very gentle. Hamlet listens to it with all the old reverence and pity—as if, for him, the moral dilemma could never be relaxed:

> Do not look upon me
> Lest with this piteous action you convert
> My stern effects . . .

In the 'Hide fox' scenes that follow immediately, Hamlet exhibits something of the violent elation and savage wit with which he greeted Horatio and the soldiers after his first meeting with the ghost. This time, however, it is shrewder, more alert and realistic; when the mood subsides and he is on his way to England, he finds a stern resolution in the self-appraisal of 'How all occasions' (IV.iv.32). The ghost's re-appearance, therefore, is a re-statement, with variations, of an earlier theme; it leads to the last movement of the play in which resolution, though tragic, is honourable.

The first scenes with the ghost, however, do not offer these modes of accommodation nor gather such strength from their dramatic con-text in the unfolding plot. Their achievement must be much more expensive. In the first place, their conceptual challenge is enormous. To apprehend and then act those 'Thoughts beyond the reaches of our souls' is something only the most gifted player can achieve. But there are acute psychological difficulties too.

Most acting requires, as I have suggested, a measure of agreeable exhibitionism which the tactful processes of art and technique trans-mute into a form of public entertainment. At some time during rehearsals these processes may prove difficult, even uncomfortable, but that is a manageable hazard, and will probably have disappeared by the time the play is being performed. But there are some states of mind, some forms of suffering, which are not so susceptible of a comfortable projection because they inevitably involve—at least in rehearsal where their challenge may, and often does, prove insuperable—an exposure of areas in the actor's personality so disordered and vulnerable that their translation into the composition and repose of a performance is both difficult and painful—so much so, in fact, that the actor may sub-consciously resist it and contract. It is not merely the discomfort of knowing the distance between the objective and the achievement; it is more than discomfort; it is a kind of distress—an inability to trust the eventual landing of the vessel of one's own inadequacies and nakedness and confusion on the shores of art and resolution. A sympathetically creative director, of course, is an invaluable helmsman, but these are rare, and if left too much to his own devices in such dangerous waters the actor may abandon his destination and settle for a smoother voyage.

Hence, I think, the paucity of tragic acting at present, and of Hamlets and *Hamlets*. Actors will not take the emotional risks.

There are extenuating circumstances. It has been said that the nuclear age is not conducive to classical tragedy; that the spectacle of indivi-duals on a course of heroic ruin has no valid place in a world on the brink of collective extinction. Such an attitude rises, I suggest, from an imperfect experience of tragedy, from a critical timidity which will not grant to tragedy the universal reverberations it ought to detonate. Or social difficulties seem to obtrude. These are perhaps more realistic. Our society does not encourage exceptional and excessive individuals, and whilst most actors are still more exceptional and excessive than other people, they cannot but be somewhat affected and reduced by the prevailing atmosphere of conformity and constraint. Thus the time and energy devoted to accepting knighthoods, and sending their children to prep. schools, investing on the Stock Exchange and turning themselves into companies and country gentlemen is time and energy taken away from meeting the highest tests of their talent.

But one should not underestimate the risk. Those who have taken it are not often very happy. By abandoning themselves to the nervous exposure and emotional peril to which the highest adventures of the imagination must inevitably commit them, they may be thrown for illusions of assurance or distraction upon alcohol or sexual panic.

Yet the immortal garland must be won; the dust and the heat cannot be avoided. Your cautious Othello may thrill his audience with the address to the senate, but he will not encompass the arrival in Cyprus or the Temptation scene: in other words, the disintegration of that nature whom passion could not shake. The unadventuring Lear cannot take in 'O reason not the need' or the intercession for the destitute, still less the re-union with Cordelia. When did we last see these great scenes assailingly played?

For Hamlet that supreme test of imaginative courage comes in the scenes with the ghost. Only by rising to that challenge can the actor work that magic on an audience which bends them where he wills. Hamlet himself understood this magic, and attests it in words to which actors cannot but feel an immediate and special response:

> I have heard
> That guilty creatures sitting at a play
> Have by the very cunning of the scene
> Been struck so to the soul that presently
> They have proclaimed their malefactions. (II.ii.617)

He that plays the prince must so strike to the soul of his audience that his conviction of life and of death is theirs and they are one with him.

And they will welcome the conviction for the assurances it brings of so much to which they could not otherwise have access: the assurance of the beauty of the world beyond the unweeded garden; of resolution rehearsing its eternal dialogue with thought; of the base uses to which we may return; of the golden fire and the congregation of vapours; of the special providence in the fall of a sparrow; of the readiness; and of all the splendour and affliction in what chances in particular men.

III

The Structure of 'Hamlet'

J. K. WALTON

★

THE question of the 'character' of Hamlet has occupied such a large place in discussions about the play that there has been comparatively little consideration of its structure. It is true that there has been much discussion about individual questions connected with structure, such as the order of scenes, the function of the player's speech, and the staging of the play within the play; but what is not so easily found is an approach to *Hamlet* which, while attempting to provide an answer to individual structural questions, is primarily concerned with the structure as a whole. Such an approach, since it is concerned above all with the relationship of the different aspects of the play to each other, is less likely to offer a one-sided interpretation than is an approach primarily in terms of character.[1]

There are two aspects of a tragedy which, in particular, concern us when we are considering its structure. One is the development of the relationship of the hero with the forces with which he is in conflict; the other is the initial situation in which he finds himself. These two are interrelated, for unless we fully understand the initial situation we are likely to misconceive the development of the relationship of dramatic

---

[1] Essays such as Granville-Barker's, which have much to say about structure, often import notions derived from critics who have approached the play mainly in terms of character. Wilson Knight (*The Wheel of Fire* (1949 ed.), p. 32) has asserted that 'the consciousness of death, and consequent bitterness, cruelty, and inaction, in Hamlet not only grows in his own mind disintegrating it as we watch, but also spreads its effects outward among the other persons like a blighting disease, and, as the play progresses, by its very passivity and negation of purpose, insidiously undermines the health of the state, and adds victim to victim until at the end the stage is filled with corpses'. This is to carry a character interpretation far beyond anything in Bradley.

forces. These are the two aspects which an interpretation largely in terms of the hero's character is most likely to underestimate because they appear most to deprive his character of its autonomy.

The importance of both these aspects is shown when we compare *Hamlet* with other tragedies of revenge. In *The Business of Criticism* (1959), Helen Gardner observes that:

> the essence of any tragedy of revenge is that its hero has not created the situation in which he finds himself and out of which the tragedy arises. The simplest of all tragic formulas, that a tragedy begins in prosperity and ends in misery, does not fit revenge tragedies. When the action opens the hero is seen in a situation which is horrible, and felt by him and the audience to be intolerable, but for which he has no responsibility. The exposition of such plays does not display the hero taking a fatal step, but the hero confronted with appalling facts.
>
> (p. 41)

But in Elizabethan revenge plays the villain is responsible not only for the initial situation but also for the situation which makes possible the dénouement. The revenger, like Hieronymo in *The Spanish Tragedy*, avails himself of an opportunity unwittingly provided for him by the villain, and forms his scheme on the spur of the moment. It would seem to have been considered a necessary part of the total effect of a revenge play that 'the villain should be to some extent the agent of his own destruction'.

If we turn to consider *Hamlet* without reference to other plays of revenge, we find that there is one feature of the initial situation which has been seriously misunderstood. Until the appearance of Dover Wilson's *What Happens in 'Hamlet'*, critics usually assumed that we are not meant to doubt the truth of what the ghost asserts; most of them therefore believed that Hamlet's failure to carry out his instructions should be sought in some weakness of character. Dover Wilson, however, has shown that owing to the advent of Protestantism differing opinions about ghosts were current in Elizabethan times, and that an Elizabethan audience, themselves puzzled by the nature of the ghost, would feel that Hamlet was justified in seeking proof the ghost was not a devil sent to damn him. The older view was that ghosts were souls returned from Purgatory. Protestants, not believing in Purgatory, could not accept this view; and those Protestants who were not sceptical about their existence (as was, for example, Reginald Scot) had little alternative but to believe that a ghost was either an angel or, more probably, a devil. We should therefore see the problem of the ghost's status as being for Hamlet a very real one, all the more so since he is a Protestant, a prince of Protestant Denmark who was educated at Luther's old University, Wittenberg, while the ghost, as we are eventually assured, comes from Purgatory. Hamlet, before he has met the ghost and received his instructions, shows himself aware of differing possibilities:

> If it assume my noble father's person,
> I'll speak to it, though hell itself should gape
> And bid me hold my peace. (I.ii.244)

His awareness of these possibilities is heightened when he first meets the ghost face to face:

> Angels and ministers of grace defend us!
> Be thou a spirit of health or goblin damn'd,
> Bring with thee airs from heaven or blasts from hell,
> Be thy intents wicked or charitable,
> Thou comest in such a questionable shape
> That I will speak to thee: I'll call thee Hamlet,
> King, father, royal Dane . . . (I.iv.39)

For Shakespeare's audience, the questionableness of the shape would have been increased by the fact that it was an innovation in the Elizabethan theatre. As Dover Wilson remarks (p. 55), 'the stock apparition of the Elizabethan theatre was a classical puppet, borrowed from Seneca'. The ghost in *Hamlet*, however, is no puppet; though moving apparently under the direction of unseen powers, it is extraordinarily lifelike and in appearance exactly resembles the dead king.

The questionable nature of the ghost has important consequences. Since Hamlet has to test the truth of the ghost's story, we cannot re-regard the play within the play as merely an excuse which he improvises in order to avoid action. Of yet greater structural consequence is the change in our view of Claudius. If we suppose that the ghost speaks the unquestionable truth, Claudius's consummate 'practice' is a comparatively trivial matter; for Hamlet then knows for sure that he is guilty of the crimes with which the ghost has charged him. But if until the play-scene Hamlet remains unsure whether Claudius is guilty, Claudius's 'practice' takes on altogether more importance. He ceases to be the 'small' villain of whom Bradley speaks, and becomes a much more formidable figure. In consequence, we can more readily describe the structure in terms of a conflict between opposing forces.

Bradley (pp. 40 ff.) attempts, not altogether consistently, so to view the structure of *Hamlet* and other Shakespeare tragedies, and he is led to the conclusion that 'our point of view in examining the construction of a play will not always coincide with that which we occupy in thinking of its whole dramatic effect' (p. 47). He argues that 'that struggle in the hero's soul which sometimes accompanies the outward struggle is of the highest importance for the total effect of a tragedy; but it is not always necessary or desirable to consider it when the question is merely one of construction'. This, Bradley thinks, is natural since 'the play is meant primarily for the theatre; and theatrically the outer conflict, with its influence on the fortunes of the hero, is the aspect which first catches, if it does not engross, attention'. In *Hamlet* 'from the point of view of construction, the fact that Hamlet spares the King when he finds him praying, is, from its effect on the hero's fortunes, of great moment; but the cause of the fact, which lies within Hamlet's character, is not so'.

In what follows, I try to show that there is no discrepancy between 'construction' and 'the whole dramatic effect' since in fact the 'struggle in the hero's soul' is always dramatically relevant to the 'outer conflict'. In other words, to see the dramatic structure in terms of a conflict between opposing forces is not to underestimate the importance of the inner struggle, but on the contrary helps us to appreciate its full significance.

*   *   *

Approaching a general view of dramatic structure, Bradley remarks (pp. 40–41) that 'as a Shakespearean tragedy represents a conflict which terminates in a catastrophe, any such tragedy may roughly be divided into three parts': the first, an exposition of the state of affairs out of which the conflict arises; the second, which deals with 'the definite beginning, the growth and the vicissitudes of the conflict'; and the third, which forms the catastrophe.[2] Since, still more than Bradley, I

---

[2] Bradley also holds (p. 51) that when a 'crisis' is well marked, as in *Hamlet*, 'it has the effect, as to construction, of dividing the play into five parts instead of

(*footnote continued on page 48*)

see the structure of *Hamlet* as consisting of conflict, this threefold
division serves to give in rough outline the view of the structure which
I propose, though Bradley suggests too absolute a division between the
parts (the conflict, for example, is already stirring early in Act I and is
not resolved until the end of the play). Any *schema* is bound to be in
some ways misleading. However the structure may also, as I suggest in
conclusion, be seen in terms of an image.

I.i and I.ii, while giving us much of the exposition, initiate the
dramatic tension. This they do not only because each may be regarded
as a self-contained dramatic unit, rising to a climax and reaching a
temporary resolution, but also because these two units, while organi-
cally linked, with I.ii developing the dramatic possibilities of I.i, are in
strong contrast to each other.

The tension appears in the first lines of the play, with the 'Who's
there?' asked not by the sentinel on duty, Francisco, but fearsomely by
the relieving sentinel, Bernardo. This inversion of the usual procedure
hints at a general inversion of the customary order of things. A new
order is suggested by the regularity with which the ghost appears for the
third night 'jump at this dead hour' (l. 65). Horatio agrees with those
who have seen it on earlier occasions that it is 'most like' the dead king
and questions it, thus beginning that process of inquiry which, in one
form or another, runs throughout the play, and which may generally
be described as an attempt to distinguish appearance from reality. The
imagery that is used by Horatio in his questioning is significant since it
introduces the theme of usurpation:

> What art thou that usurp'st this time of night,
> Together with that fair and warlike form
> In which the majesty of buried Denmark
> Did sometime march? (I.i.46)

Is the ghost in a sense a usurper? The question is related to the later
question whether the successor to 'buried Denmark', Claudius, is himself a usurper. The belief that the visitation 'bodes some strange
eruption to our state' (l.69) leads to an account by Horatio of the

three'. It will be seen that this division into five may approximate to a five-act
structure. The text of *Hamlet*, however, gives us little indication of Act division.
Q1 and Q2 have no division into Acts, while F (the First Folio) has only a
division for Act II. The subsequent Act divisions, III, IV, and V, of modern
editions are inherited from the 'Players' Quarto' of 1676, which merely represents the theatrical practice of the Restoration.

threatened invasion by Fortinbras from Norway. As we will later learn, there is danger, but it is internal rather than external, and Bernardo is wrong to associate the ghost with the threat of invasion (ll. 109–11). Appearance and reality do not correspond. When the ghost again enters, as Horatio is speaking of harbingers of disaster, it shows itself in a contradictory light, and the climax of the scene is reached. The ghost is majestical:

> We do it wrong, being so majestical,
> To offer it the show of violence... (I.i.143)

But as soon as the cock crows it starts:

> like a guilty thing
> Upon a fearful summons ... (I.i.148)

and the scene ends with references to the dawn that is breaking—which appears as a symbol of what is normal, indeed of hope, through the association of 'The bird of dawning' with 'our Saviour's birth' (ll.158–60)—and with an agreement to tell Hamlet, to whom the ghost may speak.

I.ii is in strong contrast with I.i. Here, instead of the starlit cosmic setting on the battlements, with its supernatural visitation, we have the Council Chamber. In place of the silent, unearthly, majestic, but also evidently guilty form of the dead king, there is the suave wordliness of the present ruler, who talks much in a mode of elaborate and seemingly complacent rhetoric that can hardly fail to arouse suspicion about what lies underneath:

> Therefore our sometime sister, now our queen,
> The imperial jointress to this warlike state,
> Have we, as 'twere with a defeated joy,—
> With an auspicious and a dropping eye,
> With mirth in funeral and with dirge in marriage,
> In equal scale weighing delight and dole,—
> Taken to wife ... (I.ii.8)

Having disposed of the Fortinbras threat and given Laertes permission to return to France, Claudius turns to Hamlet; but his attempt to ingratiate himself by referring to the different forms of relationship between them—'But now, my cousin Hamlet, and my son'—is self-defeating, for it is just this excess of relationship which Hamlet finds so

D

hard to bear. The struggle between the two, though it is only in its
early stage, at once becomes visible with Hamlet's aside, 'A little more
than kin, and less than kind', and his retort 'Not so, my lord; I am too
much i' the sun' to Claudius's inquiry, 'How is it that the clouds still
hang on you?'. In his speech beginning 'Seems, madam! nay, it is; I
know not "seems" ', Hamlet shows that he is aware of possible dis-
crepancies between appearance and reality. Claudius, for his part,
makes a splendidly persuasive speech against excessive mourning, and
reveals by his unwillingness that Hamlet should return to Wittenberg,
which is in contrast with his readiness to grant Laertes permission to go
to Paris, that he wishes to keep him under surveillance ('in the cheer and
comfort of our eye'). This move aimed at achieving greater security is
the first of Claudius's major mistakes, and like all else that he does,
ultimately self-defeating. Its self-defeating nature is immediately, if
only indirectly, indicated in his words which follow Hamlet's acqui-
esence when his mother pleads with him to stay:

> This gentle and unforced accord of Hamlet
> Sits smiling to my heart: in grace whereof,
> No jocund health that Denmark drinks to-day,
> But the great cannon to the clouds shall tell,
> And the king's rouse the heavens shall bruit again,
> Re-speaking earthly thunder. (I.ii.123)

The sense of these words, as understood by Claudius, is that the heavens
by respeaking what he has proposed will endorse it; there is a suggestion
that the will of Claudius and the will of the heavens speak with one
voice. But the reverberation, taken together with the recoil associated
with firing of cannon, presents, as well, an image which suggests that
deeds may return to afflict their inventors. Immediately after Claudius's
cannon-speech, the scene reaches its climax with Hamlet's first soliloquy, in which is expressed his greatest despair.

This soliloquy recalls the opening scene. The first lines,

> O, that this too too sullied[3] flesh would melt,
> Thaw and resolve itself into a dew!

where Hamlet feels trapped by his mother's corruption, recall the
resolution of I.i, with its implication of hope:

[3] I adopt the emendation 'sullied', based on the Q2 'sallied', in place of the
F 'solid' followed by the Globe editors.

> But, look, the morn, in russet mantle clad,
> Walks o'er the dew of yon high eastward hill . . .
>
> (I.i.166)

where 'dew' represents what is fresh and natural. The opening scene is also recalled when Hamlet contrasts Claudius with 'the majesty of buried Denmark'. But in this soliloquy, Hamlet himself is ignorant both of the past and of the future. His:

> How weary, stale, flat and unprofitable,
> Seem to me all the uses of this world . . .

comes largely from disgust that his mother has posted 'with such dexterity to incestuous sheets'. He refers to Claudius only because Gertrude's choice of such a husband, so inferior to his father, increases his disgust with her. He is as yet unaware that Claudius, by killing his father, is principally responsible for his own wish for death; for had not Claudius killed the elder Hamlet, Gertrude's weaknesses would not have had the opportunity of so blatantly revealing themselves. But Hamlet is also unaware of the future. He sees no end to 'things rank and gross in nature'. When he wishes that:

> the Everlasting had not fix'd
> His canon 'gainst self-slaughter . . .

his use of the term 'fix'd' in conjunction with ''gainst' shows that he is punning on the word 'cannon',[4] with a reference to the preceding speech of Claudius. The pun gives an extra dramatic point to what is anyway manifest enough, that he is unaware, like Claudius, of the self-destructive implications, developed towards the end of the play, of this cannon-speech; he is as yet not conscious of the extent to which actions may turn on their doer. In other words, instead of allowing what is 'rank and gross in nature' to contribute to its own destruction, the only solution he can think of at present is, by suicide, to destroy himself. At the end of the play this situation will have changed into its opposite:

[4] The fact that there is no specific prohibition against suicide suggests that Shakespeare went out of his way to make the pun. C. Wordsworth remarks that 'unless it be the Sixth Commandment, the "canon" must be one of natural religion'. So definite is the suggestion of a physical as well as a theological canon that Theobald felt it necessary to point out that 'canon' does not refer to a piece of artillery but to a divine ordinance. Hamlet puns extensively, including at some of the principal dramatic moments (see, e.g., V.ii.337, quoted below, note 28).

Hamlet, as we shall see, is by then aware of the self-destructive nature of such as Claudius and, far from thinking of suicide as a solution, he is prepared to wait for Providence to determine the time of his death; and he kills Claudius when he is ripe for destruction.

After the soliloquy, we are shown Hamlet for the first time with the sole person whom he can trust, Horatio. Here we have an indication that the only thing which Hamlet values is human worth. He replies to Horatio's 'your poor servant ever' (l. 162) with 'Sir, my good friend; I'll change that name with you'; and when Horatio says of Hamlet's father 'I saw him once; he was a goodly king' (l. 186), Hamlet answers 'He was a man, take him for all in all'.[5] After the supernatural of the beginning of the play, and the formality of the corrupt court, we have here, as in Hamlet's soliloquy, the essentially human. We are then reminded of the supernatural events by Horatio's account of them to Hamlet; and the scene ends with Hamlet's absolute determination to speak to the Ghost, and his conviction that:

> foul deeds will rise,
> Though all the earth o'erwhelm them, to men's eyes.

Thus I.ii, like I.i, moves through a definite progression, and ends on a qualified feeling of hope. At the beginning of the scene Claudius has the initiative, but by its end the initiative has passed to Hamlet.

It is part of the dramatic movement of the play that Hamlet should be increasingly isolated in the Danish court. In the next scene we see how the pressure of his environment, represented by the conventional advice given by both her brother and father, causes Ophelia to reject Hamlet. This advice is given because both Laertes and Polonius are incapable of estimating Hamlet at his true worth, and judge him by themselves. The fallaciousness of this advice to Ophelia is emphasised by the nature of Polonius's advice to Laertes which occurs in the central part of the scene, after Laertes but before Polonius has warned Ophelia about Hamlet. This advice to Laertes represents the height of a trivial moralising and culminates in the complacent belief, which is to be shown wrong by so many of the *dramatis personae*, that:

> to thine own self be true,
> And it must follow, as the night the day,
> Thou canst not then be false to any man. (I.iii.78)

[5] I follow the sense that the passage has in F, which has a colon after 'all'. Q2 has no internal punctuation in a sentence that clearly requires it.

In Polonius's advice to his children we have, too, a preparation, by way of contrast, for I.iv and I.v, where, in place of Polonius and his commonplace moralising, there is the ghost which shakes:

> our disposition
> With thoughts beyond the reaches of our souls . . . (I.iv.55)

The appearance of the ghost is preceded by Hamlet's 'dram of eale' speech. A common misinterpretation of this speech is that Hamlet is unwittingly referring to himself and the fatal flaw which brings about his tragedy. But Hamlet is here dealing with reputation—'the general censure' (l. 35)—and how one fault, for which perhaps its possessor is not responsible, may lead to the mistaken view that the nation or person concerned possesses no virtues but only a particular vice. By raising the general issue of appearance and reality, the speech is structurally important; it connects the question of the nature of the previously imperturbable and moralistic Claudius who, however, to-night,

> takes his rouse,
> Keeps wassail, and the swaggering up-spring reels . . . (I.iv.8)

with the question of the nature of the ghost; for the ghost appears the instant the speech is concluded, and, having at once presented Hamlet with the possibilities that it is 'a spirit of health' or 'goblin damn'd' or simply 'Hamlet,/King, father, royal Dane', it waves him on with 'courteous action'. Hamlet's great strength of will is demonstrated by his unflinching determination to question the ghost and find out, if he can, 'why is this? wherefore? what should we do?' (l. 57). He has to overcome both the internal opposition of the fears aroused by such an apparition and also the external opposition of his friends ('I'll make a ghost of him that lets me').

The ghost's instructions to Hamlet and Hamlet's response have a dramatically important congruence. After telling him that he is bound to revenge, and then providing him with details of how the crime was committed, the ghost gives Hamlet his final instructions, in which there is an appeal to passion but also to judgement. First there is the appeal to passion:

> If thou hast nature in thee, bear it not;
> Let not the royal bed of Denmark be
> A couch for luxury and damned incest. (I.v.81)

Then follows the appeal to judgement:

> But, howsoever thou pursuest this act,
> Taint not thy mind, nor let thy soul contrive
> Against thy mother aught: leave her to heaven
> And to those thorns that in her bosom lodge,
> To prick and sting her.

Hamlet's exclamation:

> O all you host of heaven! O earth! what else?
> And shall I couple hell? O, fie!

shows that for a moment—'And shall I couple hell?'—he considers the possibility that the ghost is a devil, but for the time being he generously rejects the thought as unworthy ('O fie!'). Having accepted the ghost at its face value, Hamlet then responds to the ghost's behests in a manner which suggests that in him there is a combination of passion and judgement which makes him well fitted to carry them out. First passion:

> Yea, from the table of my memory
> I'll wipe away all trivial fond records,
> All saws of books, all forms, all pressures past,
> That youth and observation copied there;
> And thy commandment all alone shall live
> Within the book and volume of my brain,
> Unmix'd with baser matter: yes, by heaven!
> O most pernicious woman!
> O villain, villain, smiling, damned villain! (I.v.98)

Hamlet's passion has, however, now moved to the point where it becomes tempered with thought, and we have the ironical detachment of:

> My tables,—meet it is I set it down,
> That one may smile, and smile, and be a villain;
> At least I'm sure it may be so in Denmark . . .

The cellerage scene, which follows, would bring into the mind of an Elizabethan audience grave doubts concerning the nature of the ghost. Here the ghost, in order to help Hamlet swear his friends to secrecy, speaks from underground; but by so doing immediately calls in question its own status, for, as Dover Wilson reminds us (pp. 81–2), Elizabethans commonly believed that under the earth was a habitat of devils. Hamlet himself at once emphasises this interpretation by treating the ghost jocularly as if it were his familiar ('art thou there, truepenny?'; 'Well said, old mole! canst work i' the earth so fast?/A worthy pioner!'). Hamlet's object, as Wilson shows, is to make more certain that Marcellus will not reveal Hamlet's encounter with the ghost, by persuading him that he has been sworn to secrecy in the hearing of a powerful fiend. But the voice from underground would be taken by an Elizabethan audience as raising doubts in Hamlet's mind, as it did in their own, concerning the nature of the ghost, doubts which Hamlet had expressed on first seeing it but had put aside by an effort of will. In other words, we have the ironical situation that by the very process of making sure that there will be no 'ambiguous giving out' about what happened, the ambiguity concerning the nature of the ghost is emphasised.

The difficulties of Hamlet's situation are indeed great. On the one hand he has been given instructions of peculiar difficulty, calling for a combination of passion and judgement, by a spirit the nature of which appears highly ambiguous. On the other hand, the adversary on whom he has been instructed to wreak vengeance, Claudius, while clearly of much inferior character to Hamlet's father, appears in his own way formidable[6] both in his handling of the business of state and in his capacity for acting the part of king.

Until after the play scene, the action from now on consists of attempts by Claudius and Hamlet to penetrate the disguise of each other. After Hamlet has been instructed by the ghost, the initiative passes to Claudius. Polonius, Rosencrantz and Guildenstern, and Ophelia attempt in turn to make Hamlet reveal the cause of his 'transformation'. Hamlet then regains the initiative with the Gonzago play.

The surveillance of Hamlet is introduced by the Polonius-Reynaldo scene, which follows immediately after the cellerage episode. Here Polonius, at the end of his instructions to Reynaldo concerning Laertes, sums up the tactics he is to employ, which are very similar to those that will be used against Hamlet:

> And thus do we of wisdom and of reach,
> With windlasses and with assays of bias,
> By indirections find directions out . . . (II.i.64)

[6] So formidable, in fact, that he has deceived some modern critics. See, for example, Wilson Knight, *The Wheel of Fire*, p. 35: 'He is—strange as it may seem—a good and gentle king'.

The Polonius-Reynaldo scene has the function of making Claudius's efforts to discover the truth about Hamlet appear as if they might possibly be the expression of a legitimate concern. Polonius's instructions and moralising are, no doubt, foolish, but they are legitimate. Polonius is Claudius's chief counsellor; and Claudius, the last time we saw him (in I.ii), was in a strongly moralistic vein, though we have later heard about his wassailing and his participation in 'the swaggering up-spring'. Immediately after Reynaldo has left, Ophelia enters and gives Polonius information about Hamlet. It must therefore have been easy for an Elizabethan audience, who had doubts about the nature of the ghost and who would not have had a modern audience's knowledge of the play, to associate Polonius's stratagem for finding out about Laertes with Claudius's for finding out about Hamlet; and they could thus appreciate, all the more keenly, Hamlet's predicament.

After Polonius has received Ophelia's report, Claudius instructs Rosencrantz and Guildenstern to draw Hamlet 'on to pleasures' (II.ii.15) and thereby find out the cause of his transformation. The Ambassadors from Norway announce that the Norwegian king agrees to Claudius's demands, and they convey the request that Fortinbras be allowed passage across Denmark to Poland. Polonius tells Claudius, as 'fruit to that great feast' of the news from Norway, that the cause of Hamlet's madness is the repulsion by Ophelia of his love. The self-defeating quality in Polonius is simultaneously emphasised in the humour of his struggle to be brief, which only makes for greater prolixity. He enunciates his simple faith—a faith which is later to conduct him to his unillumined death—that:

> If circumstances lead me, I will find
> Where truth is hid, though it were hid indeed
> Within the centre. (II.ii.157)

Then he proposes his plan to 'loose' his daughter to Hamlet, with Claudius and himself behind the arras, a plan which is not put into execution until the nunnery-scene in III.i.[7] Dover Wilson (pp. 106-8) thinks that Hamlet's abuse of Polonius in the fishmonger episode (II.ii. 170-223) is to be explained only by supposing that a stage-direction indicating Hamlet's earlier entry is missing, and that he has, in fact,

[7] In Q1, the nunnery-scene, together with the preceding soliloquy, takes place immediately after the plan has been formulated. This scene sequence has been followed in some modern productions and has some superficial attraction, though the Q2 and F sequence is dramatically preferable: see pp.62-3.

overheard Polonius propose the plot. Polonius's plottings have, how-ever, a self-vanquishing quality which makes it unnecessary to suppose anything so crude as that Hamlet actually overhears his plan. His interruption of Hamlet at his reading and his ill-judged 'Do you know me, my lord?' give Hamlet an opening. Hamlet must know that Ophelia has rejected him at the orders of her father, who thinks that her virtue is in danger. In order to mock Polonius the conventional moraliser, Hamlet therefore simply inverts the situation by describing Polonius not as the guardian of his daughter's virtue but as a pander (i.e. 'fishmonger'); and, ironically, hits in a sense on the truth, since Polonius is plotting to use Ophelia for Claudius's purposes, though Hamlet himself still thinks of Polonius as merely a tedious old fool (II.ii.223). The capacity of Polonius for self-defeat is again brought out after his question 'What do you read, my lord?', when he retreats physically as well as intellectually before the advancing Hamlet and is told that 'yourself, sir, shall grow[8] old as I am, if like a crab you could go backward' (l. 205).

Like Polonius, Rosencrantz and Guildenstern fail. Instead of dis-covering Hamlet's secret, Hamlet discovers theirs: they have been 'sent for' (II.ii.303). This information tells Hamlet little about Claudius himself, and serves at first to increase, if anything, Hamlet's melan-choly by showing him what his old friends are worth. But it begins a movement, prefigured in his encounter with Polonius, consisting of a progress in knowledge which culminates in Hamlet's discovery, by means of the experimental test of the play scene, that the ghost spoke the truth about Claudius, a discovery which ends Hamlet's melancholy and fills him with elation.

When he meets Rosencrantz and Guildenstern, Hamlet is in a melancholy mood, seeing the world in largely subjective and relativist terms and seeming to doubt the possibility of attaining to any certain knowledge of reality. After the preliminary exchanges, Rosencrantz declares that he and Guildenstern do not think, with Hamlet, that Denmark is a prison, to which Hamlet replies:

> Why, then, 'tis none to you; for there is nothing either good or bad, but thinking makes it so: to me it is a prison. (II.ii.255)

---

[8] The reading 'shall grow' is from Q2; here the Globe follows F's 'should be'.

Soon after this Hamlet forces from Rosencrantz and Guildenstern the
real reason why they have come to Elsinore. This knowledge does not
take him very far, since they might have been told to watch him for a
legitimate enough reason; and, in fact, in telling them why they were
'sent for', Hamlet largely maintains his relativist position: in theory he
is prepared to accept that the universe and men are excellent, but to him
they seem different:

> it goes so heavily with my disposition, that this goodly frame the
> earth, seems to me a sterile promontory, this most excellent canopy
> the air, look you, this brave o'erhanging firmament, this majestical
> roof fretted with golden fire, why it appeareth nothing to me but
> a foul and pestilent congregation of vapours. . . . What a piece of
> work is a man, how noble in reason, how infinite in faculties, in
> form and moving, how express and admirable in action, how like
> an angel in apprehension, how like a god: the beauty of the world;
> the paragon of animals; and yet to me, what is this quintessence of
> dust? [9]

While Hamlet exaggerates his ignorance earlier in the same speech
('I have of late—but wherefore I know not—lost all my mirth . . .'),
we have no reason to doubt that this speech as a whole genuinely
represents Hamlet's outlook at this particular point of the dramatic
action. Hamlet only is sure he feels that things are wrong, not that they
are in fact wrong. His generosity has made him instinctively ready to
accept the ghost's credentials and he thus believes himself bound to
carry out the task of vengeance. But it follows from the state of his
ignorance—or his lack of confidence in his knowledge—that he can
think of vengeance only in terms of passion. At this stage, if he is to act
at all, he has to act on passion rather than on judgement because he
does not possess enough certain knowledge to provide the material
for judgement. This is why, when the players arrive, Hamlet asks for
'a passionate speech' (l. 452). He asks for the Æneas speech in particular
because it depicts a scene of vengeance in which passion is the only
motivating factor. The speech describes a situation which has some
obvious bearing on Hamlet's as he at present sees it or would wish to
see it. There is, to begin with, an identification of passion with honour
by means of the imagery which associates the blood Pyrrhus has shed
with heraldry:

[9] This quotation is taken from Dover Wilson's edition. It follows Q2
closely.

> head to foot
> Now is he total gules; horridly trick'd
> With blood of fathers, mothers, daughters, sons . . .
>
> (II.ii.478)

There is also the spectacle of Pyrrhus pausing in his vengeance, because of a situation which seems to be caused by the very completeness of the passion with which he sets about executing it (ll. 493–504). The respite is only temporary — 'Aroused vengeance sets him new a -work'— and so, the implication surely is, Hamlet would like to think is it with himself owing to a similar excess of passion. The last part of the speech, where Hecuba is described as grieving wildly for Priam, glances partly at Gertrude's lack of feeling—this is how Hamlet would wish his mother to have grieved—and the speech ends by describing how the Gods, 'unless things mortal move them not at all', would have been stirred to passion by the spectacle of her sorrow.

The function of the player's speech, however, is to demonstrate, directly to us, the audience, but by a more indirect method to Hamlet, that passion by itself cannot form the basis for action; and thus that Hamlet, in his present lack of certain knowledge, cannot be expected to act out of passion alone. If we take the speech at its face value, its most notable feature is its complete lack of irony. There is no sense that, when passions are carried to an extreme (as they inevitably must be if unmixed with other qualities), they may have consequences different from those they are meant to bring about. Pyrrhus in rage strikes wide, but this does not matter for:

> with the whiff and wind of his fell sword
> The unnerved father falls . . . (II.ii.495)

while:

> senseless Ilium,
> Seeming to feel this blow, with flaming top
> Stoops to his base . . .

Moreover, although the 'hideous crash' of 'senseless Ilium', seemingly brought about by Pyrrhus's blow struck in rage, 'Takes prisoner Pyrrhus' ear' and his sword, declining on Priam's head, seems to stick in the air so that Pyrrhus appears merely 'a painted tyrant' and does nothing, this halt to his vengeance is only a lull before the storm. Pyrrhus's rage has neither made inoperative his vengeance nor caused it to have any other consequences than he desires. In other words, taken at its face value the speech does not reflect reality (cf. the player king's speech, III.ii.196–225, in the Gonzago play, which Hamlet, who has by then attained a higher level of consciousness, sees as a holding of 'the mirror up to nature'; here (see below, p.70) there is a strongly ironic awareness of the self-destructive qualities of passion). On the other hand, if we do not take the speech at its face value but critically —as we are invited to do by the stylistic exaggerations of the introductory part (e.g. 'eyes like carbuncles')—then we are made highly conscious of the absurdity of a view of life which holds that passion alone should be the motive for action.

But Hamlet himself cannot be shown as learning in this way, the way in which we the audience learn, for he has chosen the speech because he admired it. It comes from 'an excellent play, well digested in the scenes, set down with as much modesty as cunning' (III.ii.459), and it would be difficult to explain satisfactorily in concise dramatic terms a change in Hamlet's opinion. What therefore Shakespeare does is to alter the angle from which Hamlet regards the speech; he is not shown as being moved by the speech itself but rather by the fact that the player appears to be moved by it.

The stages through which Hamlet moves to an awareness of the inadequacy of passion are clearly indicated in his soliloquy (II.ii.576–634); we, the audience, should be predisposed, through the direct demonstration of the inadequacy of passion provided by the player's speech, to sympathise here with the development of Hamlet's consciousness. At the opening of the soliloquy it is made plain that Hamlet is moved not so much by the words of the player's speech or even by his rendering of them as by the physical changes in his appearance:

> Is it not monstrous that this player here,
> But in a fiction, in a dream of passion,
> Could force his soul so to his own conceit
> That from her working all his visage wann'd,
> Tears in his eyes, distraction in's aspect,
> A broken voice, and his whole function suiting
> With forms to his conceit? (II.ii.577)

Hamlet is still thinking in terms of passion; he is stirred that 'in a dream of passion' the actor could so change,[10] and he asks himself what could the actor do:

> Had he the motive and the cue for passion
> That I have?

By considering the matter still only in terms of passion, Hamlet is made to feel that he must be a coward, that:

> it cannot be
> But I am pigeon-liver'd and lack gall
> To make oppression bitter, or ere this
> I should have fatted all the region kites
> With this slave's offal . . .

But even as he announces that he must lack gall to make oppression bitter, he thinks of Claudius and the deadly bitterness of his reference to him shows that this is not so; and he is led to a passionate denunciation:

> bloody, bawdy villain!
> Remorseless, treacherous, lecherous, kindless villain!
> O, vengeance!

But on account of his capacity for self-criticism, passion with Hamlet is not self-defeating; it is, rather, tempered by thought. He thus proceeds:

> Why, what an ass am I! This is most brave,
> That I, the son of a dear father murder'd,
> Prompted to my revenge by heaven and hell,
> Must, like a whore, unpack my heart with words,
> And fall a-cursing, like a very drab,
> A scullion!

[10] The function of the discussion about the travelling players and the wars of the theatres is to emphasise, by an account of their professional activities, what an audience watching *Hamlet* on the stage might forget—that the players are actors and that therefore they are acting acting. The discussion also provides an opportunity for the first expression of an awareness of a process of self-defeat. Hitherto (unless we include Hamlet's words about the backward crab-like progress of Polonius) we have simply been presented with various processes of self-defeat at work. This explicit awareness is appropriately given to Hamlet, in his question about the 'little eyases': ' . . . will they not say afterwards, if they should grow themselves to common players—as it is most like, if their means are no better—their writers do them wrong, to make them exclaim against their own succession?' (l. 364). While Hamlet's question is, of course, playful in tone, the image of the bird of prey ('little eyases') which defeats its own purposes the bigger it becomes is a pregnant one. Hamlet a little later (l. 397) speaks of his enemies as birds of prey ('I know a hawk from a handsaw'). Claudius's fate is thus already foreshadowed in Hamlet's question about the 'little eyases'.

Here, the too self-critical, 'Prompted to my revenge by heaven and hell', prescribes the movement his thought will take. Since heaven and hell cannot be supposed to give the same instructions, for Hamlet to say that he is prompted by heaven and hell is practically the same thing as to say that he is prompted by heaven or hell; in other words, that he is uncertain by which. He therefore goes on to evolve the plan for the play-scene[11] in order to test Claudius, since:

> The spirit that I have seen
> May be a devil.[12]

The beginning of the next scene serves to remind us of how menacing an opponent Hamlet is considered to be by Claudius, who speaks of his 'turbulent and dangerous lunacy' (III.i.4). While Hamlet has by now come to doubt the ghost's word, Claudius is increasingly suspicious of Hamlet, and is not reassured by the report from Rosencrantz and Guildenstern that they have failed to discover his secret. He accepts, however, Hamlet's invitation to the play, and instructs Rosencrantz and Guildenstern to:

> give him a further edge,
> And drive his purpose on to these delights . . . (III.i.26)

which Claudius sees as providing for Hamlet a harmless distraction. Then follows the taking up of positions for the nunnery-scene.

The correct place for the nunnery-scene must be here, and not immediately following the formulation of the plan to 'loose' Ophelia to him, as in the bad quarto. The series of attempts to penetrate Hamlet's antic disposition are most effective if they are presented in an order of growing seriousness, from Polonius's, which Hamlet treats contemptuously, to that of Rosencrantz and Guildenstern which is more dangerous, to Ophelia's which moves Hamlet most of all and is nearly successful; for Hamlet at its end reveals himself so far as to utter a direct threat concerning Claudius (ll. 154–5). This gives Claudius a warning, so that 'in quick determination' he announces that Hamlet 'shall with speed to England'—another reason why the nunnery-scene must occur here, since it is of the essence of the presentation of Claudius that he

---

[11] Hamlet has earlier (II.ii.562) asked the players to play *The Murder o, Gonzago*, but by a theatrical convention he is to be taken, in his soliloquy, as giving us the development of his thoughts and emotions as they at first occurred: see Dover Wilson, p. 142, note 1.

[12] I follow Q2 here. The Globe, following F, has 'the devil'.

should make swift decisions, and we cannot imagine him holding his hand from the time when the scheme is concocted.[13] Moreover, the 'To be or not to be' soliloquy, which necessarily precedes the nunnery-scene, can only, as we shall see, occur at this point of Hamlet's development.

The 'To be or not to be' soliloquy has an important place in the structure. We should remember not only that the soliloquy is overheard by Polonius and Claudius, the 'lawful espials', but that just before Hamlet begins to speak we have for the first time certain knowledge, given to us in Claudius's aside (III.i.49–54), that he is guilty of the crimes with which the ghost has charged him. Hamlet's soliloquy represents a development of the doubt he expresses about the nature of the ghost at the end of II.ii. Now Hamlet is doubtful about the whole nature of the after-life, and this doubt affects his view of present existence and whether we should passively accept adversity or fight against it:

> To be, or not to be, that is the question,
> Whether tis nobler in the minde to suffer
> The slings and arrowes of outragious fortune,
> Or to take Armes against a sea of troubles,
> And by opposing, end them, to die to sleepe
> No more, and by a sleepe, to say we end
> The hart-ake, and the thousand naturall shocks
> That flesh is heire to; tis a consumation
> Deuoutly to be wisht to die to sleepe,
> To sleepe, perchance to dreame, I there's the rub,
> For in that sleepe of death what dreames may come
> When we haue shuffled off this mortall coyle
> Must giue vs pause, there's the respect
> That makes calamitie of so long life: . . .[14]

Here 'To be' involves enduring without resisting whatever blows

[13] Granville-Barker, in speaking (p. 164) of the Q2 and F scene sequence, points out that 'with the train of Hamlet's plot now about to be fired, action and counteraction can, after the discursive delays, be pressed forward together, and the story carried unchecked to its exciting mid-crisis and Hamlet's foiling and departure'.

[14] Since I do not agree with the Globe emendations in the soliloquy, the following quotations are from the most authoritative text, the good quarto. I depart from Q2 only in the addition of the words 'of vs all' (l. 83), which are taken from F.

fortune may inflict, while 'not to be' is associated with fighting
adversity, since opposition to 'a sea of troubles'—which suggests
an irresistible infinity of ills—must end in the death of the person taking
up arms against them.[15] But while these troubles will thus certainly
be ended by death, the wording leaves open the possibility that through
an epic struggle the troubles will in reality be overcome, the struggle
involving none the less the death of him who takes up arms against
them. At all events, such a person will end these troubles 'to die to sleepe/
No more'—that is, he will die to sleep no more in the sense that,
though dead, he will not be like:

> the fat weed
> That roots itself in ease on Lethe wharf, (I.v.32)

but will have for ever cast off the sloth which consists in being able to
act but failing to do so. Using the word 'sleepe' in a contrasting sense,
Hamlet contemplates being able 'by a sleepe'—the sleep of death—to
end these troubles, and is so led to think of dreams. But these dreams,
or the after-life, are unknowable and therefore to be avoided if possible.
Hamlet's thought now extends from his own predicament to that of
'the general gender';[16] for the ills he goes on to speak of are not, for
the most part, those from which a prince would suffer. Here he talks
not of active opposition which will bring death, but of suicide:[17]

> For who would beare the whips and scornes of time,[17]
> Th'oppressors wrong, the proude mans contumely,
> The pangs of despiz'd loue, the lawes delay,
> The insolence of office, and the spurnes
> That patient merrit of th'vnworthy takes,
> When he himselfe might his quietas make
> With a bare bodkin; . . .

Hamlet proceeds to identify himself closely with such through his
change from the third person to the first person, at the same time as he
refers to the 'vndiscouer'd country, from whose borne/No trauiler

[15] The epic image of fighting the sea is found in Celtic mythology. Herford
(cited Dover Wilson, N.C.S., p. 191) notes that Shakespeare might have found
it in Abraham Fleming's translation of Ælian, (1576).

[16] We are later told (IV.vii.18) that 'the general gender' (i.e. the mass of
mankind) love Hamlet—one reason why Claudius cannot proceed openly
against him.

[17] Here, according to Onions, A Shakespeare Glossary, 'time' means 'the age
in which one lives, (hence) the world, society, mankind'.

returnes', where his doubt that the ghost really is his father's spirit, a doubt amounting to positive disbelief, is given its most direct expression in the soliloquy:

> who would fardels beare,
> To grunt and sweat vnder a wearie life,
> But that the dread of something after death,
> The vndiscouer'd country, from whose borne
> No trauiler returnes, puzzels the will,
> And makes vs rather beare those ills we haue,
> Than flie to others that we know not of.

Finally, to end where he began, he refers to the question of taking up arms against a sea of troubles, when he goes on to speak of 'enterprises of great pitch and moment':

> Thus conscience dooes make cowards of vs all,
> And thus the natiue hiew of resolution
> Is sickled ore with the pale cast of thought,
> And enterprises of great pitch and moment,
> With this regard theyr currents turne awry,
> And loose the name of action.

Here Hamlet has, if not actually answered the question he asks at the beginning of the soliloquy, progressed to the point where, through seeing his own problem in relation to that of the 'general gender', he is able to analyse the situation, with its dilemma, which inhibits his particular action (taking up arms). The fact that his analysis has led him to see inaction as based on cowardice ('Thus conscience dooes make cowards of vs all') suggests that, especially as he is a prince, he is prepared to reject inaction which has such a basis. When Hamlet has, with a highly generalised mode of thought, reached this point, he catches sight of Ophelia, and she further predisposes him to action.

By implying with obvious injustice that Hamlet was the first to prove 'unkind' (ll. 99–101), Ophelia overplays her part, and immediately arouses Hamlet's suspicions ('Ha, ha! are you honest?'). Moreover, Hamlet associates Ophelia's weakness with his mother, to whom he obliquely refers ('virtue cannot so inoculate our old stock but we shall relish of it'), and, after the generalisations of the soliloquy, finds he is faced in a very specific way both with an immediate threat as well as with a situation which arouses his deepest feelings—and also his deepest suspicions, not of the ghost but of Claudius. He combines,

E

bitterly and passionately, a threat to Claudius with an answer to the question 'To be, or not to be', in his 'Get thee to a nunnery' speech (ll. 122–33) where he charges himself with the vices we least suspect him of having but which will most menace Claudius ('I am very proud, revengeful, ambitious'). The answer and the threat are repeated more directly and as specifically as is conceivable in his parting words:

> I say, we will have no more marriages: those that are married already, all but one, shall live; the rest shall keep as they are. To a nunnery, go.

This is 'not to be' both in the sense of non-existence and also in the sense that Hamlet is prepared to take up arms against a sea of troubles and by opposing end them.

In the soliloquy and the nunnery-scene Hamlet thus moves from contemplation to a preparedness for action. It is important that when the test of the play-scene comes he should be shown as ready and keen to act. The plan to use Ophelia as a decoy is self-defeating, like all the other schemes in the play, though from a short-term point of view it is successful. Claudius has received further confirmation of Hamlet's dangerous state of mind, and decides at once to send him to England. Polonius is moved to suggest his plan that Hamlet's 'queen mother' should, after the play:

> all alone entreat him
> To show his grief: let her be round with him . . . (III.i.190)

Polonius himself being placed so as to overhear what is said. Hamlet, after he has refrained from killing Claudius at his prayers, is caught by Polonius's scheme so that he becomes involved in an attempt to save his mother's soul, kills Polonius, and leaves himself defenceless against Claudius's improved version of the earlier plan to send him to England, a version according to which he is to be executed the moment he arrives. But in the long run these two plans contribute to the destruction of Claudius; for Hamlet returns unharmed, possessing a detachment of mind which allows Claudius full scope for self-defeat, while the killing of Polonius creates the conditions for the duel with Laertes and Claudius's own death.

The next two episodes, Hamlet's advice to the players and his praise of Horatio, are both important as revealing the state of his mind at the time of the crucial play-scene. Hamlet, having tempered passion with thought (in the soliloquy at the end of II.ii) and then thought with passion (in the soliloquy in III.i and the nunnery scene), is now presented as keeping a balance between them. The fact that Hamlet advises temperance to the player in his acting indicates that Hamlet's mind is now temperate. There is a strong contrast between his outlook here and at the time of the player's speech. Then he called for 'a passionate speech' and admired not the speech but the actor for appearing to be so moved by it. Now he warns the same actor that 'in the very torrent, tempest, and, as I may say, the whirlwind of passion, you must acquire and beget a temperance that may give it smoothness', though he is not to be 'too tame neither'. On the earlier occasion, Hamlet's thinking in terms of passion was based on a sense that his perception of the world was merely subjective. Now he suggests that by combining passion and judgement it is possible to achieve the purpose of 'playing'[18], which is to present an objectively correct view of things—'to hold, as 'twere, the mirror up to nature; to show virtue her own feature, scorn her own image, and the very age and body of the time his form and pressure'.

Hamlet's praise of Horatio points in the same direction. It is often said that Hamlet is Horatio's opposite and lacks just those qualities which Horatio possesses. But this is surely incorrect. Horatio is meant to remind us through his 'elective affinity' with Hamlet, of those qualities of 'blood' and 'judgement' which Hamlet displays throughout the dramatic action. Hamlet tells Horatio:

> Since my dear soul was mistress of her choice
> And could of men distinguish, her election
> Hath seal'd thee for herself; (III.ii.68)

and when Hamlet is dying, Horatio elects to follow him in death, but is prevented by Hamlet's final act of judgement. Hamlet possesses Horatio's commingling of 'blood and judgement', but in a larger and more dramatic measure. Horatio is shown as having these qualities in an abstract sense, since he is on the margin of the dramatic action throughout, with the exception of the moment when, with a temporary loss of judgement, he tries to commit suicide and is prevented by Hamlet. Hamlet throughout the play shows how 'blood and judgement' are commingled in practice. When therefore Hamlet says:

[18] As Dover Wilson observes (N.C.S., p. 196), 'playing' includes play writing as well as acting.

> blest are those
> Whose blood and judgement are so well commingled,
> That they are not a pipe for fortune's finger
> To sound what stop she please. Give me that man
> That is not passion's slave, and I will wear him
> In my heart's core, ay, in my heart of heart,
> As I do thee . . . (III.ii.73)

he is telling us about these qualities in himself. The similarity between Hamlet and Horatio is further indicated by Hamlet's request that together they will watch Claudius and:

> both our judgements join
> In censure of his seeming. (III.ii.91)

The play-scene, which follows, is constructed so as to emphasise the conflict between Hamlet and Claudius, a conflict which, though still devious, is carried on here without intermediaries for the first time since we first saw them (in I.ii), and also so as to give prominence to the long speech (III.ii.196–225) of the player king. This conflict begins in the opening lines with Hamlet's words which are both threatening and show that he is aware that he is threatened (III.ii.98–100).[19] The threat represented by the Gonzago play is increased by Hamlet's comments on it and its effects (e.g. 'they do but jest, poison in jest; no offence i' the world' and ''tis a knavish piece of work: but what o' that? your majesty and we that have free souls, it touches us not'). These comments culminate in Hamlet's exposition at the point when Claudius rises ('you shall see anon how the murderer gets the love of Gonzago's wife'). The dumb show, together with Hamlet's 'miching mallecho', fits into this pattern of sustained pressure, and we do not have to suppose with Dover Wilson (chap. V) that Claudius is otherwise occupied and that Hamlet is afraid the players will prematurely reveal his plan. Granville-Barker sees Lucianus's speech as 'the culmination of a long, tense, deliberate struggle to break down the King's composure, on his part to maintain it'. Elsewhere, he argues that a dumb show must inevitably have had, at this time, elements of the formal mime in it such as

---

[19] Dover Wilson (N.C.S., p. 198) gives a full elucidation of these lines, in which Hamlet replies to Claudius's 'How fares our cousin Hamlet?' with 'Excellent, i'faith; of the chameleon's dish: I eat the air, promise-crammed: you cannot feed capons so'. There is also the reference to the assassination of Caesar (III.ii.103–11).

'we commonly associate with ballet and the *Commedia dell'Arte*' (p. 87), and suggests that thus played (as in the 1932 *Comédie Française* revival), the meaning would be less certain. It is, in fact, dramatically most effective if the dumb show is presented in such a manner that Claudius suspects its meaning but cannot be certain until the poison is poured into Gonzago's ear and Hamlet provides explanation.

But the dumb-show has another and more technical purpose. Since the Gonzago play is to end well before its close, but more especially since a large part of what of it we are to be shown in no way forwards the action, it is desirable to have a swiftly moving presentation in dumb-show of the whole. The part of the Gonzago play which does least to forward the action is the long speech by the player king (III.ii. 196–225). The greater part of the remaining dialogue is spoken by the player queen and consists of expressions of love and anxiety together with protests that she will not marry a second husband. These expressions and protests are a necessary part of the dramatic action, but the player king's long speech is, from a narrow view of the action, absolutely unnecessary; indeed, in its well-argued distrust of the declared resolution of the player queen it depicts a state of affairs the opposite of what we have been given to understand was the case with the elder Hamlet, who was taken entirely by surprise by the behaviour of his 'seeming-virtuous queen' (I.v.46). Clearly, then, Shakespeare for his larger dramatic purposes wishes to give special prominence to the player king's speech. Since Hamlet sees the Gonzago play, when properly acted, as a holding of the mirror up to nature, we should take the generalisations enunciated by the player king—generalisations which are controverted only by the insincere protestations of the player queen— as reflecting what Hamlet sees as nature at this stage of his development,[20] a stage where he has attained a higher level of awareness. Whether or not the player king's speech represents the 'some dozen or sixteen lines' he has written,[21] Hamlet—since he arranges the pro-

[20] The couplets in which the player king's speech, like the other parts of *The Murder of Gonzago*, are written give an effect of formality and thus serve to distinguish the play within the play from the play itself. The couplets also provide an appropriate vehicle for the sententious wisdom of the player king. It is important to distinguish the style of the player's speech in II.ii from that of the Gonzago play. The player's speech is written in an inflated style which is meant to invite criticism. The Gonzago play is written in a formal and archaic style which is acceptable at its face value.

[21] I believe we are meant to see the player king's speech as representing the

duction, provides a chorus of comments, and receives from Claudius's reaction to the play confirmation of his guilt—is associated in a peculiarly intimate way with the view of life which the play puts forward.

In this speech what is chiefly significant is the development of ideas. It begins with an account of purpose seen largely in terms of passion. Purpose is 'Of violent birth, but poor validity', and through the very process of maturing becomes weakened. It is 'like fruit unripe' which:

> sticks on the tree;
> But fall, unshaken, when they mellow be.

Thus a purpose proposed in passion will end with the passion which gave it birth:

> What to ourselves in passion we proposes,
> The passion ending, doth the purpose lose.

Not only this, but the very violence of the passion will bring about its own destruction, including the decision to which the passion may have given rise:

> The violence of either grief or joy
> Their own enactures with themselves destroy ...

While this analysis of passion refers partly to Gertrude, it has a wider reference. Hamlet, unlike his mother, has not attempted to base his actions on passion alone. As we have seen, initially he responds to the behests of the ghost with a mixture of passion and ironical detachment, and in the 'O, what a rogue and peasant slave ...' soliloquy he is shown as realising in a very specific way the inadequacies of passion, while the speech to the players has provided a criticism of passion the implications of which are very similar to the generalisations of the player king. The second half, however, of the player king's speech

lines written by Hamlet. Briefly (Furness in his footnotes prints four pages of argument), the difficulty would seem to have arisen because, from a narrow dramatic viewpoint, it is desirable to suggest that the speech written by Hamlet is the one during which Claudius actually 'unkennels' his guilt, but from a larger dramatic viewpoint it is desirable to suggest that the speech written by Hamlet is the player king's. Shakespeare, wishing to have dramatically the best of both worlds, gives indications supporting each suggestion. The number, 'some dozen or sixteen', which could be a rough compromise between the length of Lucianus's speech and the player king's, tends perhaps to support this theory.

proceeds, through a discussion of love and fortune which still refers partly to Gertrude, to enunciate the view that not merely may purpose weaken or be forgotten but that a purpose may produce a result the contrary of its intention. Thus:

> who in want a hollow friend doth try,
> Directly seasons him his enemy . . .

and the general conclusion follows that:

> Our wills and fates do so contrary run
> That our devices still are overthrown;
> Our thoughts are ours, their ends none of our own:

—a conclusion which goes far beyond describing the self-defeating nature of passion, and the consequent instability of our purposes, and states the general proposition that our wills and fates are contrary. The action of *Hamlet* has already illustrated this proposition, but not so abundantly as it will in the later part of the play: here the player king's speech looks chiefly to the future. If in the earlier part of the play Hamlet realises the limitations of passion, in the later part he develops his awareness of how purposes bring about the opposite of what they intend to the point where he is able to say, 'I am constant to my purposes; they follow the king's pleasure' (V.ii.208). Both in the earlier and later parts Hamlet's ability to overcome the 'nature' to which in the play-scene the mirror is held up, is based on an awareness of its workings.

When he has learned that Claudius is indeed guilty, Hamlet, far from being depressed by the thought of the heavy task which is now indubitably laid upon him, is elated and ready for action ('O good Horatio, I'll take the ghost's word for a thousand pound. Didst perceive?'). The exchanges with Guildenstern about playing the recorder help to define Hamlet's state of mind at this stage of the action:

You would play upon me; you would seem to know my stops; you would pluck out the heart of my mystery; you would sound me from my lowest note to the top of my compass: and there is much music, excellent voice, in this little organ; yet cannot you make it speak. 'Sblood, do you think I am easier to be played on than a pipe? Call me what instrument you will, though you can fret me, yet you cannot play upon me. (III.ii.380)

These words of Hamlet do more than refer to the failure of the attempts of Rosencrantz and Guildenstern to discover his secret; there is also a reference to his commendation of Horatio, when Hamlet describes him as one of those:

> Whose blood and judgement are so well commingled,
> That they are not a pipe for fortune's finger
> To sound what stop she please. (III.ii.74)

Rosencrantz and Guildenstern are in fact earlier (II.ii.238) associated with the strumpet fortune ('Faith, her privates we'). Hamlet has a good right to see his own 'blood and judgement' as being well commingled. Not only is he able to out-manoeuvre Rosencrantz and Guildenstern (whom he will later send to their deaths through a still more obvious exercise of these combined qualities) but the very idea of 'the Mouse-trap', which has enabled him to pluck out the heart of Claudius's mystery, came, as we have seen, from such a commingling. We have no reason to doubt that, now that Hamlet knows Claudius is guilty, he could indeed:

> drink hot blood,
> And do such bitter business as the day
> Would quake to look on. (III.ii.408)

That Hamlet means this in earnest so far as Claudius is concerned is emphasised by his having to tell himself he must be restrained with his mother:

> O heart, lose not thy nature; let not ever
> The soul of Nero enter this firm bosom . . . (III.ii.411)

The counter-plot is, however, by now under way: Hamlet has been summoned by his mother, according to Polonius's plan, and Claudius, telling Rosencrantz and Guildenstern that 'I your commission will forthwith dispatch', orders them to prepare for 'this speedy voyage' to England. The counter-plot becomes formidable because it works together, if only temporarily, with a characteristic development of the action. Hamlet on his way to his mother sees Claudius at prayers. The Gonzago play has succeeded only too well. Not only has Claudius revealed his 'occulted guilt', but he has taken the matter so much to heart that he is moved to prayer not knowing that Hamlet is watching him. The whole basis of the play-test of Claudius was that Hamlet should 'observe his looks' (II.ii.625) in 'censure of his seeming' (III.ii.92). By the same logic, Hamlet must now take seriously Claudius's 'seeming'. He is thereby presented with a terrible dilemma, which is summed up in

> Now might I do it pat, now he is praying;
> And now I'll do't. And so he goes to heaven . . .

When we last saw Hamlet, at the end of III.ii, he was prepared in a passionate mood to kill Claudius; and when therefore he now enters and makes ready to plunge his sword into the murderer, we are meant to see him as being on the point of passionately carrying out his task. But in Hamlet, as in Horatio, 'judgement' is commingled with 'blood'; and in the following lines he realises, at the turning point of the dramatic action, the self-defeating nature of the act. It is a realisation for which the later part of the player king's speech, with its account of how purposes may produce their contrary, prepares us. That Claudius, after Hamlet has gone, should exclaim 'My words fly up, my thoughts remain below' does not mean that Hamlet was wrong not to kill him; it means rather that the irony whereby Hamlet has to accept his 'seeming' here, as in the play-scene, is deepened.

The indications that Hamlet is not here merely finding an excuse for inaction are reinforced by the remainder of his soliloquy. Hamlet's reference to his father's purgatorial sufferings recalls I.v. The emphasis which these sufferings are given there by the ghost, together with the ghost's horror at being 'Cut off even in the blossoms of my sin', indicate that we are meant to take Hamlet's concern in the prayer-scene with the future state of Claudius as genuine. Moreover, the later lines of the soliloquy, which Dr. Johnson and others have found 'too horrible to be read or to be uttered' (ll. 88–95), reveal a hatred of Claudius of such a degree as to suggest that it has been given an added intensity because Hamlet has been forced to forgo killing him. This intensity is communicated especially in the line 'Then trip him, that his heels may kick at heaven', where there is a peculiarly apposite inversion of the thought that by killing Claudius now he may merely send him to heaven, though the idea itself is conventional enough.

But at the same time, Hamlet must also be taken as thinking, if only incidentally, that there is something ignoble in killing a defenceless man, on his knees and with his back turned. Shakespeare's whole presentation of Hamlet makes it inconceivable that he would perform such a base act. That Hamlet considers that it would be base is, moreover, indicated in the text. The Q2 reading, 'Why, this is base and silly, not reuendge', which I take to be a Shakespearian first attempt, contains an explicit reference to baseness; and the suggestion that the act would be ignoble is included within the scope of the folio reading 'hyre and Sallery' which replaces 'base and silly' and is preferred by editors. Although to a modern audience Hamlet's motive here may appear very different from his refusal to kill Claudius because his soul might go to heaven, both are meant to be seen as the product of a highly developed moral awareness, an awareness which so largely informs his judgement.

We are helped in assessing this central structural point, if we compare Hamlet here with his foil, Laertes, in IV.vii. There, when Claudius asks Laertes what he would do:

> To show yourself your father's son in deed
> More than in words?

he replies that he would cut Hamlet's throat 'i' the church' (IV.vii. 127). Laertes' response is essentially stupid, for 'to cut his throat i' the church' would mean that in all probability his own soul would be damned and that of his victim saved, and thus his purpose of revenge entirely self-defeated. The contrast between Laertes' blindness and Hamlet's awareness is made all the greater because Laertes' reply follows a speech by Claudius in which, in a preamble to his already quoted question, he lectures Laertes on how things contain within themselves their own destruction. Although Claudius's words here are in the first instance about Laertes' love for his father, Polonius, they are developed so as to have a wider application:[22]

> There lives within the very flame of love
> A kind of wick or snuff that will abate it;
> And nothing is at a like goodness still;
> For goodness, growing to a plurisy,
> Dies in his own too much: that we would do,
> We should do when we would ... (IV.vii.115)

Laertes' self-defeating response, that he is prepared to go to any lengths in committing an act of physical revenge, is clearly compared with Hamlet's attitude in the prayer scene, where the same moral sensibility that makes him take the words of the ghost so much to heart, and test

---

[22] They can be taken as applying to Claudius's own death, as well as to Laertes' (see below, p. 82).

them in the play-scene, prevents him from killing Claudius—and thus, in not too recondite a sense, 'dies in his own too much'. (Here, as often in Shakespeare, 'his' = 'its'.) This dying 'in his own too much', common to Laertes and Hamlet, makes all the greater the contrast between them since opposing qualities are involved.

But in order fully to appreciate the central point of the dramatic structure when Hamlet and Claudius meet, Claudius not knowing that Hamlet is present and Hamlet not knowing what is taking place in Claudius's mind, we have to remember that each is aware of the self-defeating nature of what he himself is about to do. The more Claudius struggles to repent, the more clearly he realises that unless he gives up those 'effects' for which he did the murder ('My crown, mine own ambition and my queen')—effects which he does not contemplate abandoning—he cannot truly repent and cannot therefore be pardoned. This realisation culminates in the cry:

> O limed soul, that, struggling to be free,
> Art more engaged! (III.iii.68)

Claudius has, in fact, placed himself in a position where both of the only two courses open to him are self-defeating. If he repents and gives up the effects for which he did the murder, this will be a self-defeat on a material, though not spiritual, level. If he is not prepared to give up the effects, then the more he struggles for forgiveness, the more clearly will he realise the spiritual hopelessness of his position and the more his 'limed soul' will be engaged. Hamlet, on the other hand, has not so much placed himself as been placed in a position where, likewise, both of the two courses open to him are self-defeating. If he kills Claudius when he is praying, he will be self-defeated both in the sense that, so far as he can know, Claudius's soul will go to heaven, and also in the sense that he will, through the baseness of the act, have violated his own nobility of nature. If he refrains from killing Claudius, he will be self-defeated, but only in a more immediate and transitory physical sense. It is an important point of dramatic contrast that, while Claudius and Hamlet both should have an awareness of the processes of self-defeat, Claudius's awareness is inadequate, since, by praying for forgiveness without being ready to abandon the effects of his crime, he attempts to act in defiance of this awareness, whereas Hamlet by refraining from killing Claudius behaves in a way that is in keeping with the awareness which he possesses.

In the closet-scene, which follows, Hamlet is caught in the toils of
the counterplot: it is quite wrong to think that he here vents his
indignation on his mother merely in order to evade action. His feelings
about his erring mother are exacerbated because she dares, in accordance with Polonius's instructions, to tax him with his behaviour
towards Claudius. Hamlet replies to such effect that the Queen is so
alarmed that she calls for help, a call which is taken up by Polonius,
who is the first victim of his own stratagem. In evaluating Hamlet's
conduct at this point, we must not fall into the error of those who tend
to think of Polonius as being indeed an 'unseen good old man' rather
than as the willing, if not entirely witting, tool of a murderous usurper;
and we should see the speed with which Hamlet acts partly as a response
to a threatening danger and partly as an eagerness, arising from the
fact that he has just forgone killing Claudius at his prayers, to seize the
opportunity of killing him at a more propitious moment. His killing
of Polonius leads his mother to further attack him ('O, what a rash and
bloody deed is this!'), and her attack in turn leads him to his great
remonstration (III.iv.40–51 and 53–88) in which he makes her, evidently for the first time, see into her very soul (l. 89). The culmination
of this remonstrance comes when Hamlet discourses on 'blood' and
'judgement'. He supposes that:

> You cannot call it love; for at your age
> The hey-day in the blood is tame, it's humble,
> And waits upon the judgement . . . (III.iv.68)

but he is forced to conclude that 'rebellious hell' can indeed 'mutine in
a matron's bones', and that with Gertrude 'reason panders will' (l. 88),
a conclusion which represents the moment when his mother at last
recognises the foulness of her sin. Her admission, however, that when
Hamlet turns her eyes into her very soul she sees:

> such black and grained spots
> As will not leave their tinct . . .

carries Hamlet, who has been discoursing on the need for the supremacy
of judgement over blood, beyond the point where his own judgement
controls his blood. His remonstrance, like the Gonzago play, has worked
only too well, since he now, through Gertrude's admission of the existence of the 'grained spots', is led to contemplate his mother 'in the
rank sweat of an enseamed bed', and so to a passionate denunciation of
Claudius, 'A cutpurse of the empire and the rule', in which he unpacks

his heart with words just as in the soliloquy in II.ii. This causes the ghost to appear, though Hamlet, before the ghost speaks to him, is able to see the fault in himself which makes necessary the visitation:

> Do you not come your tardy son to chide,
> That, lapsed in time and passion, lets go by
> The important acting of your dread command?
> O, say!
>   GHOST. Do not forget: this visitation
> Is but to whet thy almost blunted purpose. (III.iv. 106)

As Dover Wilson observes (N.C.S., pp. 213–14), 'lapsed in time and passion' means 'arrested' or 'taken prisoner' by the conditions of the moment (circumstance) and passion. Hamlet sees clearly that passion by itself can only defeat his purpose—it is never passion that he lacks— and is so immediately recalled to his senses. Noticing the state of Gertrude, who, because she is unaware of the ghost's presence, thinks that Hamlet is mad, the ghost asks Hamlet to 'step between her and her fighting soul' and to 'speak to her'. Hamlet obeys by asking 'How is it with you, lady?', and Gertrude's answer (ll. 116–24) makes it clear that her 'amazement' comes from the fact that Hamlet, as she thinks, holds discourse with 'the incorporal air' (l. 118). The ghost is horrified that her inability to see him is the cause of her 'amazement'; and with a look at Hamlet so piteous that it threatens, by converting Hamlet's 'stern effects', to defeat the purpose of the visitation, the spectre 'steals away'.[23]

It is, therefore, wrong to suppose with some critics that Hamlet in this scene loses control of himself and goes against the ghost's earlier instructions that he is not to:

> let thy soul contrive
> Against thy mother aught: leave her to heaven
> And to those thorns that in her bosom lodge,
> To prick and sting her . . . (I.v.85)

---

[23] According to Der Bestrafte Brudermord, the reason why Gertrude cannot see the ghost is that she is 'no longer worthy to look on his form'; and Dover Wilson suggests (N.C.S., pp. 214–15) that the notion was a common one of the period. Even if this is not the reason implied at this point in Hamlet, the realisation of the ghost that Gertrude cannot see its presence may be taken as indicating to it the gulf, spiritual as well as physical, which lies between them.

and that the ghost appears to Hamlet partly to remonstrate with him for disobeying these instructions. Hamlet has not been 'contriving' anything against his mother in the sense in which the ghost employs the word, when it tells Hamlet, in effect, not to plan revenge on her. He has contrived only against the soul of Claudius, by refraining from killing him. Now, except when he is overcome by passion on hearing his mother's confession, Hamlet is engaged in the rational task of trying to save her soul. Clearly, Gertrude here requires help, for hitherto she has been presented as complacently accepting the new state of affairs since her marriage with Claudius, and her conscience begins to prick and sting her only when it has been awakened by her son. Hamlet proceeds systematically in his task. Having first made her realize the nature of her sin, and then, after the visitation of the ghost, having called on her to repent to such effect that she exclaims, 'O Hamlet, thou has cleft my heart in twain', he gives her sound practical advice on how to use 'that monster, custom' in the service of virtue. That Gertrude does, at least partly, repent is indicated by the fact that she does not betray Hamlet, by her reference (IV.v.17) to her 'sick soul' and 'sin's true nature', and by her disinterested grief for Ophelia's death, of which she gives a poignant account (IV.vii. 167–84).

Hamlet's control of his faculties in the closet-scene is further suggested by the fact that at its close he twice expresses a mode of thought which indicates he is able to learn by experience, that of others as well as his own, and possesses an increased consciousness of how purposes may bring about a result the opposite of what is intended. At the central point of the play he has been aware that it would be self-defeating to kill Claudius at his prayers, and at the beginning of III.iv he has seen Polonius in a large sense the author of his own death. At the end of the scene, Hamlet ironically advises his mother to act 'like the famous ape' and bring about her own destruction by betraying him to Claudius; and he then proceeds to show assurance in his ability to deal with Rosencrantz and Guildenstern by means of having them hoist with their own petar.

But while Hamlet is in control of his faculties during nearly all the closet-scene, he is not in control of the situation. As Hamlet has put himself in Claudius's power by killing his counsellor, Polonius's machinations have worked better than Polonius himself can have hoped. From the end of the closet-scene to when Hamlet leaves for England, a double movement takes place. On the one hand, the net closes on

Hamlet with increasing speed, which Claudius sees as the prime essential the situation demands. He tells Gertrude that

> The sun no sooner shall the mountains touch,
> But we will ship him hence . . . (IV.i.29)

and in IV.ii Rosencrantz and Guildenstern, together with a guard (implied in Q2, but not in F), discover Hamlet and order him to reveal the whereabouts of the body of Polonius and to go with them to the king. When Hamlet runs out exclaiming 'Hide fox, and all after', they pursue him. In IV.iii Rosencrantz is able to inform Claudius that Hamlet is 'Without . . . guarded, to know your pleasure'; and at the end of the scene Claudius, having told Rosencrantz and Guildenstern 'I'll have him hence to-night' (l. 57), reveals in his soliloquy that the letters to England contain instructions for Hamlet's immediate death. But at the same time as Claudius and his agents close in on him, another and very different movement occurs. This consists of the increasing contempt with which Hamlet, directly and to their faces, treats Claudius and his creatures, who consequently take on an increasingly ignoble appearance at the same time as the menace they present becomes greater. In IV.ii Hamlet tells Rosencrantz that he is a sponge, that the king keeps such officers as himself 'like an ape, in the corner of his jaw', that the king himself is 'a thing. . . . Of nothing'. In IV.iii he instructs Claudius 'how a king may go a progress through the guts of a beggar', tells him if his messenger cannot find Polonius in heaven, 'seek him i' the other place yourself', remarks ironically of his purposes 'I see a cherub that sees them', and departs, very pointedly failing to take leave of him.

Hamlet's soliloquy 'How all occasions do inform against me' (IV.iv. 32–66) occupies an important place in the dramatic structure, although it has been cut from the Folio text. This soliloquy, which occurs just before Hamlet disappears from the audience's view for the longest period in the play, refers both to the past and the future, summing up what is past and adumbrating what is to come. It is desirable to indicate that although Hamlet is being sent off to England, he is still determined on revenge, to which he is now prompted by 'excitements of my reason and my blood', and not merely by passion as in the earlier part of the 'O, what a rogue and peasant slave ...' soliloquy in II.ii. The soliloquy also helps us not to have forgotten Fortinbras when he reappears at the end of the play. Moreover, for an Elizabethan audience, who more than a modern audience would appreciate the need for Hamlet to verify the ghost's story and who would better appreciate his reluctance to send Claudius to heaven, it was desirable to raise once more the the question of why Hamlet delays. We should not take his statement that he has 'cause and will and strength and means/To do't' as indicating that at this very moment he possesses all these prerequisites. Clearly he is now under guard, and has been since the discovery of the death of Polonius. The passage in which the statement occurs should be taken as referring in a general sense to Hamlet's situation since he has received confirmation of the ghost's charges against Claudius.[24] Hamlet sees the cause of his delay in some inadequacy of his reason:

> What is a man,
> If his chief good and market of his time
> Be but to sleep and feed? a beast, no more.
> Sure, he that made us with such large discourse,
> Looking before and after, gave us not
> That capability and god-like reason
> To fust in us unused. Now, whether it be
> Bestial oblivion, or some craven scruple
> Of thinking too precisely on the event,
> A thought which, quarter'd, hath but one part wisdom
> And ever three parts coward, I do not know
> Why yet I live to say 'This thing's to do;'
> Sith I have cause and will and strength and means
> To do't.

Here, the 'beast' is taken to represent what is purely animal and devoid of reason (cf. 'a beast, that wants discourse of reason,/Would have mourn'd longer'). Hence, when Hamlet speaks of 'bestial oblivion', he is referring to the kind of oblivion which arises from an absence of that 'large discourse' which looks 'before and after'; and when he speaks of 'some craven scruple/Of thinking too precisely on the event', he has in mind a reason which is inadequate because it is one-sided, because, so to speak, it looks only 'after' and not 'before'. In the later part of the play, from the graveyard-scene onwards, Hamlet shows that he is capable, with large discourse, of looking before and after, and so is able to avoid, though only at the expense of his own life,

[24] Cf. Hamlet's 'O, what a rogue and peasant slave . . .' soliloquy which, as already suggested (above, note 11), should be taken as referring to Hamlet's thoughts and emotions at an earlier point.

being trapped by 'time' (the conditions of the moment) and by passion.

From IV.v to IV.vii the action moves swiftly in presenting the working out of the fate of Ophelia, together with the related matter of the return of Laertes and his conspiracy with Claudius to dispose of Hamlet. But at the same time, although Hamlet is not present during this part of the play, the action contributes to his presentation. Having abandoned her judgement to her father, in obeying his instructions to avoid Hamlet, Ophelia, now that her father is dead, is 'divided from herself and her fair judgement' (IV.v.85); and her 'Lord, we know what we are, but know not what we may be' (IV.v.42) is thus a poignant variation on the player king's 'Our thoughts are ours, their ends none of our own', for Ophelia now no more knows what she is than previously her thoughts were her own and not her father's. Her state in IV.v should help us to distinguish Hamlet's condition, in which his judgement refuses to leave him, from that of real madness. Laertes, Hamlet's foil, is prepared, unlike Hamlet, to consign 'conscience and grace' to 'the profoundest pit' (IV.v.132), and, full of passionate determination, he asserts the absolute primacy of his will (KING: Who shall stay you?/LAERTES: My will, not all the world), but, also unlike Hamlet, is soon twisted by Claudius round his finger.

During this part of the play (IV.v to IV.vii) when Hamlet does not appear, Claudius is faced by a series of crises. There is Laertes' return and his passion at the death of his father and the madness of Ophelia; then, more menacing still, there is the news of the return of Hamlet. Claudius appears able to surmount these difficulties. He even, as befits an adversary worthy of Hamlet, shows himself aware, like him, of how an act can turn back on itself. He speaks of how 'the great love the general gender' bear Hamlet would mean, if he tried to proceed openly against him, that:

> my arrows,
> Too slightly timber'd for so loud a wind,
> Would have reverted to my bow again,
> And not where I had aim'd them . . . (IV.vii.21)

though here Claudius, with a suggestion of self-deception, thinks of the arrows as returning in a miraculously harmless fashion. Again, we have seen how Claudius, in giving an account to Laertes in IV.vii of how love dies, goes on to generalise (for Claudius, like Hamlet, can generalise) by observing that:

F

> nothing is at a like goodness still;
> For goodness, growing to a plurisy,
> Dies in his own too much . . .

so that his words may be taken as referring, unknown to Claudius, to
the central moment in III.iii when Hamlet spares his life. The beauty
of this generalisation is that, in addition, it looks forward, also unknown to Claudius, to his death; for Claudius is to be included among
that which 'dies in his own too much'. Thus when he tells Laertes how:

> with ease,
> Or with a little shuffling, you may choose
> A sword unbated, and in a pass of practice
> Requite him for your father. (IV.vii.137)

Laertes, carried away by the idea of treachery, adds that he will anoint
his sword with poison; and Claudius, to make treble sure, tells how he
will have prepared for Hamlet 'A chalice for the nonce'. It is just this
superfluity of the means of death which creates the situation that
enables Hamlet to kill Claudius. But Claudius's 'too much' has, as we
have seen, taken several forms from the moment when he first appears
and wishes, for his greater security, to keep Hamlet at Court.

The graveyard-scene is, structurally, highly important. Here we see
Hamlet for the first time since his return to Denmark 'looking before
and after' and developing with 'large discourse' and to a higher degree
than before two aspects of his thought which are themselves more
closely interrelated here than they have hitherto been: his sense of a
common humanity independent of rank or property, and his awareness
that man's fate may be so contrary to his will that, in the words of the
player king, 'Our thoughts are ours, their ends none of our own'.
The first of Hamlet's suppositions concerning the skulls the gravedigger
is engaged with contains the idea of self-defeat and includes the case of
Claudius, if it does not indeed refer to him:

> That skull had a tongue in it, and could sing once: how the knave
> jowls it to the ground, as if it were Cain's jaw-bone, that did the
> first murder! It might be the pate of a politician, which this ass now
> o'er reaches; one that would circumvent God, might it not? (V.i.83)

Claudius, guilty of a brother's murder, himself refers in the prayer-
scene to Cain (III.iii.37-8) and in the same place tries to circumvent
God. He is also a 'politician' in the sense both of a crafty intriguer
and of 'one practically engaged in conducting the business of the state'

(N.E.D. permits both meanings). According to legend, Cain did the first murder with the jaw-bone of an ass. Thus the inversion in 'It might be the pate of a politician, which this ass now o'er reaches' suggests that the politician, with whom Cain is identified,[25] had over-reached himself. Hamlet, continuing to look 'before and after', next supposes the skull might be that of a courtier ('here's fine revolution, an we had the trick to see't'); and then, of another skull, that it might be that of a land-buying lawyer.

The final skull to be contemplated is Yorick's. This contemplation is given special prominence by being preceded by the dialogue which establishes Hamlet's age as thirty and thus specifically supports the suggestions that Hamlet is now more mature than he was before he left for England, when most critics (e.g. Bradley, pp. 407–9) have the impression that he is about five years younger. In the contemplation of the other skulls, Hamlet deals chiefly with the development through which they may have gone, and the discrepancy between will and fate which the development reveals; although this discrepancy has egalitarian implications, a sense of egalitarianism has been directly expressed only by the introductory talk of the gravediggers (Adam 'was the first that ever bore arms'). In the contemplation of Yorick's skull, however, Hamlet explicitly combines a sense of development and of egalitarianism. Yorick is well chosen, for not only is he 'of infinite jest' (cf. 'What a piece of work is a man ... how infinite in faculties'), but, though humble, he shared in life a community of mirth with King and court ('Where be ... your flashes of merriment, that were wont to set the table on a roar?'); and now in death, while he continues, macabrely, to grin, he can find no answering response ('make her laugh at that') on account of his similarity to what my lady will become. This awareness of a similarity between the destinies of high and low appropriately culminates in a comparison of the fates of Yorick and Alexander. Hamlet's capacity for looking in this fashion at Alexander helps to raise him above his immediate circumstances. The greater includes the less, and Claudius, already glanced at in the politician, occupies an ignoble place in Hamlet's vision of mankind and its manifold contradictions. The graveyard-scene as a whole is crucial for an understanding

----

[25] As Dover Wilson observes (N.C.S., p. 235), Cain was the first 'politician', since 'he denied that he was his brother's keeper, and when God asked him where Abel was he quibbled'.

of why Hamlet should feel able to stand back and await with confidence
the moment when Claudius shall have matured for destruction.

As soon, however, as Hamlet is shown as achieving the height of
perspective of the graveyard-scene, he is faced with an immediate test
of his state of mind, a test as severe as may be conceived, by the entry of
the funeral of Ophelia and by the attack of Laertes. This episode has
been misunderstood by many critics, since they follow the bad quarto
stage direction, 'Hamlet leapes in after Leartes'. There is no such direction
in the authoritative texts, Q2 and F. This absence is, admittedly, not
decisive, for there are many similar omissions, when the direction is
none the less implied in the text. But, as Granville-Barker observes
(p. 139, note 19), the text supplies two indications that Hamlet does not
leap into the grave. He can do so only at one point—upon his announce-
ment, 'This is I,/Hamlet the Dane', where the royal dignity of the phrase
is quite out of keeping with the action. Moreover, it is plain that
Laertes is meant to be the aggressor. He is the first to attack both
verbally ('O, treble woe/Fall ten times treble on that cursed head'), and
physically (Hamlet tells him, 'I prithee, take thy fingers from my throat').
What happens, therefore, is that Laertes leaps out of the grave when he
exclaims, 'The devil take thy soul!'. Since graves in Elizabethan times
were much shallower than they are to-day,[26] there is no difficulty in
supposing that Laertes leaps out of one.

We should therefore see at the outset of this encounter not a distraught, hysterical Hamlet but a Hamlet who tells Laertes with an
ironical scorn that, in order to demonstrate grief, he will perform as
well as he any extravagance of deed or word. We should not be
misled by the comments of Claudius and Gertrude, both of whom
assert Hamlet is mad. Each wishes for different reasons to mislead;
Gertrude so as to protect Hamlet, Claudius because he wants to restrain Laertes from acting prematurely ('Strengthen your patience in
our last night's speech'). The point of the scene is, by comparing Hamlet
and Laertes, to emphasise Hamlet's restraint, a restraint in which
passion, though 'towering' (see V.ii.80), is tempered by a deep sense of
irony. Hamlet's final words:

---

[26] See Dover Wilson, N.C.S., p. 239. On the Elizabethan stage, the open
'trap' would represent a grave. Dover Wilson, pointing out that graves were
wider as well as shallower, argues that we may thus more readily conceive of
Hamlet leaping into one and there fighting with Laertes.

> Let Hercules himself do what he may,
> The cat will mew and dog will have his day ...

represent a continuation of the justifiably lofty attitude of spirit which
he displays as he earlier ponders on how mortal are the various forms of
greed and ambition of politician, courtier, and lawyer.

The beginning of V.ii, which follows, has puzzled many critics who
find it hard to understand why Hamlet's account of how he has dealt
with Rosencrantz and Guildenstern should be so long delayed. L. L.
Schücking (in R.E.S. (1935), pp. 129–38) has found this delay so
improbable that he maintains that the entire graveyard-scene was an
afterthought. But, as we saw, the graveyard-scene has an important
place in the dramatic structure, and there are good reasons why
Hamlet's account should occur immediately after the graveyard-scene
and immediately before the challenge and duel. The graveyard-scene,
which must come first because it sums up Hamlet's development since
he left for England, provides an explanation in general terms why he
should feel able to wait till Claudius is ripe for death; and it is desirable
that there should follow a specific account of the aspects of his adventures
which have contributed most to the forming of this feeling. The account
of how Hamlet dealt with Rosencrantz and Guildenstern shows us
Hamlet the man of successful action, but of action which is successful
because it is sudden and not the result of 'our deep plots' (which 'pall').
Hamlet is thus led on to his reflection on the discrepancy between what
we will and the outcome of what we will:

> There's a divinity that shapes our ends,
> Rough-hew them how we will ... (V.ii.10)

These words refer us back to the words of the player king (quoted
above, p. 71) with their suggestion that intentions bring about their
opposite. But in Hamlet's account of the death of Rosencrantz and
Guildenstern there is also a direct illustration of intentions bringing
about their opposite and an illustration in particular of self-defeat. As
Hamlet explains to Horatio,

> Why, man, they did make love to this employment;
> They are not near my conscience; their defeat
> Does by their own insinuation grow ... (V.ii.57)

This suggests that so too it may be with Claudius, who is referred to in

the following lines, where Hamlet, by recapitulating the reasons he has
for killing him, shows he is still determined to carry out his task; and
we are clearly not meant to question this determination, since we have
just heard how capably he has dealt with Claudius's creatures.[27] When
Horatio tells Hamlet that the news of the death of Rosencrantz and
Guildenstern will shortly be known to Claudius, Hamlet can thus reply
with a justified confidence:

> It will be short: the interim is mine;
> And a man's life's no more than to say 'One'.
>
> (V.ii.73)

It is therefore a serious misinterpretation to see Hamlet here as pre-
varicating. The account which he gives of these past actions prepares
us for his actions yet to come.

The dialogue with Osric, who brings Claudius's message, is at first
sight surprisingly long (over a hundred lines), but it has an important
function. Claudius's messenger is a link between the graveyard-scene
and both Claudius and the duel.   Since Osric is so obviously a courtier,
without any other qualities to recommend him, he has already been
anatomised when Hamlet in the graveyard speaks of courtiers (V.i.90–
101). Osric is also connected with the graveyard because, when he first
appears, Hamlet tells Horatio that:

> He hath much land, and fertile: let a beast be lord of beasts, and his
> crib shall stand at the king's mess: 'tis a chough; but, as I say,
> spacious in the possession of dirt. (V.ii.87)

The fact that the 'crib' of one who is 'lord of beasts' will 'stand at the
king's mess' suggests that we see Claudius and the court hierarchy in
terms of a beast image which, through the words 'spacious in the
possession of dirt' (cf. 'fine pate full of fine dirt', V.i.116), is connected
with the graveyard-scene. Again, Osric's description of Laertes, whom
he praises preparatory to delivering the challenge ('an absolute gentleman, full of most excellent differences'), recalls the second gravedigger's
question about Adam, 'Was he a gentleman?'.

The function of the second messenger sent by Claudius is to give
Hamlet the opportunity of making the solemn declaration which
clearly goes beyond the immediate circumstances:

[27] Hamlet is entirely justified in dispatching Rosencrantz and Guildenstern
to their deaths: he cannot know whether they know of Claudius's instructions,
and he must so act from self-defence.

I am constant to my purposes; they follow the king's pleasure: if his fitness speaks, mine is ready; now or whensoever, provided I be so able as now. (V.ii.208)

Here is demonstrated not only Hamlet's undefeated constancy, but also his strategy, which has already been implied in so much of what he says, of waiting till Claudius is ripe, through an inner self-defeating process, for destruction.

Hamlet's sense that the occasion may involve more than a mere fencing match is emphasised by his dialogue with Horatio when, for a moment, they are left alone. Although he tells Horatio he is confident he will win the match 'at the odds', he adds that 'thou wouldst not think how ill all's here about my heart: but it is no matter'. When Horatio suggests that if he has misgivings he should withdraw on the excuse that he is not 'fit', Hamlet refuses; his fitness and the fitness of Claudius at last agree:

Not a whit, we defy augury: there's a special providence in the fall of a sparrow. If it be now, 'tis not to come; if it be not to come, it will be now; if it be not now, yet it will come: the readiness is all: since no man has aught of what he leaves, what is't to leave betimes?
(V.ii.230)

The last words, 'since no man . . . betimes?', refer us back to Osric but also to the graveyard-scene, and, through it, to the earlier part of the play. These words mean 'since no man really possesses what he has when he is living, what is it to leave early?'. Osric may be 'spacious in the possession of dirt' but he remains Osric; 'they are sheep and calves which seek out assurance' in the possession of property. We have only our human worth, but 'the drossy age' dotes on the worthless (V.ii.197); and:

> in the fatness of these pursy times
> Virtue itself of vice must pardon beg,
> Yea, curb and woo for leave to do him good. (III.iv.153)

In 'these pursy times' we do not even in the full sense possess our good qualities, for they are traitors to us in that they bring about our doom: as Adam says to Orlando in *As You Like It*:

> your virtues, gentle master,
> Are sanctified and holy traitors to you.
> O'what a world is this, when what is comely
> Envenoms him that bears it! (II.iii.12)

Hamlet's ' . . . what is't to leave betimes' is followed by the entry of
Claudius, Gertrude and the Court, together with Laertes; and, as a
prologue to the duel, Hamlet asks forgiveness of Laertes. This asking of
forgiveness, together with Hamlet's praise of Laertes, emphasises that
Hamlet is indeed, as Claudius earlier (IV.vii.136) says, 'most generous
and free from all contriving', and that it is because of these noble
qualities that he will not 'peruse the foils' and that he will so make it
possible for his enemies to destroy him. But within the framework of
the duel-scene, which can take place only on account of his 'traitorous'
virtue of magnanimity, Hamlet shows another quality, a commingling
of passion and judgement which here, unlike earlier in the drama, does
not cause him to delay but ensures that he closes with Laertes, that
Claudius 'dies in his own too much',[28] that Horatio lives to report his
cause aright, and that the future of the state is provided for.

But at the same time that Hamlet, within the framework of the duel-
scene, is successfully exercising passion and judgement, Laertes and
Claudius are, like Rosencrantz and Guildenstern, hoist with their own
petar. Hamlet alone finds happiness ('Absent thee from felicity
awhile . . .') here where his tragedy is consummated. Immediately
before the duel Claudius gives the order that:

> If Hamlet give the first or second hit,
> Or quit in answer of the third exchange,

then:

> let the kettle to the trumpet speak,
> The trumpet to the cannoneer without,
> The cannons to the heavens, the heavens to earth . . .

As when Claudius announces that, because Hamlet agrees to stay in
Denmark, the cannon shall be shot off for each health he drinks
(I.ii.125–8), the reverberation from the heavens to earth suggests that
the heavens endorse Claudius's will, but also that the acts of Claudius
may return on his own head. At the deaths of Laertes and Claudius
the idea of self-defeat is prominent. Laertes sees himself as 'a woodcock
to mine own springe' (l. 317), acknowledges 'I am justly kill'd with
mine own treachery', declares that:

28 In the pun that Hamlet makes as he forces the poison down Claudius's
throat,

> Is thy union here?
> Follow my mother . . .

the irony is clearly a product of looking before and after, and is an expression
of Hamlet's judgement which is joined to his passion.

> the foul practice
> Hath turn'd itself on me;

and says of Claudius when Hamlet has forced him to drink from the cup:

> He is justly served;
> It is a poison temper'd by himself.

The image of a shot is used once more, though in a variant form, when Horatio, in summing up for Fortinbras and the English ambassadors what has happened, tells them they will hear of:

> in this upshot, purposes mistook
> Fall'n on the inventors' heads ... (V.ii.395)

With the concluding line of the play, 'Go, bid the soldiers shoot', and the sound of cannon which follows, we are reminded of the struggle in which Hamlet has been engaged and that he has well merited that 'the soldiers' music and the rite[29] of war' should 'speak loudly for him'; but we have, as well as an image of the struggle in which Hamlet's will has prevailed, a last iteration of the image of an act turning back on the doer. In an important sense the whole structure of the drama is contained within the image of the shooting off of cannon and its reverberation; and after the final 'Peale of Ordenance',[30] the rest—for us, as earlier for Hamlet—is silence.

[29] I follow Q2 ('right') here. The Globe, following F, has 'rites'.
[30] The final stage direction in F (omitted in Q2) is ' ... *a Peale of Ordenance are shot off*'.

IV

The Heroism of Hamlet

G. K. HUNTER

★

THE period 1599–1602 seems to show Shakespeare much interested in
the nature of heroism. Comedies apart, the plays usually assigned to this
time—*Henry V*, *Julius Caesar*, *Hamlet*, *Troilus and Cressida*—all raise a
question about it in one form or another. And at the end of the period
we have two plays, *Othello*, and *King Lear*, which show a new and
markedly less cerebral handling of the qualities that make for greatness.
It may be possible to regard these as the fruits of a preceding time of
intense and restless searching (whose crown is *Hamlet*). It is my argument that this search can be seen as proceeding through the repertory
of traditional kinds of heroism, seeking human values that will endure
—endure, that is, against such forces as are represented by the corrosive
cynicism of Thersites and the no less corrosive hedonism of Falstaff.

In any view of life (literary or non-literary) the *hero*, if he is able to
make an important stretch of action meaningful to us, must seem to us
to be (in himself) an important kind of person. Bowra sums this up very
well when describing the epic hero:

> He gives dignity to the human race by showing of what feats it is
> capable; he extends the bounds of experience for others and en-
> hances their appreciation of life by the example of his abundant
> vitality.

The tragic hero would seem only to be a special case of this generic
kind of heroism. A. H. Thorndike provides a suitably simplified view
of his function when he says that 'a typical tragedy is concerned with
a great personality engaged in a struggle that ends disastrously'.[2] It is

[1] *Heroic Poetry* (1952), p. 4.
[2] *Tragedy* (1908), p. 9.

not true, of course, that all tragic actions revolve round the figure of a hero; but some awareness of responses to the created situation that are larger than the ordinary certainly seems to be required. Our lives are caught up into a larger and more violent course of action; the tragic hero conveniently focuses this for us because he is 'like us'; but he is also greater than us, an image of the fullness of human capacity, so that we cannot patronise his failure and his fall, cannot suppose that we would have done better. We become aware that even in this fullness humanity can only resist fate, not conquer it; but the vitality displayed in the struggle remains a magnificent extension of our own being, and we continue to respond to its vibrations, even in defeat.

But what qualities make a man seem 'important' enough to us to have this effect? Different actions as well as different ages involve different conceptions of heroism; the hero of the battlefield may be the fool of the council-chamber; the 'great personality' may be insufficient in terms of mere human understanding to impress us more than partially. In tragedy, we not only measure the heroism of the 'hero' (meaning protagonist) in terms of the challenges that the play itself puts forward, but all the time we are also measuring the adequacy of these challenges to represent the worst that life can offer. In the period of Shakespeare's writing around *Hamlet* it is the question of this general adequacy that seems to be at stake; three principal traditions of heroism (which I may define very briefly here as an admirable posture of the will, directing effort and action) revolve within the poet's mind, under the pressure of an increasingly vivid sense of evil. These are (1) the power to command and control human affairs (leading to deserved social eminence), (2) goodness (however defined), and (3) force of personality. They may be recognised as being embodied typically in the king, the saint and the soldier. We may begin by examining how these modes of heroism appear in Shakespeare's work of the period 1599–1602.

The long concern with plays about English history (the most sustained effort of Shakespeare's lifetime) had made prominent in his world the virtue of the leader of men who, however limited in goodness (seen as a private virtue), knows how to preserve the well-being of the state. *Henry V* is obviously the climax of this interest and must have been designed to be so for a long time before it was written. It is clear enough from the two parts of *Henry IV* that Hal was intended to be a hero in the round (in contrast to the merely military Hotspur). Here was to be a generosity of interest: 'Sirrah, I am sworn brother to a leash of drawers and can call them all by their christen names', disciplined by self-awareness and proper reverence for his own destiny. As we all know, the resulting paragon is, however, strangely cold and hollow, and men have usually preferred the characteristics that bring defeat (in Falstaff) to those that give victory to Hal. And in spite of Falstaff's absence from the play of *Henry V* it remains difficult, even there, to give full assent to the heroism of a leader who is so much the puppet of his own propaganda. Henry tells us that it is not Ceremony that is the soul of kingship, but it is not clear what else is. One who wears the public mask as gracefully as this king is bound to make us suspect the reality of his face; it is hard to trust the man whose conquest of environment is unsupported by any suggestion of struggle against the baseness of his own human nature.

It would be tendentious to suggest that it was any sense of this limitation in England's paragon that sent Shakespeare to look through Plutarch's picture-gallery of antique heroes. But it is true that the ending of the English history cycle in *Henry V* coincides with a renewed interest in Plutarch. The Amyot/North Introduction makes it sound as if Plutarch's interest was in the external histories of successful statesmen like Henry V, relating (as it says) 'the speciall actes of the best persons, of the famosest nations of the world'. But if Shakespeare picked up the *Parallel Lives* with this in his mind he must soon have changed it, reading a passage like:

> The noblest deedes doe not alwayes shew mens vertues and vices, but oftentimes a light occasion, a word, or some sporte makes mens naturale dispositions and maners appeare more plaine, then the famous battells wonne, wherein are slaine tenne thowsande men, or the great armies, or cities wonne by siege or assault.... they must geve us leave to seeke out the signes and tokens of the minde only, and thereby shewe the life of either of them, referring you unto others to wryte the warres, battells and other great thinges they did. ('Life of Alexander.')

Plutarch's interest is in the very thing that was missing from *Henry V*— the inner shape of greatness—that form of which success is only the shadow, and which can exist without the outward evidence of success to support it.

That Shakespeare was prepared to go straight to the heart of this view of heroism as an inner integrity, and set it against the public view that pervaded *Henry V*, is implied by the choice of material from Plutarch for his next play, *Julius Caesar*. For Brutus is, of all the characters in Plutarch, the one who is most clearly admired for what he was rather than what he did, a man whose action was (pragmatically judged) disastrous, but who is redeemed by the ruthless sense of duty that drove him to it. Julius Caesar, on the other hand, is not only a transcendent Henry V, the master statesman of the Western World, but a sharper image of imperious self-ignorance than patriotism could allow in English monarchy. Shakespeare is well known to have strengthened the contrast between the sublimity of Caesar, the vessel of *Imperium*, and the weakness of Julius, a body. He seems in fact to have sought to create in this play two contrary images of heroism, allowing them to compete with one another for our admiration, and our distaste. But the play does not seek to force a choice between these images; the ethical genius and the political genius face one another across a chasm of valuation that action, however violent, cannot bridge. That third kind of heroism that I have mentioned above (that of the soldier) appears here only in the figure of Antony, passionate, affectionate, powerful, but eventually (under the shadow of Octavius) morally unstable. But the play does not develop any action that can be seen as originating in the will of Antony, so that his heroism here remains potential rather than actual.

Shakespeare's concern with these varieties of human capacity appears even more clearly in the other antique drama which he wrote in this period, in *Troilus and Cressida*, which may be taken to reflect an appeal to the most celebrated fictional heroism (in the *Iliad*) as *Julius Caesar* to the most resounding historical one. In *Troilus* we meet heroism as integrity (Hector), heroism as passionate battle-prowess (Achilles), heroism as rational control (Ulysses) and, joined to these as reflector, the passionate and attractive inexperience of the lover-hero Troilus. And once again, the variety of heroic attitudes in the play points to an analytical rather than synthetic interest in this material; the play seems more concerned to set the attitudes against one another than to make any one central. *Troilus and Cressida* is closer to *Hamlet* than is *Julius Caesar* (largely because of the figure of Troilus, with his capacity to change or grow); but, like *Julius Caesar*, it lacks the essential focus of choice between its different conceptions of greatness. In *Julius Caesar* the different heroisms are left in separate (ethical and political) compartments; the play does not show us Brutus tempted to behave

like Caesar, nor Caesar as envious of Brutus. In *Troilus* the values appear
in a world which supports none of them, enclosed in a narrative which
betrays them all. Choice between them is impossible, for each is
presented as the delusion of an individual mind: Troilus' Cressida and
Diomed's Cressida are different people, the products of different out-
looks, and no compromise between them is possible.

But in *Hamlet* all the possibilities reflect back to the hero; we are
asked to note not only the variety of potentially heroic attitudes, but
also to consider their relationship within one mind, and the possibility
of choice between them. *Hamlet* implicates us as readers or (even more)
as audience, where *Troilus* can only intrigue us; for we feel ourselves
caught, with Hamlet, by the currents of attraction and repulsion which
the polarities of heroism exercise upon him. The yearning of the self-
conscious mind to be other than it is, the potentiality of choice between
personae, the doubt concerning choices made—all this catches us with a
personal acuteness that the other plays cannot rival. The central focus
which is lacking in *Julius Caesar* and *Troilus and Cressida* is here found in
the mind of the prince; his self-consciousness (especially seen in the
soliloquies) is the means by which Shakespeare is enabled to collate
and compare modes of heroism which (objectively considered) are
essentially disparate; for their fields of activity are here less important
than the feelings about them in the central observing mind.

The range of potential heroism observed by Hamlet is, however,
just what Shakespeare had measured in the other plays I have discussed.
The same norms of success, integrity and passion appear here, but not
simply (as in the other plays) as separate figures—Fortinbras, Horatio
and Laertes in this case—but as figures whose meaning depends on
their relationship inside the observing and discriminating mind of
Hamlet himself.

Heroism of the Henry V kind, competence in the management of
affairs, capacity to seize opportunity and skill to turn it to advantage,
control over passion coupled with power of passionate display at
precisely the right moment—these leader's gifts appear not only in
Claudius (whose competence Hamlet can hardly be shown to envy)
but also in Fortinbras, whose relationship to father and uncle enforces
comparison with Hamlet. The admirable qualities in Fortinbras are
focused in the final soliloquy, 'How all occasions do inform against
me', and it is clear enough from this why Hamlet admires Fortinbras
(or 'strong-in-the-arm'); but one can also see from it why Fortinbras

cannot be the hero of this play. Even in Hamlet's praise there are ambiguities enough to start counter-currents in our minds. Fortinbras is presented as all air and fire, all aspiration, in Hamlet's image of

> a delicate and tender prince
> Whose spirit with divine ambition puff'd
> Makes mouths at the invisible event, (IV.iv.48–50)

and this is admirable enough when set in opposition to the heavy sloth that Hamlet imputes to himself in *dull . . . sleep and feed, a beast, no more . . . bestial oblivion.* But what looks like 'divine' aspiration from a subjective point of view may look like culpable levity when seen objectively. The idea of *puff'd* is carried on in *egg-shell . . . straw . . . fantasy and trick of fame,* where the subjective valuation (*fame*) is seen as unrelated to the facts, and the aspiration begins to appear as the kind of expensive princely folly that Montaigne never tires of exposing. Shakespeare had made this undercut explicit enough, before the soliloquy began, in Hamlet's

> This is th' imposthume of much wealth and peace,
> That inward breaks, and shows no cause without
> Why the man dies. (IV.iv.27)

But the prince's own mind does not take up this objective valuation. Rather he picks up the idea of fame and honour as the essential element in 'rightly to be great'; he presents 'greatly to find quarrel in a straw' as the natural corollary of 'capability and godlike reason'. This is a strange line of reasoning, though critics seldom question it, supposing that Shakespeare is wholly with Hamlet in his conclusion:

> My thoughts be bloody, or be nothing worth.

There is danger, of course, in imputing modern squeamishness to an Elizabethan play; but there is also the danger of suppressing Shakespeare's human responses lest they seem too humane. Tillyard has pointed out the close parallel between this soliloquy and the Trojan council scene in *Troilus and Cressida,* and, in view of the general relationship between the two plays, we ought to allow this to affect our view of Shakespeare's intentions in *Hamlet.* The Trojan scene shows Hector defending the reason that looks 'before and after' and deriding that subjective valuation of experience that makes 'honour' the key to right conduct:

'Tis mad idolatry
To make the service greater than the god;
And the will dotes that is attributive
To what infectiously itself affects,
Without some image of th' affected merit. (II.ii.56)

The whole course of *Troilus and Cressida* supports this separation of subjective and objective valuation. And in *Hamlet* too, the Reason that controls the daylight world of action, and the Honour that means following one's dream, even one's nightmare, and accepting *its* logic— these are just as hard to reconcile. Hamlet wishes to reconcile them, of course, and the soliloquy suggests a short cut, an assimilation of Hamlet's mind and Fortinbras' action. But surely we are meant to see the discontinuity in this, even though Hamlet cannot. The prince's blindness should not blind us to the limitations of Fortinbras' heroic will. Henry V was presented in a play that showed off his capacities; Fortinbras appears in one mainly focused by individual self-scrutiny, and in this context his range of abilities is bound to seem shallow and opportunist.

He appears again, at the end of the play, knowing how to speak the proper consolations, but moving very quickly to matters more close to his heart:

For me, with sorrow I embrace my fortune:
I have some rights of memory in this kingdom,
Which now to claim my vantage doth invite me.
(V.ii.399)

We may feel satisfied that he will tidy up efficiently the remaining uncertainties in Denmark. But the power to order what has been achieved and the power to live through and redeem the unjointed time are seen as quite different in dimension; and in the life of the play Fortinbras' efficient kind of heroism is fairly insignificant. In any case, as I have noticed above, the heroism of public success is already devalued in the play by the success of Claudius and his henchman Polonius. The rottenness of their rule lies precisely in the divorce of public statement (or 'painted word' as Claudius calls it) from personal value; and Fortinbras has no equipment for combatting such corruption. We can hardly regret that Hamlet has failed to be like him.

In Laertes we meet other characteristics that Hamlet feels to be heroic, and absent from his own character. Laertes is a passionate young man whose passions carry him towards irrevocable action; and since his main action concerns revenge for a murdered father, we are obviously intended to contrast his behaviour with Hamlet's. Laertes (unlike Hamlet) is always ready with a passionate speech and a big theatrical gesture in response to emotional stimulus:

> To hell, allegiance! vows, to the blackest devil!
> Conscience and grace, to the profoundest pit!
> I dare damnation. To this point I stand,
> That both the worlds I give to negligence,
> Let come what comes; only I'll be revenged
> Most thoroughly for my father. (IV.v.131)

Hamlet is guiltily aware that he does not have this capacity. When he returns to Elsinore, to find the burial of Ophelia in execution, it is the sound of Laertes' passions that stimulates him to leave Horatio and the quizzical observer's role, and compete in rhetorical self-expression:

> I loved Ophelia: forty thousand brothers
> Could not, with all their quantity of love,
> Make up my sum. What wilt thou do for her?
> . . .
> Woo't weep? woo't fight? woo't fast? woo't tear thyself?
> Woo't drink up eisel? eat a crocodile?
> I'll do't. Dost thou come here to whine?
> To outface me with leaping in her grave?
> Be buried quick with her, and so will I:
> And, if thou prate of mountains, let them throw
> Millions of acres on us, till our ground,
> Singeing his pate against the burning zone
> Make Ossa like a wart! Nay, an thou'lt mouth,
> I'll rant as well as thou. (V.i.292)

But in the very act of competing, Hamlet reveals his awareness that this is absurd, and in the Hamlet-world such direct self-expression is bound to be absurd; nothing can be improved by it. And that Shakespeare intends us to see this as self-evident seems to be indicated both in the career of Laertes and in the parallel situation of *Troilus and Cressida*. In *Troilus* the 'valiant ignorance' Achilles, and the 'beef-witted' Ajax, 'with too much blood [i.e. passion] and too little brain', are 'bought and sold among those of any wit'. The passion of Laertes is likewise the mere plaything of the magnificently competent Claudius. Within

G

the space of some thirty lines or so, his rebellion has been scotched and
he, the leader, has become principal agent in the king's own policy.
It is clear that passion alone would not take Hamlet very far in the
battle against such a 'mighty opposite'.

Hamlet's relationship to the passionate ideal of conduct is kept before
our eyes in the middle scenes of the play by the further parallel of
Pyrrhus engaged in revenging *his* father. The player's speech describing this passionate revenge (proper enough for the son of Shakespeare's Achilles) gives rise to Hamlet's longest single meditation on
the attractiveness of the ideal—the soliloquy 'O, what a rogue and
peasant slave am I'.

As in the soliloquy facing Fortinbras, Hamlet here sees his inaction
only as sloth:

> yet I,
> A dull and muddy-mettled rascal, peak,
> Like John-a-dreams, unpregnant of my cause. (II.ii.593)

But the soliloquy as a whole hardly supports the view that the power
of passionate self-expression would give answer to his difficulties. The
words of passion come, but only in the accents of a 'very drab', 'a
stallion'. And if we call Laertes 'theatrical', what words shall we use
for the first player? The cue for passion that Hamlet hears is not to be
answered by simple violence of response. Hamlet's obliquity, his
hesitation, his awareness of complexity and ambiguity, argue him
fully human in a way that the two-dimensional proponents of Passion
can hardly be; and this, given that he carries forward the struggle to
realise his "duty" as unrelentingly as they do, argues him 'not less but
more heroic.'

A norm that is more difficult to place in relation to Hamlet is
represented by Horatio,

> one, in suffering all, that suffers nothing;
> A man that fortune's buffets and rewards
> Hast ta'en with equal thanks . . . not a pipe for fortune's finger
> To sound what stop she please. (III.ii.71)

Hamlet's praise of Horatio is warm and unqualified, and, even more
telling, is not accompanied by incredible self-accusations (for sloth is
the last quality anyone could impute to Hamlet). It is clear that
Horatio's virtue is close to Hamlet's own mind; they share that vein of

THE HEROISM OF HAMLET

University philosophising which looms out of the Wittenberg past and into the disillusioning present. But the disillusioning present has brought out differences between Hamlet and the standard philosopher-hero which are important to any consideration of his heroism. Horatio, on the other hand, remains well inside the best Christian-Stoic tradition; he guards his integrity with *apatheia* (what Charron[3] calls 'a courageous insensibility in the suffering of injuries') — what enables a good man to survive with his virtue intact even in the wickedest of times (under a Nero or a Claudius). And this means, of course, that Horatio, like other passive heroes, like the Stoic commentators in Jonson's *Sejanus*, cannot move beyond the sidelines. He will not commit himself to the misrule of passion; but at the same time as this makes him virtuous it renders him incapable of controlling any fate other than his own. 'More an antique Roman than a Dane', he believes in the Stoic's final freedom, the freedom to commit suicide; but even this is seen here as a limitation; there are better things for a man to do:

> As th'art a man,
> Give me the cup: let go; by heaven, I'll have't.
> . . .
> If thou didst ever hold me in thy heart,
> Absent thee from felicity a while,
> And in this harsh world draw thy breath in pain,
> To tell my story. (V.ii.353)

Even while it is more violently disillusioned, Hamlet's wider vision remains more freely optimistic about possible success in action and the advantage of involvement. And this is not simply because he is commanded to revenge and therefore has to believe that he is moving towards a climactic action. The whole bias of his mind is towards the passionate exploration of unknown modes of being, an exploration that draws its impetus from Hope, a virtue unknown to Stoicism.

> He falls to such perusal of my face
> As he would draw it. Long stay'd he so (II.i.90)

says Ophelia, reporting her interview with the prince. It is one of the principal ironies of the play that not only this but every exploration is turned back upon himself; the more he searches for external contact, the more he is driven into isolation. But this is not the isolation of the defeatist; only that of the frustrated man of action.

[3] P. Charron, *Of Wisdom*, tr. S. Lennard (n.d.; entered S.R., 1606), III.xxxiv.

In 'to be or not to be' Hamlet begins by taking up the Stoic potentialities of his own situation; he begins (I suppose that he is here talking
about action against enemies, not about suicide) by asking where true
nobility lies—in passive endurance ('suffer the slings and arrows of
outrageous fortune') or in action. But by line four he has left *apatheia*
behind him; the rest of the soliloquy, however inconclusive, is concerned with the possible results of action against evil, not with the
capacity to endure it.

The contrast between Hamlet and Horatio is neatly caught by the
difference of their response to the ghost. The first we ever hear of
Horatio is that he 'will not let belief take hold of him', and the first
independent line he speaks is

> Tush, Tush, 'twill not appear. (I.i.30)

He is harrowed by the strangeness of it when he can no longer dis-
believe it, but his rational mind soon encompasses the fear in explanation:

> But in the gross and scope of my opinion,
> This bodes some strange eruption to our state. (I.i.68)

It is an explanation which refers the apparition to the world outside
the beholder's mind, limiting its power to disturb:

> A mote it is to trouble the mind's eye.

But Hamlet, though aware of its potential evil, strains towards
involvement with the ghost ('would the night were come'); seeking not
so much to explain it as to find in it an explanation of his own intuitions (or 'prophetic soul'). When he decides to follow it and (as it were)
take the experience into his being, Horatio can only suppose that he
waxes desperate with imagination.

But Hamlet welcomes *strangeness* (as, later, *rashness*) where Horatio
would avoid it:

> HORATIO: O day and night, but this is wondrous strange!
> HAMLET: And therefore as a stranger give it welcome.
> There are more things in heaven and earth, Horatio,
> Than are dreamt of in your philosophy. (I.v.164-7)

'Philosophy' here presumably means 'rational explanation'; the philosophical mind is presented as a closed or a reductive kind of mind, as in *All's Well* (II.iii.1–5):

> we have our philosophical persons to make modern and familiar, things supernatural and causeless. Hence is it that we make trifles of terrors, ensconcing ourselves into seeming knowledge when we should submit ourselves to an unknown fear.

It is only the mind that is not philosophic (in this sense) that can bring a full response to the new categories of experience, the 'unknown fear' that divide Elsinore from Wittenberg.

Not only in the contrast with Horatio (though most obviously there) but throughout the play, Hamlet seems almost deliberately designed as a counterblast to the received figure of the Christian-Stoic hero. We meet him first in a situation that was the standard setting for philosophic 'Consolations'—that of a bereaved son. He is showered with standard advice:

> Fie! 'tis a fault to heaven,
> A fault against the dead, a fault to nature,
> To reason most absurd, whose common theme
> Is death of fathers. (I.ii.101)

Claudius' sentiments here are entirely within the gospel of the times. Charron has a long chapter (Bk. I, cap. xxxi) on the enervating effects of sadness 'against nature':

> it polluteth and defaceth whatsoever Nature hath made beautiful and amiable in us, which is drowned by the force of this passion . . . we go with our heads hanging, our eyes fastened on the earth, . . . turned (as the Poets feign) like *Niobe* into a stone by the power of this passion. Now it is not only contrary and an enemy unto Nature, . . . but a rash and outragious complaint against the Lord and common Law of the whole world, which hath made all things under the Moon changeable and corruptible.

In terms of these vulgate values Hamlet certainly stands condemned.

And there are more respects than this in which Hamlet is set against the Christian-Stoic ideal of the philosopher hero. The use of maxims or *sententiae*, and of a 'table-book' in which to record these and other moral matters, was standard practice for those who wished to arm themselves against the vicissitudes of fortune. But when Hamlet meets the ghost he throws away this armoury:

> Yea, from the table of my memory
> I'll wipe away all trivial fond records,
> All saws of books, all forms, all pressures past
> That youth and observation copied there,
> And thy commandment all alone shall live
> Within the book and volume of my brain . . .
> O villain, villain, smiling damned villain!
> My tables, meet it is I set it down
> That one may smile, and smile, and be a villain.
>
> (I.v.98)

As the power to speak 'consolations' is left to Claudius, so the power to dole out maxims is left to Polonius. What Hamlet writes down in his table-book is a paradox whose implications are so staggering that they make set advice irrelevant; it is indeed essentially the same paradox as confounds Troilus:

> If there be rule in unity itself
> This was not she; O madness of discourse,
> That cause sets up with and against itself!
> Bifold authority! where reason can revolt
> Without perdition, and loss assume all reason
> Without revolt. (V.ii.141)

In the world of experience that Hamlet must live through, appearance and reality, subjective and objective truth, have fallen apart; nay more, one thing may both be and not be at the same time, may be both 'the royal bed of Denmark' and 'a couch for luxury and damned lust', both 'man, how noble!' and 'this quintessence of dust'. One vision presents simultaneous 'school-fellows' and 'adders fanged', the 'fair Ophelia, nymph at thy orisons' and the archetypal wanton, 'you jig, you amble, and you lisp, you nickname God's creatures and make your wantonness your ignorance', simultaneous queen-mother and 'most pernicious woman'.

In this landscape of paradox the philosophy that is founded on the 'rule of unity', the assumption of coherence in experience and the capacity to generalise—this is bound to collapse. Troilus escaped from such 'knowledge enormous' into a subjective fury which really fulfilled Hamlet's:

> From this time forth
> My thoughts be bloody or be nothing worth, (IV.iv.65)

but the play of *Troilus* presents this as escapism, as an unthinking anger which is more bestial than admirable, perhaps heroic but certainly not fully human, and therefore not one which could be counted a full response to the *Hamlet* situation. A more painful and more difficult course of action is laid out for Hamlet (native and indued to paradox as he becomes—an innocent murderer and a sane madman); he is asked by Shakespeare to retain a sense of divine ordinance, of an objective meaning that validates experience, even amid the ruins of his own world of meaning, and to act out of this perilous intuition, to know and feel from this indescribable centre. Shakespeare raises the idea of escape on several occasions; the idea of suicide obviously attracts Hamlet; but the continuing sense of supernatural sanctions, existing and objective, forbids him to indulge his personal desires. 'Must I remember?' he asks at the beginning of the action; and pat comes the answer in the ghost's 'remember me', which Hamlet takes as his motto. It is, however, a motto for a madman, for only in the added freedom of madness can the mind 'distracted with contrariety of desires', as Dr Johnson finely puts it, *remember* the blackness of the ghost's vision while looking at the 'eyes assured of certain certainties', the daylight simplicities of Denmark. Of course, even in the first soliloquy, placed strategically just before he hears of the ghost, Hamlet is aware of the gap between the inner landscape of his own mind,

Fie on't! ah fie! 'tis an unweeded garden,

and the outer world of efficient government and family solicitudes. But this division is one which, however strongly felt, cannot at this point be bridged by expression, let alone action. 'I have that within which passeth show', he tells the court; and this I take to mean not that it would be impolitic to show his feelings, but that no expressive means of communicating them can be imagined—and again, at the end of the soliloquy: 'But break my heart, for I must hold my tongue.' This is one resolve whose non-fulfilment every critic of *Hamlet* would agree about. For the ghost provides a language as well as a resolve; but it is the language of madness.

If the nightmare landscape of paradox requires the response of madness to carry the human mind through it, then we must recognise the madness as part of a heroic struggle—a struggle to remember the evil that interpenetrates our being, even while living in the ordinary world

of action and anticipation. And this is an heroic struggle which none of
the established modes of heroism could encompass. It is not enough for
Hamlet to be *angry* (like Achilles), or self-contained, or competent,
though he must remain aware of these as potentialities in himself.
He must possess, and be seen in the play to exercise, a unique capacity
to face and absorb into his purpose every experience that comes his
way, however strange (or mad). What the Stoic would reject, the
passionate man brush aside, the man of affairs organise out of existence,
he continues to accept, modifying his consciousness to incorporate it,
and struggling all the time for purposive mastery over the chaos of
his perceptions.

*   *   *

I have presented Hamlet as a hero whom we admire because he keeps
facing up to and (however desperate) maintaining some control over
the flux of action that he stirs around him, though sometimes he maintains it only by the inner turbulence of madness. We admire him
because he is never merely passive, or escapist or cowed in a situation
which presses him all the time to be one (or all) of these. His will
remains pointed in a single direction, though his movement is laby-
rinthine. He has integrity, but it is an integrity that depends on no
exclusion of sympathies or passions, but on a fully human response to
the implications of his deeds, so that he may say with Macduff:

> I shall [dispute it like a man] . . .
> But I must also feel it like a man. (*Macbeth*, IV.iii.220)

He has passions, but the force of his feelings does not over-simplify
the actions in front of him. He even has competence, but it is not
competence that he is prepared to exercise in the service of an ideal
that he has never examined.

His struggle is, in fact, a struggle to remain fully human, and yet
capable of controlling a time that is out of joint. It is not (in spite of
what the critics say) simply a struggle to bring himself to obey the
ghost; but rather a struggle to act, which means to *translate* the ghost's
absurdly simplified command into the terms of daylight and responsible actions. He is presented by the play as caught between two equally
impossible courses: to give in to the ghost's command, reverberating
out of that region where truth is never less than absolute (and so lose

control that way), or to give in to the world of social and political truth, meaning expediency, the world which has charge of all the sane language in Elsinore. The former alternative exercises a continuous and appalling pressure on his mind; but the latter is real, and all around him every day; and both would be equally destructive of his individual life.

It is this, far more than any strategy of revenge, that marks the difference between the play of Hamlet and such 'primitive' revenge plays, as Kyd's *The Spanish Tragedy* or Marston's *Antonio's Revenge*. In these, the hero's (and the audience's) sense of the difference between right action and wrong action is often obscured, but is never ultimately in doubt. Hamlet, however, is not allowed to go on drawing strength from the certainty of this distinction, which is lost among the competing formulations of his mind. In none of these plays is the revenge simply a matter of striking a blow; in all of them it involves moving into a position where the blow is most meaningful. In *The Spanish Tragedy*, however, the meaning is created for Hieronimo by the supernatural chorus, permanently on the stage. In *Antonio's Revenge* it is created, not so much by the ghost (whose supernatural authority has somewhat waned since the time of Kyd), as by the political image of Piero as a tyrant, against whom political retribution is inevitable. But Hamlet is deprived of both supernatural and political certainty; he has to create the sense of meaning in his action out of himself, out of his hard-fought-for grasp on what is right action and what is wrong. It is this absence of external standards that makes it so difficult to define the nature of Hamlet's heroism. Hamlet is immensely articulate; but the many words he expends, defining his relationship to the various representatives of heroic conduct in the play, are mostly words which separate him from these norms. Hamlet is defined less by his own actions and opinions than by his reactions to others—to the Queen, the ghost, Ophelia, Claudius, Laertes, Fortinbras. And these reactions involve, in nearly every case, a complex response of attraction *and* revulsion; the play seems designed to prevent Hamlet from finding any external model or simple solution for conduct, driving him into a version of heroism which depends less upon acting or even knowing than upon *being*. And this is appropriate enough to a play which shows evil, for the first time in Shakespeare, and one of the earliest times in European literature, not as a class of activity but as a description of being. For the notice of what Claudius has done comes into the play only to confirm what is seen as logically prior—the kind of man he is. And for

the rest—Gertrude, Polonius, Rosencrantz and Guildenstern—evil is
something that hangs around them like a cloud rather than an activity
they engage in.

But the play of *Hamlet* can only be seen as a study of Being if it is
followed as an action. The continuity of the action cannot be ignored
or subordinated, and it may seem that the formulation of Hamlet's
heroism which I have given so far ignores the action by pursuing a line
of interest that is largely complete before the enactment of revenge.
If the central movement of *Hamlet* were a movement to acquire standards by which the final action could be meaningful, we would expect
the revenge to stem from some advantage that these standards gave.
And this is not at all evident. To quote Dr Johnson again, 'his [Claudius']
death is at last effected by an incident which Hamlet has no part in
producing'. A gap would seem to be left between the inner history of
Hamlet's mind and the outer development of the action, a gap that has
often been used to prise the play apart, and could be used so again. But
the sense that Hamlet is passive in the last Act where he ought to be
active, the victim where he ought to be the master of the situation,
depends perhaps on a view of these polarities markedly simpler and
very different from those of the Elizabethans. The age was well acquain-
ted with the stories of martyrdoms; is the martyr passive or active, the
victim or the victor? Eliot's St Thomas notes the complexities:

>   Neither does the agent suffer
> Nor the patient act. But both are fixed
> In an eternal action, an eternal patience.

Even the allegedly 'simple' revenge play is marked by this complexity.
Revenge plays very regularly move on to the plane of ritual for their
final scenes; and ritual involves actions for which the person acting
cannot be held entirely responsible. *The Spanish Tragedy* set the fashion;
Hieronimo's fatal playlet of Soliman and Perseda formalises and simpli-
fies the relationships of the central characters. Belimperia (chaste and
resolute) plays 'Perseda chaste and resolute'; Balthazar, the princely
lover who hopes to win Belimperia from her common love, plays
Soliman the Emperor who hopes to win Perseda from her common
lover. The Bashaw (or Pasha) who organises the crimes and killings
(and then kills himself) is played by Hieronimo. Thus we have the
sense of each of these characters being absorbed into a pattern which
acts out their just relationship for them, almost without their volition.
In *Antonio's Revenge*, by a tissue of ironies, the murder is given the formal

structure of a wedding masque; the ghost of Andrugio takes the role
of Master of the Revels, and tells us,

> Now downe lookes providence,
> T'attend the last act of my sons revenge.

By vesting Hamlet's heroism in the fullness of his human response,
Shakespeare has denied himself the opportunity to use this formula.
Hamlet cannot, without loss of his kind of heroism, be absorbed into a
framework of meaning outside himself; his personal quest for standards
of being cannot be dropped and then replaced by an impersonal action;
in any case, the moral relationships of *Hamlet* are too complex to be
fulfilled by a simple plot of the 'Soliman and Perseda' kind. No more
can he be allowed to make his exit as an explicitly Christian hero. The
performance of his final actions as the accredited agent of God would
remove the tragic element in his relationship to death. A similar reason
can be invoked against a final appearance of the ghost; the point of the
dénouement must be not that the ghost is satisfied, but that Hamlet is
fulfilled.

Shakespeare relies on none of these ways to create a fusion of active
and passive responses. And yet few would deny that there are elements
of all these in the final scene of the play. Hamlet is not made a Christian,
and yet he is given sentences (the famous ones about the divinity that
shapes our ends, and about the fall of a sparrow) which strongly suggest
the patience of the Christian martyr, awaiting the blow. He does not
foreknow the plot that is laid against him, and yet he is given an
intuition of it, a kind of awareness, in 'the interim is mine' and 'but
thou wouldst not think how ill all's here about my heart'. But these are
not allowed to carry the action; they are overscored by the foolery
with Osric and the merely courteous relationship with Laertes. Again,
the sword-play with Laertes is far more formalised than we usually
remember. The Q2 Entry should give us a lead: *A table prepard,
Trumpets, Drums and officers with Cushions, King, Queene, and all the
state, Foiles, daggers, and Laertes.* This, with the judges, the wagers,
draughts of Rhenish, the kettle-drums braying and cannon sounding
off, creates a ritualistic framework for the realism ('fat and scant of
breath') of the fencing-bout itself. Hamlet himself shares some of this
ambivalence. Throughout the Act he has been rather like an actor
waiting in the wings for the call that he knows will come. He does not
know that it has come when the sword-play begins, but he is remark-

ably detached from his own interests, and when the moment of truth
arrives, there is a notable absence of rant, shock or exclamation. His
mind seems well prepared for what has happened; he leaps forward
triumphantly, and with overmastering wit, into the role he has so long
been waiting for:

> The point envenomed too!
> Then, venom, to thy work.
>
>   Is thy union here?
> Follow my mother.

And in the imperious eloquence of his speech from the throne,

> You that look pale and tremble at this chance,
> That are but mutes or audience to this act,
> Had I but time . . .

with its self-conscious use of theatrical imagery, we may feel that the
personal and ritual roles, the active and the passive, have at last, however momentarily, combined. This play, no less than the Mousetrap,
has become Hamlet's. Claudius may have organised it, but it is Hamlet
who has taken control of it and made it his own. But even this, it is
important to recognise, does not bring the play to rest in ritual or
impersonality. Horatio sees Hamlet's death as that of a Christian soul,
but twenty lines later Shakespeare, ambivalent to the last, makes him
express the course of events, not as due to Providence but as 'accidental judgments, casual slaughters', as the production of chance.

It seems possible to see what Shakespeare is doing here, in this final
scene, in relation to what I have said about Hamlet's heroism. He is, I
suggest, doing everything in his power to blur the merely personal
responsibility of Hamlet for acting or not acting, everything, that is,
short of infringing his hard-won individuality. In *Othello* and *Lear* he
was to present a different final battle, a battle against oneself and what
one has made of life, where both victim and victor are inside the single
heroic individuality. Never again was he to seek to combine this battle,
the struggle to absorb and transmute evil, with the physical action to
overthrow it. Never again was he to make the final tragic movement
out of the hero's battle against an external enemy. And one can see why.
Hamlet represents an enormous and convulsive effort to move forward
to the heroism of the individual, without abandoning the older social
and religious framework of external action. And one cannot say that

the effort failed, though the length and complexity of the play are unparalleled. If we feel disposed to regret that it has not the formal unity and perfection of *Othello*, we should remember that without the convulsion of *Hamlet* the later (and unique) Shakespearian kind of tragedy could not have come into being.

V

The Morality of Hamlet—
'Sweet Prince' or 'Arrant Knave'?

PATRICK CRUTTWELL

*

WAS Hamlet a good man or was he a bad one?

I cannot think it illegitimate to ask that simple question (though, of course, the answer need not be simple); it is, I believe, a question which every reader or playgoer 'uncorrupted by literary prejudices' asks himself, and which the play as a whole insists that we should ask. But the answers it has received range no less widely than those given to the other questions which play and characters provoke; for the one thing about Hamlet (prince as well as play) on which all writers are in agreement is the unique extent of their disagreement. And disagreements about Hamlet seem to have been of a special kind. They have involved a transference to ourselves, to within ourselves, of problems which should exist only inside the play, with the consequence of an all-befogging emotional subjectiveness. It is plain that this subjectiveness, and the consequent fogging, are often wilful. Many critics have been helpless and puzzled before *Hamlet* because they wanted to be helpless and puzzled, because they found it emotionally pleasurable. Some of them have rationalised this by arguing that it is also aesthetically justifiable, for such was the author's intention—but, be that as it may, this puzzlement about Hamlet has certainly caused, and been caused by, a habit of expanding him from a specific character in a specific play to something wider and vaguer. Hamlet=Everyman; Hamlet=Shakespeare: these have been the favoured expansions—and one may be right in suspecting that lying behind both of them has often been another: Hamlet=Me. The appeal of this last is not hard to guess. Partly a projected masochism—how many of us, in our adolescent moods, have taken to our own wounded sensibilities the cursed spite and the time out of joint!—and partly a projected vanity; for that

Hamlet is a 'genius' is a conviction no less widespread than that he is Shakespeare or Everyman. The conviction, I suspect, is largely derived from this sensed kinship with our own self-mirroring daydreams; for, without that aid, would one see more in him than great charm, quick wit, a ranging curiosity of mind and a remarkable articulateness? At least it should rouse our suspicions when we see that the kind of genius which intellectuals attribute to Hamlet is precisely the kind appropriate to intellectuals: what Coleridge called 'the prevalence of the abstracting and generalising habit over the practical'. And one loses count of the later critics who have simply paraphrased Coleridge.

What it all amounts to, then, is that Hamlet is one of the handful of literary creations which have turned into something more than simply characters in a novel or poem or play. He has become a figure of myth; and just as Odysseus is the myth-character of the Traveller, Faust of the Seeker, Quixote of the Knight, and Juan of the Lover, so Hamlet has been made the myth-character of the doubting, self-contemplating Intellectual. It is only appropriate, then, that his outlines should be so much hazier than those of the other myth-characters. The haziness is inherent in the myth and in the manner by which the myth has been made, for Hamlet, the puzzled self-contemplator, has been created through the self-projections of a long line of puzzled self-contemplators. Everything about him has for long been hazy; and why should we expect an exemption from haziness in the moral judgements which men have passed on him?

*　　*　　*

For the first decades of the play's existence we have no direct evidence; but P. S. Conklin is surely correct in suggesting that 'the early prince was most decidedly a malcontent avenger who still kept the markings of his Kydian ancestry'[1]—for however great or little importance we ascribe to the undoubted existence of that earlier play and earlier prince, it can hardly have had no effect at all. The transforming of the malcontent avenger, 'often bitterly sarcastic, cynical, cruel and obscene' (as Conklin—p. 13—describes the type) into a character basically sympathetic must have been gradual. One can hardly imagine an actor daring suddenly to present a Coleridgean or Goethean Hamlet,

---

[1] P. S. Conklin, *A History of 'Hamlet' Criticism*, 1601–1821 (1947), p. 9.

even if he could have conceived it; for I doubt if audiences of the seventeenth century were as ready as are (unfortunately) audiences of the twentieth to accept Shakespearian productions which work on the principle: 'Let's see what the text obviously calls for and then do the opposite.' Gradual the transformation must have been, but not really slow. As early as 1709, it looks as if the seed of a sympathetic Hamlet has been sown; for in that year Steele is talking of his 'noble ardour' and 'generous distress at the death of Ophelia' and praising the veteran Betterton, still acting the part 48 years after Pepys had seen him, for representing *virtue* . . . on the stage with its proper ornaments'. Through the eighteenth century the debate continued. Johnson assumes that Hamlet is 'represented as a virtuous character', but is aware that some of his actions—notably his stated reason for sparing the king at prayer and his mendacious excuses to Laertes for his behaviour at Ophelia's funeral—are difficult to reconcile with the assumption of goodness. But Johnson does assume this; what he blames is Shakespeare's inconsistent character-drawing. Akenside, as reported by George Steevens, was categorically on the opposite side: 'The conduct of Hamlet was every way unnatural and indefensible, unless he were to be regarded as a young man whose intellects were in some degree impaired by his own misfortunes'—and Steevens supported him, talking of 'the immoral tendency of [Hamlet's] character'. But in spite of Akenside and Steevens, the general run of eighteenth-century comment was towards the totally sympathetic Hamlet of Goethe and Coleridge and the nineteenth century as a whole; this is foreshadowed, as one might expect, by Henry Mackenzie, the Man of Feeling, who talks in 1780 of the prince's 'delicate sensibility'. Through the romantic and Victorian years this tune is sustained, with whatever variations. Hamlet is deeply admired—more than that, he is loved, as the Shakespeare- and Everyman- and Me- identifications thicken and intensify— and as for the awkward episodes, especially his behaviour to Ophelia, these are usually dealt with by accepting Akenside's hint and assuming that Hamlet's madness was not always or altogether feigned.

Thus the Hamlet of nineteenth-century romanticism was largely the 'sweet' and angel-borne prince of Horatio's farewell. Our own age has queried this, and the Hamlet who is now presented, both on stage and in print, is a figure whose moral effect is much more dubious. In part, no doubt, this has been caused by—or at least gone together with —a revised opinion of the play itself as a work of art. The consensus of earlier judgement gave it as Shakespeare's masterpiece; most of us today, if we don't go as far as Eliot's 'most certainly an artistic failure' (*Selected Essays*, p. 143), do tend to agree with Knights's: 'In the twentieth century, *Hamlet* has yielded to *King Lear* the distinction of being the play in which the age most finds itself' (p. 11). (The present writer feels inclined to disagree—or at least would like to add: 'So much the worse for "the age".') And the fact that the total effect of the play is undoubtedly centred on the namepart to a degree unique in Shakespeare (a fact noted as early as 1710, when Shaftesbury said it had 'only ONE *Character*')—this has meant that any shift in attitude, any uneasiness, towards the play (or the prince) involves a corresponding shift towards the prince (or the play). The moral shift with regard to the prince may give the superficial effect of a return to the original Hamlet, the 'malcontent avenger' of Conklin, and it is true that this figure has been revived, brought back to our notice, whereas for Goethe and Coleridge he had entirely disappeared. But this is only superficial, this impression of a return to the seventeenth century; for although we have readmitted intellectually and recognised historically the 'malcontent avenger', it is quite impossible for the twentieth century to respond to such a type as we may imagine the seventeenth century responded. The latter seems to have regarded the 'malcontent avenger' —Tourneur's Vendice is the perfect specimen—as a type almost on the edge of caricature, to be taken at times with a shudder, at other times with a giggle, but almost never with that fellow-feeling, that degree at least of moral admiration, which true tragedy is usually thought to call for. You could admire a Vendice for his wit, his panache, his conspiratorial ingenuity, and his quickness with dagger or sword; but you did not admire his goodness, and when he came to his own sticky end you felt that he had earned it no less, though no more, than the scoundrels he himself had disposed of. A response as simple as that is not possible for Hamlet.

The question to be asked, I repeat, is the question: Was Hamlet a good man or was he a bad one? I shall look at this as it appears in most of the play's major episodes; but underlying it throughout, and decisive for our answer, are two other questions. How do we take his madness —feigned or real, or, if mixed, mixed in what proportions? And how do we take the obligation of revenge laid on him by the ghost—as a true moral duty, recognised as such by the prince himself and to be accepted as such by us, or as a temptation to wrongdoing?

H

The former is clearly paramount in deciding Hamlet's moral responsibility. When, for example, he says to Ophelia: 'I loved you not', but to Laertes, over her dead body: 'I loved Ophelia'—when he behaves to her as we see him doing in the nunnery-scene but also as she reports him to have done before—then surely the natural and immediate response of most of us is that unless we can allow him a degree of genuine mental disturbance, the only possible verdict is Johnson's 'useless and wanton cruelty'. (But the 'natural and immediate response' is not always the right one.) And a survey of *Hamlet* commentators would show, I believe, a certain correlation. Those who like the prince and admire him as a good man will tend to see a part at least of his madness as genuine; those who do not will see it all as feigned. We assume, of course, that in the lost 'Kydian' *Hamlet*, the hero simply put it on as a trick. But Kyd's own example, *The Spanish Tragedy*, is enough to show how easily that can slide into something more than a trick: for the 'mad Hieronymo' of the later additions makes an effect dramatically indistinguishable from the effect of the real thing. (Compare Edgar as Tom a'Bedlam: how many producers, how many actors, how many audiences, really remember that he is perfectly sane?) The earliest references to 'mad Hamlet' seem indecisive on the question of real or feigned, but they imply beyond doubt a great deal of thoroughly extreme behaviour. 'His shirt he onely weares, Much like mad-Hamlet, thus as passion tears . . .' (1604). 'If any mad Hamlet hearing this smell villany and rush in by violence . . .' (1609). Conklin suggests (p. 12) that the character as originally played must have had 'comic overtones' when putting on the 'antick disposition', and there is probably a relic of this as late as 1765, in Johnson's surprising remark: 'The pretended madness of Hamlet causes much mirth.' What seems undeniable is that the prince as originally conceived and played behaved for quite long stretches in a manner utterly different from his behaviour at other times. Whether an audience thought his madness feigned or real—and remember we are criticising a play, not a treatise of psychiatry—the effect was bound to be: 'This isn't the *real* Hamlet!' And for such a way of playing, for such violent alternations of behaviour, the text gives ample warrant, indeed specific instructions. From Hamlet's own 'put an antick disposition on' through Ophelia's description of neglected clothes, physical collapse ('pale as his shirt, his knees knocking together'), hysterical gestures and deep sighs, and the king's 'transformation, sith nor the exterior nor the inward man

Resembles that it was', to the Queen's 'mad as the sea and wind when they contend', and in many other places, the text is insisting on an extravagance of behaviour which could scarcely be overacted. But no contemporary actor that I have seen—and not many contemporary critics that I have read—pay more than token attention to these unequivocal textual instructions. The modern tendency is to present not a Hamlet who is at times perfectly sane and at other times perfectly lunatic, or behaving as if perfectly lunatic, but a Hamlet who is all the time just a trifle and part of the time more than a trifle—neurotic. This, I suppose, in the age of Freud, may be expected. Ernest Jones is quite clear about it—'Hamlet's behaviour is that of a psychoneurotic'— and though Knights may not accept Jones's fully psycho-analytical reading, he can begin a sentence: 'As in many neurotics, Hamlet . . .' (*Explorations*, cited in Williamson, p. 753)—as if this were to be taken for granted. It is, in my own judgement, almost totally wrong.

Right or wrong, it has had a curious effect on the moral issue. If one imagined Hamlet as a real person, outside the theatre and the play, then clearly his moral responsibility would be greatly lessened if he could be thought of as all the time mentally and emotionally disturbed. But the effect of this *in the play* is to keep him all the time before us as a person behaving, if not quite normally, then at least within sight of normality and therefore within reach of moral judgement; whereas if he is allowed now and then to rant and caper, heave profound sighs and wear his stockings down-gyved to the ankles, we forget, in practice, that this is 'feigning' and simply discount it. If—to take a concrete instance—the scene with Ophelia can be played as Aaron Hill in the early eighteenth century suggested—that is, Hamlet must quite unmistakably 'act mad' when she is watching but look sanely miserable when she doesn't see him—then his behaviour to her becomes perfectly plausible. But no modern actor does play the scene in that way. The reasons are clear. Partly it is that our greater reluctance to accept on the stage a 'make-believe' we would not credit offstage renders an acted madness unacceptable; partly that our greater sensitiveness to mental illness makes the mere idea of pretending to be mad more than a little distasteful. So in the names of realism and sensitiveness, Hamlet is never allowed to behave as practically everyone in the play (including himself) assures us he does frequently behave. And this implies a very different Hamlet. Instead of a man sufficiently in command of himself to sustain for long periods an exceedingly difficult masquerade, and sustain it well enough to deceive everybody, we have someone always on the edge of breakdown and sometimes over it. The former, I believe, is a great deal nearer than the latter to Shakespeare's conception: though I must agree with Waldock that here Shakespeare himself is partly to blame.[2] He has not completely 'assimilated, re-explained' the inherited theme of feigned madness into his own creation.

To this it may be said that after all Hamlet does complain, more than once, of 'melancholy'; he does express a deep disgust and weariness of life; and that this indicates a degree of 'madness' that is not 'feigned'. But, as B. L. Joseph[3] and Lily Campbell point out, melancholy to the Elizabethan mind did not necessarily imply a condition in the least resembling what we would call a state of 'neurosis'. It was simply a variety of temperament. It might occur in a thoroughly vigorous and decisive man of action—though perhaps (this is my own impression) it was thought more likely to be the temperament of the scholar, the meditative man. This is the sense still current in Milton's *Penseroso*, and that Hamlet was of that kind may have been signalled to an Elizabethan audience by his 'intent in going back to school in Wittenberg'. (Most of the contributors to this volume are probably melancholiacs in the Elizabethan sense—but not, I trust, neurotics.) Shakespeare does show characters who are what we would call neurotic—Don Juan of *Much Ado*, Jaques, Angelo, Leontes, Apemantus—and these are truly unbalanced in ways that Hamlet is not. They show it by an alienation from reality which breeds irremovable delusions, violently anti-social behaviour, and above all a tendency to shun and hate their fellow-creatures. In none of them are the easy sociability, the unforced authority, the capacity to love and be loved, which Hamlet shows. And as for the disgust for life which Hamlet expresses, isn't this very adequately accounted for by what happens to him? Eliot's famous remark, that 'Hamlet . . . is dominated by an emotion which . . . is in *excess* of the facts as they appear' (*Selected Essays*, p. 145), has always, I must confess, filled me with stupefaction; for when I consider the 'facts' as they did 'appear' to Hamlet—the sudden death of a much-loved father, followed immediately by the indecently hasty and incestuous remarriage of his mother to a man whom Hamlet hated and despised and who then proceeded to cheat him out of the throne, this followed in turn by the supernatural reappearance of his late father with

---

[2] A. J. A. Waldock, '*Hamlet*': *A Study in Critical Method* (1931), p. 68.
[3] See *Conscience and the King* (1953), p. 26, etc.

the information that Hamlet's stepfather was his father's murderer
and the peremptory command that he, Hamlet, should set to work at
once on vengeance—when I consider all this, I find it hard to imagine
any degree of emotion which ought to be censured as 'excessive' and I
am deep in admiration for the high behaviour-standards of those
critics who find in Hamlet's occasional outbursts of hysteria evidence
that he must be neurotic. This seeing Hamlet's emotion as 'excessive'
and irrational is part, I believe, of that tendency to expand his character
outwards from the play in which it should remain embedded; what has
happened is that because Hamlet has become the great type-figure of
intellectual *Weltschmerz*, the very embodiment of 'ich weiss nicht was
soll' es bedeuten, dass ich so traurig bin', the fact that he has very good
factual and individual reasons for feeling 'traurig' has to be forgotten,
and the passages in which disgust for life is most powerfully expressed
are read as if they were odes by Leopardi or lyrics by Housman instead
of dramatic utterances conditioned by particular moments in a sequence
of dramatic events.

    If, then, we conclude that Hamlet is not a neurotic, he is a normal
man in a situation of intense strain, what effect will this have on the
moral question? It must clearly make Hamlet a good deal more
culpable when he misbehaves, at least when we reflect about him afterwards, if not when we are actually seeing him on the stage. We can
rescue him only on one assumption—that he has had laid on him a
moral duty so stern and undeniable as to excuse any behaviour which
is directed to its performance. And this brings us to the question of
revenge.

    The original Hamlet, there is no doubt, was almost nothing but an
embodiment of Revenge. Shakespeare's play, as Conklin says, 'had
merely made more proverbial still a "Hamlet revenge" fixation which
the popular mind already possessed' (p. 11)—a fact attested by a wealth
of contemporary allusion on the lines of that in *Westward Ho*: 'Let
their husbands play mad Hamlet and cry Revenge.' We cannot tell
for how long this Ur-Hamlet held the stage instead of—or together
with—his more complex descendant; it looks as if for a time there
must have been one Hamlet for the groundlings and another for the
highbrows. Waldock seems to me in the right when he suggests (p. 66)
that in Shakespeare's handling of his inherited story 'the revenge theme
has been considerably damaged'; but, damaged or not, it is still very
much there. We cannot ignore it, we must not play down its sometimes

unpleasing effects—or play them up, given them a quality of moral repulsiveness which may not have been meant—for it is this, more than anything else, which has divided the prince's interpreters. Was he right to take the command 'Revenge!' as a true moral duty? Does the play as a whole insist that we should agree with this—as powerfully as the *Choephori*, for instance, insists that Orestes must take vengeance for his father's murder? There is a whole spectrum of answers to these questions—of which we may take Joseph as representative of the one end, Knights and Wilson Knight of the other. Joseph, accepting the revenge-ethic as the ethic which governs the play, argues that 'in a revenge play a nobleman was bound to kill Claudius, and many of Shakespeare's first audiences would have expected this in real life as well' (p. 24). Knights's disagreement is specific: 'We may be told, in *Hamlet* Shakespeare is using the conventions of the revenge play. . . . This has always seemed to me a very rum argument indeed . . .'[4] Joseph argues that Hamlet is a character 'in the renaissance tradition of honourable and noble behaviour', that in the whole play there is no 'overt statement' against revenge, and that when Hamlet accepts the ghost's command to forget everything but the duty of taking vengeance he is performing a symbolic 'act of forgetting' (pp. 37, 44, 80). Knights replies that a ghost who 'clamours for revenge' must be a ghost concerning whom Shakespeare entertains 'grave doubts' and that Hamlet's acceptance of his command is simply a yielding to temptation (pp. 46–8). Wilson Knight agrees; the ghost's command was 'devilish', he was 'a portent not kind but sinister'.[5]

Disagreement could hardly be more absolute. It is part, of course, of a wider disagreement. Joseph sees the character relatively, in terms partly historical, Knights and Wilson Knight absolutely, in terms entirely moral. My own verdict inclines to agree with Joseph, mainly, I think, because this reading seems to stay more scrupulously within the play itself and within the framework of time and form in which the play was made. Knights's reply to this is that he *is* seeing the play within a 'framework'—and the framework is that of Shakespeare's other plays written in the same period as *Hamlet*. These, he thinks, enforce a morality which exposes the inadequacy, the wrongness of the revenge-ethic; and would Shakespeare, at about the same time, write a play to the opposite effect? But this, I believe, falls into two errors. It mini-

[4] L. C. Knights, *An Approach to 'Hamlet'* (1960), pp. 45-6.
[5] *The Wheel of Fire* (1959 ed.) p. 42.

mises the difference between an imaginative artist and a moralising arguer; and it is based on selective reading. We may be entitled to draw from Isabella's pardoning of Angelo and Cordelia's of Lear the message that forgiveness is better than vengeance; but surely it is equally true that the whole moral weight of *Macbeth* is behind the personal and bloody vengeance which Macduff vows and takes on the man who has killed his wife and children, and the whole moral weight of *Lear* is no less behind Edgar's challenging and killing of Edmund. (Not to mention the action of Lear when he 'killed the slave that was a-hanging' Cordelia.) This reluctance to believe that Shakespeare could possibly have conceived a character who was 'represented as virtuous', in Johnson's words, but who also pursued revenge as a moral duty—and even greater reluctance to believe that Shakespeare could have thought such a character right to do so—springs, to my mind, from the very powerful quasi-pacifist emotions of many twentieth-century liberal intellectuals and especially of those literary critics whose preoccupations are more with morality than with history. They hate the use of physical force; they are enormously suspicious of what were once called the 'military virtues'; they do not like the idea that a poet whom they admire could have admired a fighting-man. It is this which distorts Leavis's view of Othello and Traversi's of Henry V, and it is this which I detect in Knights's phrase 'the *murder* of Rosencrantz and Guildenstern' (p. 33). Murder? Well, yes, in a sense I suppose it was; but I fancy that most readers, when they come to that word, are brought up with a shock—a shock of spontaneous disagreement—which, if they reflect on it, they will explain in words like these: 'Knights has forgotten something. He has forgotten that *Hamlet is at war*.' Shakespeare did his best to remind him, with pointed use of military imagery— 'the enginer/Hoist with his own petar' and 'the pass and fell incensed points/Of mighty opposites', both of which refer directly to Rosencrantz and Guildenstern—but I suspect that these signposts failed to show the right way because, for this critic, 'war' and 'murder' are emotionally synonymous. They were not so for Shakespeare; nor for Hamlet. And revenge, in effect, was a private war. Does not Bacon's 'wild justice' really say the same?

But could it not still be argued that even if Hamlet, and even if the play of *Hamlet*, accept revenge as a moral duty, nevertheless its execution, and the nasty things that must be done on the way to it, do in fact degrade and contaminate the prince? This is Kitto's argument. Hamlet, he thinks, is paralysed and 'left prostrate' by 'his comprehensive awareness of evil' and 'the destructive power of evil'.[6] Knights finds this inadequate. Part of the corruption is in Hamlet himself, not all in the world around him, and the play 'urges' us to question and criticise 'the attitudes with which Hamlet confronts his world' (p. 34). Does it? I wish I could see just where the play is 'urging' this. The only unequivocal urgings that I can see are those which—through Hamlet himself—are urging him to get on with the job; otherwise, I should have thought, the overall tone of the play is urging us very strongly to admire this prince, and to sympathise with him, at least, all through. Denial of this implies, of course, that the ending of the play must be totally ironic: not merely Horatio's elegy—which I suppose may be discounted (though against the emotional grain) as the words of a deeply moved friend—but also the verdict of the uninvolved Fortinbras:

> For he was likely, had he been put on,
> To have proved most royal . . . (V.ii.408)

He could never have said that of Knights's Hamlet.

Nor can I believe, in any case, that Elizabethan minds would accept the proposition that a man who pursues a cause just in itself can be corrupted by the pursuit of it. Their minds were more theological than ours, more closely keyed to an ultimate destiny of total black or white, damned or saved. *Respice finem*, they would have said, in every sense; Macbeth and Lady Macbeth are totally ruined, Othello and Leontes temporarily ruined, not because of the terrible things they do, but because the ends for which they do them are wrong. If then we accept, as I have argued we must, Shakespeare's acceptance in *Hamlet* of the ethic of revenge, we must accept also that the man who follows this ethic with courage and responsibility cannot be doing wrong, whatever mistakes or inevitable damage to others may befall him on the way. And Hamlet does show responsibility, when he doubts the *bona fides* of the ghost and arranges that its story shall be tested. (If only Othello had tested Iago's story with as much responsibility—!)

Nevertheless, it would be absurd to argue that Shakespeare's Hamlet —prince *and* poem—can yield a moral effect as simple as that of *The Spanish Tragedy* or, we may presume, of the original Kydian *Hamlet*. Waldock and Joseph are right, I believe, when they point out (p. 22, etc.; p. 37) that there are no signs from Hamlet of conscientious

---

[6] H. D. F. Kitto, *Form and Meaning in Drama* (1960), pp. 290, 327-8.

scruples about undertaking the task of revenge, and no other expressions of such feelings in the play: but is it not strange that there should be none? For both play and character are notably Christian. The ghost's speech about Purgatory; the wonderful lines of Marcellus describing the miracles at Christmas; the King at prayer; the burial of Ophelia; Hamlet's references to Christian doctrine on suicide: these give the play terms of reference much more specifically Christian than those of the other tragedies. And yet the completely anti-Christian ethic of revenge is never, as it were, tested by, never even brought up against, this Christian world in which it lives. It is this which makes the moral effect so much more ambiguous than that of a play which is revenge-play and nothing else, such as *The Spanish Tragedy*; for in that the moral universe is completely pagan, and the fact that the story is supposed to be set in Christian Spain is simply forgotten. This, too, invalidates Kitto's reading of *Hamlet* as a 'religious drama', one which shows 'the natural working-out of sin' and the 'operation of the divine laws' (pp. 329–30). Such words would apply only to dramas where the religious basis was clear-cut and single; but what we have in *Hamlet* is an extraordinary muddle of *two* moralities, one avowed, the other not avowed, but both playing heavily and continuously on the central character. This, I believe, is very largely responsible both for Hamlet's own confusions and for the confusions of his critics; it is certainly responsible for one or two crucially ambiguous episodes—and above all for that in which Hamlet spares the King at prayer because he thinks that if he kills him then, his victim will go straight to heaven. Nothing poor Hamlet ever did has brought down on his head so much critical obloquy as the not-doing of this. Johnson was deeply shocked: 'too horrible to be read or to be uttered' was his verdict on the speech—and if we believe, as we certainly should, that Hamlet meant what he said, then we ought indeed to be shocked. But the irony is that Hamlet is here behaving as he does because he is a Christian, convinced, as most believers then were, of the vital importance of 'dying well'. The pagan revenger could have taken his vengeance then and there—the only vengeance available to a pagan, the bringing to an end of bodily life—if he were not also a Christian believer.

How aware was Shakespeare of this moral muddle at the core of his play? And how aware was Hamlet that his behaviour as revenger and his beliefs as Christian were scarcely compatible? We shall never be able to answer these questions; but it is a fact that in the Renaissance the

Christian ethic which says: 'Vengeance is mine, saith the Lord; I will repay' and the ethic of personal revenge co-existed side by side not merely as ways in which men actually behaved but as accepted, one might almost say respectable, moralities. (They continued to do so, of course, till much later: revenge became duelling, a narrower code but recognisably the same.) Whether the play intends this or not, the curious spectacle it presents of two rival moralities going their ways apparently without noticing each other is no bad representation of the actual contemporary state of affairs outside the theatre; and Hamlet himself, morally divided so perfectly that he does not seem aware of the division, may have seemed to many young men of the early 1600s a remarkably penetrating analysis of a young man like themselves. It is certain that his character 'caught on' with a speed and intensity unrivalled by any other dramatic creation of the age; his presence, his attendant aura of madness and mortality, and his peculiar tone which blends wit and pathos, cynicism and sentiment, brutality and tenderness, are everywhere in the Jacobean poets and dramatists. When a character 'catches on' like this, it is safe to assume that it does so because some element in the age feels itself fixed or embodied in this character. The level on which this is felt may be entirely superficial, of no permanent interest; and then one has the kind of creation (Byron's Corsair, for instance, and perhaps Osborne's Jimmy Porter) which enjoys at first a great brief vogue and baffles posterity ever after. But in any case the understanding of such characters should start from understanding their original affinities; and one may begin to understand the 'moral flavour' of Hamlet's personality by trying to see him as he may have been seen by the well-born young intellectuals of the early 1600s. What would they have found interesting and notable in this figure of the theatre? Where might they have thought themselves represented?

*   *   *

They might have noted at once that Hamlet is a student as well as a prince—and not only a temporary, youthful student but one who, at the age of thirty and when heir presumptive to the throne, is still anxious to go 'back to school in Wittenberg'. This would have been unusual in any age; it may have seemed even more unusual then, when the division between university and world, scholar and man of the world, still had much of the medieval strictness. Here, perhaps, was a sign pointing to a temperament which did not naturally crave a life of activity but rather one of contemplation. The strange action with which Hamlet strives to control his hysteria immediately after the ghost has left him—the taking out of his tables and writing in them—and the imagery he uses at the same moment—'within the book and volume of my brain'—these may have seemed entirely appropriate to such a temperament. Only a very powerful conviction of duty would induce a man like this to embark on a course of action and violence; he was all the more to be admired for forcing himself to do it. When the story moved on to the 'delays' and to Hamlet's self-reproaches for them, a contemporary audience would not, I think, have responded as Goethe and Coleridge did and concluded that Hamlet was *unfit* for action. They would have seen, on the contrary, just as Fortinbras did, that he was thoroughly fit for it; they would have concluded—correctly, to my mind—that what Hamlet showed, because of his temperament, was an unusual degree of reluctance and repugnance rather than unfitness. For another thing they would have noted was Hamlet's fastidiousness; this they would have picked up early on from the prince's disgust at the drunkenness of the Danish court, and that would have helped them to see him, for a certain disdain for the life of the court was one of the marks of the years round 1600. It can be found in Donne's lines of reminiscence written to Sir Henry Wotton:

> Beleeve mee Sir, in my youths giddiest dayes,
> When to be like the Court, was a playes praise,
> Playes were not so like Courts, as Courts' are like playes,

and again through Donne in such a 'Paradoxe' as the one entitled *Why are Courtiers sooner Atheists than Men of other Conditions?* In expression, at least, this disillusion was ironic and 'sophisticated' rather than serious, though perhaps it was a symptom of something serious. It mocked rather than sought to reform; it would have been sorry at heart to lose its targets. Its characteristic tone was exactly that of Hamlet on Osric and Polonius—the satire of one who is, or poses as, an insider, mocking what he is part of. When this spirit ranged wider than the court, one finds a 'no-nonsense' Old Tory pose in comment on social changes; Hamlet has it in his jest about the toe of the peasant and the courtier's kibe, and below this lay a bewildered disgust, as in Raleigh's *The Lie*, Shakespeare's own 66th Sonnet ('Tir'd with all these . . .'), and Hamlet's 'Denmark's a prison'. But this was rarely allowed free and simple expression. In a manner which may be thought very upper-class English, it hid itself as a rule under an edgy flippancy, of which Hamlet's talk with Rosencrantz and Guildenstern gives the tone— quick, bawdy, cynical. It was based, like Donne's poems, on a parody of scholastic chop-logic, as Hamlet recognises when he gives it up with 'by my fay, I cannot reason' (II.ii.272); and the flippancy was always liable to suggest—as does 'Denmark's a prison'—that it might be more than flippancy. This was the characteristic mood of the intelligent young men of the time—a mood which is always uncertain what attitude to take or what pose to strike. Knights notes it in Hamlet—with great dislike—when he talks (p. 65) of his taking 'refuge in postures' and being rarely sincere; but this seems to me unnecessarily hostile, for it is a matter of uncertainty rather than of insincerity.

It is when involved with sex that the uncertainty shows itself most vividly; and this may explain—if not entirely excuse—Hamlet's behaviour to Ophelia and his mother. He has for women that extra-ordinary mixture of attitudes—some completely incompatible with each other but all, it seems, held together by the same person—of which the classic expression is Donne's *Songs and Sonets*. (I trust these references to Donne will not lead me to be accused of saying that Hamlet—or Shakespeare—is 'like' Donne; his name recurs simply because we know far more about him, he has left incomparably more lively evidence behind him, than any other young man of his kind and time.) Among this chaos of contradictory attitudes were these. There was a cynical disbelief in the possibility of women's being chaste. There was a contempt for the old-style high-falutin lyrical courtship— Hamlet's 'Doubt that the stars are fire . . .' is his mocking expression of that—but there was certainly also a sneaking regret for the loss of it. There was a habit of confident generalising about the nature of women; Hamlet's 'Frailty, thy name is woman' (I.ii.146) comes from the same stable as Donne's 'No where Lives a woman true, and faire'. All this was sometimes conventional jesting; sometimes the desperate lashing-out of men who had been really hurt; sometimes an understandable and salutary reaction from the absurdities of 'courtly love'; sometimes the degenerate descendant of the anti-feminism of the medieval church. The language and tone of the last were certainly used, whether or not the thing was believed in, to give a quasi-theological justification; when Hamlet says to Ophelia: 'Get thee to a nunnery: why wouldst thou

be a breeder of sinners?' (III.i.122), he is giving advice which many a
Father of the Church had given before him, and for the same reason.
(Incidentally, it is quite wrong to think that Ophelia's unhappiness
during this dialogue is caused by her thinking the prince is behaving
cruelly. He may be doing so; but she does not think so. She is unhappy
because she thinks he is mad.) Similarly with Hamlet's response to his
mother's remarriage. What really catches him on the raw about this is
neither its incestuousness (though that certainly counts for more than
the modern reader is likely to allow), nor the fact that it is with a man
whom he detests, but the fact that it, and its hastiness, prove Gertrude's
sexuality to be rampantly alive. When he says to her: 'You cannot call
it love, for at your age The hey-day in the blood is tame, it's humble . . .'
(III.iv.68), he is saying what he desperately wishes were true, but knows
is not true. We tend to interpret this disgust on Freudian lines, as if it
were entirely caused by Gertrude's being Hamlet's mother; but in fact
this feeling that there is something wrong, something indecent, in a
middle-aged woman's having sexual desires was very strong and widespread. It is expressed directly in Lear's hysteria:

> Behold yond simpering dame,
> Whose face between her forks presageth snow,
> That minces virtue, and does shake the head
> To hear of pleasure's name:
> The fitchew, nor the soiled horse, goes to it
> With a more riotous appetite . . .

It was part of the traditional medieval-clerical way of feeling about
sex; it is given savagely disgusted expression in Dunbar's *Twa Mariit
Wemen and the Wedo*, and the Wyf of Bath's prologue is one long
comic refutation of it. And even in our own time, only a few years
ago, a Pope gave it as his opinion that though widows were allowed to
remarry, it would be better if they didn't. A reader of the twentieth
century is certainly entitled to feel, if he wishes, that the responses to
sex which Hamlet's behaviour seems to show were deplorable and
wrong; I do not think he is entitled to conclude that Hamlet himself
was peculiarly culpable or unbalanced, or that Hamlet's creator intended him to appear so.

In some other things less vital, the young men of the time might have
found themselves in Hamlet. There is his lively, intimate, very knowledgeable interest in the popular theatre—yet it is an interest spiced

with the highbrow's mockery. When he says: 'The adventurous knight shall use his foil and target; the lover shall not sigh gratis; the humorous man shall end his part in peace; the clown shall make those laugh . . . etc.' (II.ii.334), we are prepared for his preferring the play which 'pleas'd not the general' but did please Hamlet himself and an élite of 'others'; and the combination is exactly that of—shall we say the egghead of 1963 who professes an admiration for *Coronation Street*?—well, certainly, it is exactly the combination of the young gentlemen of the Inns of Court round the year 1600. So, I suspect, is Hamlet's attitude to war and the military qualities. This comes out, of course, in the scene (IV.iv) in which he meets the captain of Fortinbras's army. His response to that is curious. It is partly critical, that all this courage and all this bloodshed should be for what is not worth more than an 'eggshell'. But together with the criticism, and apparently overcoming it, are agreement and admiration; for the action of this army is seen as an example of the use of 'that capability and god-like reason' which Hamlet feels he himself is not using. Knights is quite sure (p. 81) not only that Hamlet himself is wrong to feel this, but that Hamlet's creator agreed and intended us to agree. It is possible, though personally I doubt it, for I do not think that Shakespeare regarded his creations in the critical evaluating way suggested by Knights's phrase for Hamlet's soliloquy in this scene; it 'contains', he thinks, 'a firm though implicit placing judgement'—of Shakespeare on Hamlet, that is, as if Shakespeare were a contributor to *Scrutiny* and Hamlet were Dylan Thomas. But what I do feel clear about is that Hamlet is here responding exactly as the young volunteers who pestered Elizabeth's military expeditions responded; he dreams of a military simplicity and certainty as solution for the complexities of his problem just as Donne, in *The Calme*, meditated on what might have been his reasons for joining the Islands Voyage:

> Whether a rotten state, and hope of gaine,
> Or to disuse mee from the queasie paine
> Of being belov'd, and loving, or the thirst
> Of honour, or faire death, out pusht mee first . . .

One of the odd things about Hamlet's character—and one of the things which makes it so often possible to compare him with a real person such as Donne—is that in practice we continually forget that *he is a prince*. Something seems to have almost obliterated that great difference between royalty and the rest which real life, at that time, certainly preserved and which is normally visible even in the Shakespearian drama itself. We do not have with Hamlet, as we do with Prince Hal, a deliberate 'stepping-down', and in fact we are never able to forget Prince Hal's rank, for he himself never forgets it. It is a matter with Hamlet of a relaxed informality of manner and an easy colloquialism of tone; they contrast very strongly, as I am sure they are meant to, with the formality of Claudius, the affectations of Osric, and the pomposity of Polonius. A great deal of Hamlet's attractiveness has always depended on this; all through the centuries readers and spectators alike have felt for him, as for no other character, I suspect, a delusion of equality and intimacy, and they have been all the more pleased with this delusion because they remembered, at moments, whom they were feeling it for. (We can be snobs in our imaginations just as much as in our lives.) We nowadays may take this rather for granted; but for Hamlet's first audiences it must have come as something of a shock and a great deal of a delight. He must have seemed in this respect a remarkably, perhaps a daringly, 'contemporary' creation, an embodiment of that phenomenon which men in the last years of Elizabeth and first years of James were all aware of, whether they approved of it or not: a loosening of the old-style formality, a relaxing of the starched Tudor stiffness. There is no need to believe the old story that Polonius was intended as a caricature of Burghley in order to feel that he could well have been played so as to suggest it.

Hamlet, then, was a very 'contemporary' character. But this character Shakespeare put in a setting almost as incongruous as he could have found. Whether he did this knowingly or not, no one can say. I should say not; it was rather the inherent effect of taking over an old story for new times. But I am sure that it is here, in this continuous incongruity between central character and setting, that the clue lies to the moral problems which play and character present. For, first of all, he is made a prince, heir presumptive to the throne; the would-be scholar, the quick-witted affable talker, is put in a position where tradition required of him gravity, haughtiness, aloofness. (Of which expected distance Polonius's warning-off of Ophelia is a symptom: 'Lord Hamlet is a Prince, out of thy star' (II.ii.141).) And then he is placed, this fastidious hater of debauchery and lover of the theatre, in a court peculiarly sombre, sordid and tasteless; and there, against his expressed desire, he is forced to remain. There comes to him next a direct supernatural intervention—one which he must and does believe in (for under his flippant wit he is a believing Christian) but which shocks him with doubts and questions as it would not have shocked the credulity of earlier ages or simpler types. And finally, there is imposed on him the demand of Revenge. This he accepts as a moral duty, for he has enough in him of the inherited concept of a prince's and a gentleman's honour; but though his reason and his conscience tell him Yes, his nerves tell him No. It is not that he cannot do it; he can, and knows he can. Nor is it that he does not want to through some delicate reluctance to kill in general or some Freudian reluctance to kill his 'father-uncle' in particular. It is the whole life of action, violence, intrigue and public duty that he is reluctant to enter; he would rather be in Wittenberg, with his books. What he really is, is a conscript in a war. He has done things, as we all do in wars, he would rather not have done; but he believes it to be a just war, and all in all, he has borne himself well. That this was how Shakespeare saw it, the ending of the play convinces me; for why else should

> The soldier's music and the rite of war
> Speak loudly for him?

VI

The Politics in 'Hamlet' and 'The World of the Play'

E. A. J. HONIGMANN

★

'THE constitution of the state of Denmark is vital to our conception of the drama as a whole.' With these words J. Dover Wilson embarked upon one of the most influential studies of *Hamlet* of the present century, and within a few pages indicated how the politics of the play strike deep into its moral structure: 'Hamlet was the rightful heir to the throne and Claudius a usurper', and 'usurpation is one of the main factors in the plot'. For, in Wilson's eyes, 'Hamlet is an English prince, the court of Elsinore is modelled upon the English court, and the Danish constitution that of England under the Virgin Queen'.

Behind these far-reaching claims there lies an assumption to which many modern critics still subscribe: that Shakespeare's plays, whatever part of the world they are set in, always portray England and Englishmen:

> Nothing is more certain than that Shakespeare has England chiefly in mind in other plays. The scene may be Rome, Venice, Messina, Vienna, Athens, Verona, or what not, and the game of make-believe may be kept alive by a splash of local colour here and there, but the characters, their habits, their outlook, and even generally their costumes are 'mere English'.

A most misleading doctrine, for it reduces the creative imagination to something uncomfortably close to photography. And a doctrine very easily exploded, for who would call Othello, or Shylock, or Ariel and Caliban, 'mere English'? Or, to take a further step, Cleopatra, Iachimo, or Coriolanus? Even if Shakespeare never left the shores of his native England, there existed opportunities in London for meeting Moors and Jews and Indians—and even fairies. Anyone as interested as the

J

author of *Henry V* in the 'foreignness' of foreigners could also interrogate travellers, or dip into the publications of the many predecessors of Hakluyt and Coryate. It is therefore important not to overemphasise the anachronisms and 'Elizabethanisms' in Shakespeare's plays—and of course there are many—at the expense of the often all-pervasive special colouring or foreign flavour which, acting more delicately, will be more easily missed.

At the very time when Wilson laboured at his indispensable books on *Hamlet* a new critical method was being explored, a method which has probably put an end to the once-popular identification of Shakespeare's 'play-worlds' and contemporary England. Wilson Knight described 'the *Lear* Universe' and 'the *Othello* Music', Miss Spurgeon explained 'the influence and presence of the moon' in *A Midsummer Night's Dream*, Charlton concentrated on the special moral qualities of the various tragedies, and innumerable books and articles helped to demonstrate that for every one of his mature plays Shakespeare created a unique 'world' or 'universe' or 'pattern'—through the imagery, the names, the local colour, the 'address to the world', the manipulation of ideas, and in a thousand other ways. The distinctness of each play-world, we now know, is not just a matter of atmosphere: it is an organic principle that extends to the personal relationships of the characters, to social organisation—and even, when the subject comes sufficiently into the foreground, to politics.

According to Wilson—and I think that he is right—the politics in *Hamlet* occupy part of the foreground, since 'the constitution of the state of Denmark is vital to our conception of the drama as a whole'. If so, it seems unlikely that the Danish constitution will simply reproduce that 'of England under the Virgin Queen'—for the form of the play will translate its materials to satisfy its individual needs.

To put it at its simplest, we have to ask whether Hamlet was 'the rightful heir to the throne' after his father's death, or whether an elective system made it possible for Claudius to become king quite legally. A great deal hangs upon this point, as Belleforest's Hamlet explained to his mother:

if I lay handes upon Fengon [=Claudius], it will neither be fellonie nor treason, hee being neither my king nor my lord, but I shall justly punish him as my subject, that hath disloyaly behaved himselfe against his lord and soveraigne prince.[1]

Belleforest's Hamlet took it for granted not only that he was 'the rightful heir to the throne' but that he was king *de jure*, and that Fengon, who occupied the throne, was an impostor. No such certainty is entertained by Shakespeare's hero, who admits that he expected an election after his father's death: Claudius, he says, 'Popp'd in between th' election and my hopes' (V.ii.65). As I read it, this means that Hamlet does not regard himself as the only possible successor to his father. Wilson, on the other hand, held that 'however it be looked at, the elective throne in Shakespeare's Denmark is a mirage'.

'There is no question of an elective monarchy in either Saxo or Belleforest', Wilson assures us, for 'Amleth's father and uncle were governors or earls of Jutland appointed by the King of Denmark'. In fact Hamlet's father and uncle, and he himself, are frequently referred to as kings by Belleforest, and the subject of their *election* arises at a critical juncture in the story which Shakespeare—unlike his modern commentators—will hardly have overlooked. Justifying the violent death of his uncle, Hamlet addressed a lengthy oration to the Danes (subtitled by Belleforest 'Harangue d'Amleth aux Danoys') and concluded with the appeal 'chuse me your king, if you think me worthy of the place' ('meslisez pour Roy, s'il vous semble que j'en sois digne'). 'This oration of the yong prince so mooved the harts of the Danes . . . [that] al with one consent proclaimed him king of Jutie and Chersonnese, at this present the proper country of Denmarke' (pp. 280–3).

It was a serious misrepresentation to say that 'there is no question of an elective monarchy' in the sources. In his valuable but, I believe, misdirected opening chapter Wilson also failed to bring forward some relevant evidence from within the play. If 'Shakespeare and his audience thought of the constitution of Denmark in English terms', how did they think of that of Norway? In Norway, as in Denmark, a king's son was passed over in the succession in favour of his uncle[2]: is old Norway, 'impotent and bed-rid', another usurper—and young Fortinbras a second Hamlet, a prince too 'tender' to seize his own? Admittedly

---

[1] *The Sources of 'Hamlet': With Essay on the Legend*, ed. Israel Gollancz (1926), pp. 225–7. All my quotations from Belleforest are taken from Gollancz's reprint of the seventeenth-century English translation, except where there is a special reason for quoting the French original (also reprinted by Gollancz), which was either Shakespeare's immediate source, or the source of his source.

[2] A. C. Bradley noticed this 'curious parallelism' (*Shakespearean Tragedy*, 1904, p. 90).

Fortinbras will have been a child when his father died (Hamlet himself was born on that very day, and Fortinbras will hardly be much older than Hamlet[3])—but in countries where primogeniture is the rule even the unborn son of a deceased king would take precedence over his uncle. Clearly in the Scandinavian 'world' of *Hamlet* a son did not always succeed his father: Fortinbras, who could 'find quarrel in a straw', would have proceeded with his lawless resolutes against his uncle, rather than against Denmark and Poland, if he thought himself cheated of his inheritance.

What Fortinbras, a very minor character, would or should have done at a point in the story lying well outside the play will seem to some readers totally irrelevant. Not so: though Bradley and his predecessors have been rebuked for speculating about characters and events 'outside the play', the reaction against conscientious prodding into the darker corners of Shakespeare's dramaturgy has been carried to quite un-healthy extremes. For, as one more recent critic contended, we must often imagine incidents that occur off-stage between scenes:

> some attention to these periods *in absentia* is absolutely necessary to an understanding of the scenes actually shown. We are justified in trying to fill these lacunae in the action so long as our observations have some basis in the play itself; only when we speculate upon possibilities not indicated in the text do we forget the author's intention. . . .[4]

I would extend the range of this counter-argument to include events before the commencement of the play 'so long as our observations have some basis in the play itself' and are 'indicated in the text'. After all, why should events taking place off-stage before Act II be thought more pertinent, and more legitimately discussible, than events taking place off-stage before Act I? Despite all the sarcasms at Bradley's expense he was surely right, and his opponents wrong, to wonder about 'Hamlet as he was just before his father's death', and 'the real Hamlet'.[5] Shakespeare alludes again and again to Hamlet's early life and behaviour because the character of the prince is his centre of interest: the 'real

[3] Cf. V.i.153–62. Both princes are given the same epithet—'young Fortinbras', 'young Hamlet'—and the play generally suggests that they are of roughly the same age.

[4] Hankins, p. 11.

[5] Bradley, *op. cit.*, pp. 103, 107, 108, etc.

Hamlet', as distinct from the distraught Hamlet presented more directly to our view, is one of the cardinal facts of the play.

I am forced to say a word in defence of Bradley because 'the politics in *Hamlet*' invite Bradley's critical method. Shakespeare 'plants' constitutional ideas which suggest Hamlet's lost opportunities and thus have an obvious bearing on the play's main action—as on its moral texture. What is more, these ideas are worked into a coherent picture, and one which seems to be Shakespeare's invention, not just a straight transference from the sources. Even though some of them lie, in a superficial sense, 'outside the play', we may insist that they 'have some basis in the play itself' and deserve scrutiny.

For a brief example of Shakespeare's adept 'planting' I return to the Norwegian succession. That Old Fortinbras was actually King of Norway emerges only once:

> Such was the very armour he had on
> When he the ambitious Norway combated; (I.i.60)

'Norway' must refer to the king, especially as Shakespeare immediately reverts to the Norwegian's ambition and challenge:

> Fortinbras of Norway,
> Thereto prick'd on by a most emulate pride, (I.i.82)

In the next scene we learn that 'Norway', the present sovereign, is 'uncle of young Fortinbras' (I.ii.28)—which completes the 'Hamlet parallel'. Shakespeare, however, limned in the Norwegian dynasty as an addition to Belleforest who, it will be remembered, mentioned the 'battaile' between 'Collere, king of Norway' (=Old Fortinbras) and 'Horvendile' (= Old Hamlet), but gave Collere neither a son nor a brother. In adding these two, Shakespeare, it may seem, also added an inconsistency, in so far as he states (i) that the loser of the Old Fortinbras-Old Hamlet combat should 'forfeit, with his life, all those his lands Which he stood seized of' (I.i.88); (ii) Old Fortinbras was defeated and in fact Norway was dispossessed of 'those foresaid lands' (I.i.103); (iii) yet the kingdom of Norway fell, apparently, not to the crown of Denmark but remained under the rule of the Fortinbras family. Nevertheless, despite his indifference to inconsistencies elsewhere, Shakespeare left none in this case—though he might be convicted of 'ambiguity'. Editors usually gloss 'seized of' (in 'all those his lands Which he stood seized of') as 'possessed of', yet it appears from Belleforest that a less comprehensive notion may be intended. In the source the Norwegian king envies the Dane's reputation as the greatest pirate of the seas, and for this reason challenges him, 'with conditions, that hee which should be vanquished should loose all the riches he had in his ship' (p. 183). Shakespeare dropped the piracy motif, but his 'seized of' could also refer to lands seized by the two kings in war— and then would not include the whole of Norway.

It suited Shakespeare to build up the 'Fortinbras story', for a number of excellent reasons. The open rivalry between Old Fortinbras and Old Hamlet contrasts with Claudius' secret rivalry; young Fortinbras, like Hamlet, lost his father by violent means, as also lands which he expected to possess, and circumstances compel him to delay taking the law into his own hands; the political issue of the succession is the same in Norway and Denmark.[6] To make so much of the bare mention of the 'battaile' of the two kings Shakespeare had to plan ahead very carefully: his 'plot' hangs together, and therefore we have to take account of it. The possibility of 'electing' a king also receives a bare mention in Belleforest—and similarly becomes something much more important, part of a network of 'political' cross-references woven through the moral fabric of the tragedy. Wilson, of course, denied this. Having missed the crucial passage in Belleforest he argued that the allusions to an 'elective' constitution in Denmark come far too late in the play and cannot mean what to the simple-minded reader or audience they seem to mean:

> it is absurd to suppose that he wished his spectators to imagine quite a different constitution from that familiar to themselves, when he makes no reference to it until the very last scene. It is plain to me that, in using the word 'election' . . . in act 5, scene 2, he was quite unconscious that it denoted any procedure different from that which determined the succession in England.

Shakespeare introduced the audience to 'a different constitution from that familiar to themselves' by means of the parallel of the Norwegian succession, which occupies a considerable amount of space in the first two scenes.

Comparing Shakespeare's Denmark and contemporary England in order to show that in both states a 'succession problem' would be

[6] For the contribution of the 'Fortinbras story', cf. also Hankins, pp. 244–5.

solved according to the same procedure, Wilson then brought forward an 'exact parallel' which would move any lawyer to indignation.

After all, was not the throne of Elizabeth and James an 'elective' one? The latter monarch, like Claudius, owed his crown to the deliberate choice of the Council, while the Council saw to it that he had the 'dying voice' of Elizabeth, as Fortinbras has that of Hamlet.

Hankins added the 'not very different' instances of 'the claims of Henry VIII's two daughters', and the abdication of Mary Stuart in favour of her son, enforced by the Scottish lords.[7] But in these three more or less 'contemporary' cases a female heir, or the absence of an indisputable heir, created a situation completely different from that in *Hamlet*, where the deceased sovereign left a son. If we are looking for an 'exact parallel' we should ask, instead, whether there was any question of an 'election' or a 'dying voice' when Charles I followed James I, or when Henry VIII succeeded Henry VII.

To continue on the theme of inheritance, could a Macbeth have been crowned, in early seventeenth-century England, in the lifetime of the legitimate sons of the deceased monarch? This happened during the Wars of the Roses, but never with general consent. Even in 1657, when Cromwell contemplated such a step, he met with implacable opposition and had to draw back: and by then the 'constitution' was far less rigid than in Shakespeare's day. Could Henry VIII have sliced up England among his three children after the manner of King Lear? Much as it has taught us, 'historical criticism' fails when it offers such unsubtle equations of the real world and the imagined.

Unlike present-day theatrical audiences, peeping through the 'fourth wall' at dramas which are billed up as 'significant' or 'up-to-date' or 'sordid' (all labels that mean merely 'realistic'), Shakespeare's public was not encouraged to think that it eavesdropped upon 'real people'. The vocabulary of the theatre[8] was frequently employed together with

[7] Hankins, p. 96. Unlike Wilson, Hankins recognised 'that the Danish king was chosen by some group', but, like Wilson (whose discussion of the same subject Hankins seems to have overlooked), he interpreted the politics of the play from a too inflexibly 'historical' viewpoint.

[8] E.g. Shakespeare brings in at regular intervals words like act, scene, stage, prompt, cue, tragedy, etc. Cf. S. L. Bethell's admirable account of the 'unreality' of Shakespeare's plays, *Shakespeare & the Popular Dramatic Tradition* (1944).

other devices to remind the audience that it *was* an audience, a collection of 'Elizabethans' at the Globe watching a play: the unreality of the play was thus emphasised, or rather, its special reality, its otherness, its unique 'world'.

At the performance of any play of Shakespeare's, and especially of one starting as mysteriously as *Hamlet*, a good audience takes nothing for granted, but feels its way into the story as this unfolds. Actors appear on the stage, yet the audience may not even assume that they represent human beings until told to do so, for they could be fairies, or weird sisters, or even (as in one Stratford production of *The Tempest*) the waves of the sea. Similarly, a good audience will not import into a play contemporary ideas about the laws of inheritance or about politics, but will wait for the dramatist to define these subjects according to his own requirements. Sometimes the definition will be clear-cut from the beginning, sometimes it takes shape only gradually in the course of the play, and sometimes it may remain blurred at the very end—deliberately blurred, for one of the secrets of Shakespeare's wonderfully irradiating art was his mastery of the subordinate art of shadowing. [9]

How, then, is the constitutional problem introduced to the audience? We learn in the second scene that the brother of the late King of Denmark has married 'The imperial jointress of this warlike state', and ascended the throne, the 'better wisdoms' of the nobles—presumably the Council[10]—having 'freely gone With this affair along'. At the same time it transpires that in Norway, as in Denmark, a deceased king's son did not succeed his father, an 'impotent and bed-rid' uncle reigning there; and a little later that Claudius officially recognises Hamlet as 'the most immediate to our throne' (l. 109). The king himself offers all this information—which, to be sure, Hamlet greets with sour hostility, but challenges neither openly nor in soliloquy for several

---

[9] Cf. H. D. F. Kitto, *Form and Meaning in Drama* (1956), p. 258: 'But surely it does not follow, as Wilson says it does, that Shakespeare must have composed the scene with the English constitution in mind. . . . It is surely the common experience that we go to the theatre willing to accept, without prepossessions, what the dramatist offers us . . . since nobody in the audience knew or cared what the Danish constitution was, in whatever century this is supposed to be, the dramatist could go ahead and assume what suited him best.'

[10] The good Second Quarto includes the Council in the stage-direction for I,ii: 'Florish. Enter Claudius, King of Denmarke, Gertrad the Queene, Counsaile . . .'

acts. As Blackstone observed, Hamlet's long silence indicates acquiescence: the prince admits that the king's position is now unassailable.

> I agree with Mr. Steevens, that the crown of Denmark (as in most of the Gothick kingdoms) was elective, and not hereditary . . . . Why then do the rest of the commentators so often treat Claudius as an *usurper*. . . .? Hamlet . . . never hints at his being an *usurper*. His discontent arose from his uncle's being preferred before him, not from any legal right which he pretended to set up to the crown . . . .[11]

In fact, Blackstone erred in declaring that Hamlet never hints at Claudius being a usurper. In the closet-scene Hamlet describes Claudius as a 'cutpurse of the empire' who 'stole' the precious diadem (III.iv. 99–100): to this otherwise unrepeated charge of usurpation I shall return in a moment. Let us note at the same time that Acts II and III are filled with cryptic statements anent Hamlet's ambition and thwarted hopes which keep alive the subject of the succession, and the mystery surrounding it: 'O God, I could be bounded in a nutshell and count myself a king of infinite space, were it not that I have bad dreams. GUILDENSTERN. Which dreams indeed are ambition . . . . (II.ii.260 ff.); 'Beggar that I am, I am even poor in thanks . . . .' (II.ii.280 ff.); 'He that plays the king shall be welcome; his majesty shall have tribute of me. . . .' (II.ii.332); 'their writers do them wrong, to make them exclaim against their own succession' (II.ii.367); 'I am very proud, revengeful, ambitious, ...' (III.i.126 ff.); 'I eat the air, promise-crammed: you cannot feed capons so' (III.ii.99–100); 'Sir, I lack advancement' (III.ii.354). Together these innuendoes may be called the second phase in the unfolding of the Danish constitution.

A third phase comes in Act IV, which discloses the part played by the rabble in the king's calculations.

(i) How dangerous is it that this man goes loose!
Yet must not we put the strong law on him:
He's loved of the distracted multitude. (IV.iii.2)

(ii)   The other motive,
Why to a public count I might not go,
Is the great love the general gender bear him;
Who, dipping all his faults in their affection,
Would, like the spring that turneth wood to stone,

---

[11] Quoted in Malone's Variorum *Shakespeare* (1821), VII, 200.

> Convert his gyves to graces; so that my arrows,
> Too slightly timber'd for so loud a wind,
> Would have reverted to my bow again. (IV.vii.16)

The fourth and final phase arrives in Act V, Scene ii, where, for the first time, Shakespeare alludes directly to an 'elective' system:

(i)   He that hath kill'd my king and whored my mother,
      Popp'd in between th'election and my hopes (V.ii.64)

(ii) But I do prophesy the election lights
      On Fortinbras: he has my dying voice (V.ii.366)

(iii) Of that I shall have also cause to speak,
      And from his mouth whose voice will draw on more.
                                                    (V.ii.402)

We can now, I think, retrace Shakespeare's steps and his 'audience-psychology'. In the council-scene (I.ii) he conveys the impression that a smooth and plausible Claudius has seized the throne—legally, but not perhaps without some sharp practice. Since, according to the *Oxford English Dictionary*, the word 'jointress' first occurs in *Hamlet*, the audience would not know certainly what was implied by 'The imperial jointress of this warlike state'—any more than we do today.[12] It would gather, however, that the new king's swift marriage to his recently-widowed 'sometime sister' was, at least in part, a political move; and that the 'better wisdoms' of the council obliged Claudius by bringing 'this affair' to a satisfactory culmination. The disgruntled behaviour of the dead king's son raises further doubts, in so far as the Elizabethans would expect the son to succeed the father in their own 'world': but

---

[12] 'Claudius's description of Gertrude (I.2.9) as "imperial jointress" is important . . . since the phrase signifies, not joint-monarch as some editors explain, but a widow who retains the jointure or life interest in the crown, and so points to the legal argument or quibble by means of which Hamlet was supplanted' (Wilson, p. 38). Even if 'jointress' later acquired the meaning advocated by Wilson (cf. *O.E.D.*), this tells us little about Shakespeare's meaning, especially if, as seems likely, he invented the word. In Belleforest, incidentally, Old Hamlet and Claudius are joint governors ['Rorique . . . donna le gouvernement de Jutie . . . à deux seigneurs . . . nommez Horvvendille et Fengon' (p. 180)], which might have suggested joint monarchs for the play. But clearly Shakespeare wished only to stir vague thoughts about Gertrude's rights, not to define them meticulously.

the 'world of the play' need not correspond to theirs, as the 'Norwegian succession' confirms, therefore the audience will not rush to conclusions. All in all, this second scene continues a process begun in the first, even though superficially contrasting with it. In the first we enter a gloomy region of shadows, a ghost rises, questions are asked but no answers given; in the second a state occasion translates the scene from the shadows to a brilliant public spectacle, and instead of questions there ensue explanations. But the explanations only operate at one level. Claudius intends in his long first speech to present his accession as natural and 'this affair' as closed; yet behind Claudius Shakespeare suggests that 'this affair' is not quite straightforward. Very different as it shows outwardly, the second scene has one important function in common with the first: it mystifies.

Hamlet, of course, consists of a number of interlocking and gradually revealed mysteries. We only become sure of Claudius' guilt in Act III, and of Gertrude's innocence of murder in Act III, Scene iv; an end is put to speculation about Hamlet's ability to revenge his father only in the very last scene, while the ghost remains an enigma even after Hamlet decides that he will take its word for a thousand pound.[13] In a play that follows as many threads as expertly as *Hamlet* it should therefore come as no surprise that the mystery of the Danish succession only yields its secret in Act V, Scene ii, even though Wilson (cf. p. 134) thought such a belated unravelling 'absurd'. Shakespeare kept alive our mild suspense by allowing Hamlet to flash into resentment at his uncle's succession (Acts II and III), and by making Claudius admit the dangers of Hamlet's popular appeal (Act IV). Then, in Act V, he provides a key to the mystery—the 'elective' constitution, which he alludes to three times to ensure that the audience takes it in.

From the vantage-point of Act V most of the earlier references to the succession fall into place. Normally, one assumes, the death of a Danish sovereign leaving a son, a brother and an 'imperial jointress', would lead to an election; Claudius, who dared not risk an election opposed to a rival as popular as Hamlet, managed to by-pass the usual processes by winning over the 'better wisdoms' of the nobility, and by

[13] 'It is permanently ambiguous. Indeed the very word "ghost", by putting it into the same class with the "ghosts" of Kyd and Chapman, nay by classifying it at all, puts us on the wrong track. It is "this thing", "this dreaded sight" . . .' (C. S. Lewis, *Hamlet: the Prince or the Poem?* (in *Proceedings of the British Academy*, 1942), p. 147).

marrying his sister-in-law.[14] When later, on a single occasion, gripped by an agonising passion, Hamlet cries that Claudius *stole* the precious diadem, the audience believes this literally no more than that the king resembles a 'mildew'd ear' and a 'king of shreds and patches' (III.iv.64, 102)—for, after all, Claudius has by this time established his dignified and indeed commanding presence in various ceremonial and also private scenes. In determining what weight should be attached to this single charge of an illegal accession we shall do well to bear in mind A. C. Sprague's rule 'that the more dramatic should give place, as evidence, to the less'.[15] Hamlet rants

> A cutpurse of the empire and the rule,
> That from a shelf the precious diadem stole

at one of the most 'dramatic' climaxes in the play, in one of the two or three passages when we see him at breaking-point—immediately before the reappearance of the ghost, a possibly self-induced hallucination. Comparably overwrought speeches are found after the ghost has told its tale (I.v.92 ff.), after the king's flight from the play (III.ii.282 ff.), and, perhaps, in Ophelia's grave (V.i.297 ff.: though here Hamlet's 'mouthing' and 'ranting' is partly deliberate). At these times of high tension Hamlet exaggerates, and the audience instinctively distrusts his 'testimony'.

In broad outline Shakespeare's 'Danish constitution' hangs together. Nonetheless, as one would expect, some details are never fully integrated in the general scheme. Who, for instance, voted at the Danish elections? Hardly, one imagines, the 'multitude'—and yet Hamlet's popular support perhaps inclined him to think well of his chances in an election, if only retrospectively, for he seems to have lacked powerful friends at court. Possibly Shakespeare thought of 'the noblest' as the electors, but,

[14] 'The elder Hamlet had died two months before, at which time his son was presumably at Wittenberg . . . it is probable that in Hamlet's absence he [Claudius] had taken over control of affairs' (Hankins, p. 98). Bradley, however, has shown that at the time of his father's death Hamlet was almost certainly not at Wittenberg (*op. cit.*, Note B). It therefore seems more likely that the shock of his mother's marriage stunned Hamlet's interest in the succession; but this matter lies genuinely 'outside the play', and so cannot be pursued.

[15] Cf. Sprague, *Shakespeare and the Audience: A Study in the Technique of Exposition* (1935), p. 243, and the excellent section on 'Testimony'. Bradley (p. 168) thought Claudius 'courteous and never undignified' as a king, an opinion that is, I believe, the accepted one.

if so, he did not bother to make this manifest.[16] Consequently we too need not bother to prod into such 'wingy mysteries' and 'airy subtleties'.

As I have indicated, Shakespeare dwelt on the 'Danish constitution' not only for its own sake but partly to bring into sharper focus the morality of the play; and, similarly, he uses it to direct the play's moods. In the opening scenes uncertainty about Hamlet's and Claudius' rights to the throne links with larger moral uncertainties—for, as C. S. Lewis succinctly phrased it, 'The Hamlet formula, so to speak, is not "a man who has to avenge his father" but "a man who has been given a task by a ghost" '—by a ghost that remains 'permanently ambiguous'.[17] The ghost is not only a doubtful quantity in itself but, to adapt Falstaff, the cause that doubt creeps into men, and into all the familiar appearances of life: doubt becomes a generalised mood in this part of the play.

Likewise the references to Hamlet's popularity in Act IV connect with an atmospheric presence. Not just the 'distracted multitude's' love of Hamlet (IV.iii.4, IV.vii.18) but also the distraction of the multitude now interests Shakespeare.

(i) 'Twere good she were spoken with: for she may strew
    Dangerous conjectures in ill-breeding minds. (IV.v.14)

(ii)   the people muddied,
     Thick and unwholesome in their thoughts and whispers,
     For good Polonius' death. . . . (IV.v.81)

(iii)   The rabble call him lord;
      And, as the world were now but to begin,
      Antiquity forgot, custom not known,
      The ratifiers and props of every word,
      They cry 'Choose we: Laertes shall be king.' (IV.v.102)

True, earlier parts of the play also animadvert upon the foolishness of 'the million . . . the general' (II.ii.456) and the 'groundlings' (III.ii.12)—

[16] Hankins (p. 96) felt that when Fortinbras called 'the noblest to the audience' (V.ii.398) this 'indicates that the kingdom's affairs were handled by a council of nobles'. In Belleforest, on the other hand, Hamlet is chosen king after his *Harangue* 'en l'assemblee des citoyens' ('among the multitude of people') (pp. 264, 265).

[17] *Op. cit.* p. 147. After Lewis' lecture the 'mystery' and 'doubt' in *Hamlet* received even greater emphasis, in D. G. James' *The Dream of Learning* (1951), chapter II ('The New Doubt'), and in Mack's 'The World of *Hamlet*'.

through Hamlet and, by the bye, quite unlovingly—but without political implications. In Act IV the 'general gender' loses its head, to the extent of making a completely 'unconstitutional' attempt to dethrone Claudius. This casts doubt retrospectively upon the absolute legality of his succession, and at the same time distends the act's over-all mood of 'distraction', a growing force in the play which spreads from Hamlet to engulf Ophelia, Laertes (in his ill-considered uprising), the 'multitude'—and even assails the king himself (IV.v.77 ff.).

The references to Hamlet's popularity in Act IV connect with still another emergent force.[18] After the moment of truth in Act III, when Hamlet finds proof of Claudius' guilt and Claudius discovers that he must strike or be struck, the law and legal form suddenly become important as instruments of policy. Claudius writes to England to order the legalised murder of his nephew (IV.iii.60 ff.); he offers to submit Laertes' grievances to arbitration (IV.v.202 ff.); he plans to get rid of Hamlet in a duel, a perfectly 'legal' way of despatching one's enemies; and both his allusions to Hamlet's popularity lead to the reflection that it prohibits resort to 'the strong law' (IV.iii.3) and 'a public count' (IV.vii.17). We get a clear indication of the way his mind works in his soliloquy, when he reflects that in this world, if not in the next, one can 'buy out the law' (III.iii.60). As the pressures build up against him his desire to operate within the bounds of law and, where possible, to make the law his tool, gives further substance to the impression that Claudius did not boggle to take advantage of the law in seizing the crown—an impression that helps to define the special rottenness of Denmark. (Later, in V.i, Shakespeare demonstrates at some length how the court wrests the law: as the gravedigger says, 'the more pity that great folk should have countenance in this world to drown or hang themselves, more than their even Christian', or, more plainly, in the words of the priest, 'great command o'ersways the order'.) Claudius knows exactly how far he may push the law, yet before the end he becomes a prisoner to his respect for 'the appearance of legality', just as Hamlet is a prisoner of his 'morality', and thus the law defeats him.

[18] Probably a technical reason also dictated the allusions to Hamlet's popularity in Act IV. In several tragedies Shakespeare felt a need to rehabilitate his hero in the audience's sympathy at this point, partly, perhaps, because the tensions of Act III brought into notice some of the hero's less amiable qualities. Thus he invented Brutus' solicitude for the sleepy boy Lucius in *Julius Caesar* (IV.iii.231 ff.), and underlined Lear's humility in his reunion with Cordelia.

Similarly, the 'elective constitution' reinforces generalised thoughts upon which Shakespeare wishes to fix attention in Act V.[19] All through the play the difficulties of 'election' or moral choice are kept in mind, yet in the last act there comes a shift in emphasis—conveniently illustrated by the two main discussions of suicide. The first puts the question 'To be, or not to be' on a purely personal level, the very possibility of an after-life being seen initially merely in terms of the individual ('To die, to sleep: To sleep: perchance to dream'); and even as Hamlet's mind plays on the theme it never rises above the personal, or to the truly religious, in 'the undiscover'd country, from whose bourn No traveller returns'. When the two grave-diggers resume the subject, however, it is in the language of 'crowner's quest law' and with a three-fold iteration of the phrase 'Christian burial', a phrase instantly placed before the audience in that pregnant first speech: 'Is she to be buried in Christian burial *that wilfully seeks her own salvation?*' Shakespeare now looks at suicide and other 'elections' from a social and religious viewpoint, underlining time and again the fallibility of the individual:

> Rashly,
> And praised be rashness for it, let us know,
> Our indiscretion sometimes serves us well,
> When our deep plots do pall: and that should learn us
> There's a divinity that shapes our ends,
> Rough-hew them how we will,— (V. ii.6)

Not a whit, we defy augury: there's a special providence in the fall of a sparrow. If it be now, 'tis not to come; if it be not to come, it will be now; if it be not now, yet it will come: the readiness is all. . . . (V.ii.230)

> so shall you hear
> Of carnal, bloody, and unnatural acts,
> Of accidental judgements, casual slaughters,

[19] The technique is not unfamiliar. Kitto wrote: 'We have to observe first how Shakespeare uses his Clowns much as the Greek dramatist used his Chorus; for they fill our minds with generalised thoughts about mortality and the vanity of human life, before we are brought, as by a gradual contraction of the focus, to the particular tragedy' (p. 283). Mack also explored 'umbrella speeches', 'mirror situations' and that 'inward action' which fills 'our minds with impressions analogous to those which we may presume to be occupying the conscious or unconscious mind of the hero' ('The Jacobean Shakespeare' in *Stratford-Upon-Avon Studies I*, 1960).

Of deaths put on by cunning and forced cause,
And, in this upshot, purposes mistook
Fall'n on the inventors' heads. . . . (V.ii.391)[20]

It enlarges the area of fallibility to suggest that Claudius 'popp'd in'
before Denmark, or the Danish nobles, could exercise the right of election, for thus the state is placed in much the same position as Hamlet,
who also found it difficult to 'elect' his future. Shakespeare, in fact,
mirrors the moral confusion of his hero in the public mind, a confusion
mentioned in the first scene (where the 'romage in the land' puzzles
ordinary men like Marcellus), but rising to the proportions of a
rebellion in Act IV, and in the final scene to the extraordinary behaviour
of the courtiers, who cry 'Treason! treason!' when Hamlet stabs the
king but, apparently, do nothing thereafter to prevent him from
forcing Claudius to drink the poison. One might almost say that
through the momentary indecision of the courtiers the audience
glimpses 'the Danish election', for they hold back partly because in
doubt as to who is or should be king.

★   ★   ★

As soon as it grew fashionable to analyse Shakespeare's play-worlds,
the 'world' of *Hamlet* became, as one would expect, all things to all
men. One held that 'the idea of an ulcer or tumour, as descriptive of the
unwholesome condition of Denmark morally, is, on the whole, the
dominating one' of its atmosphere; another found in the tragedy a
'central reality of pain', yet sketched in 'the *Hamlet* universe' as 'one of
healthy and robust life, good-nature, humour, romantic strength, and
welfare';[21] a third, Mack, submitted that 'the world of *Hamlet*' has as
its attributes 'mysteriousness', uncertainty about appearance and reality,
and 'mortality'; a fourth, Foakes, that the 'court of Elsinore is . . . at the
same time a place of nobility, chivalry, dignity, religion, and a prison,
a place of treachery, spying and, underlying this, corruption'. Still
another possibility, and a very popular one, is to compare the 'two

[20] Shakespeare also forces us to take note of misguided 'elections' in such
memorable lines as 'Why, man, they did make love to this employment'
(V.ii.57), and the Queen's 'I will, my lord; I pray you, pardon me' (V.ii.302),
when warned not to drink.

[21] Cf. Caroline F. E. Spurgeon, *Shakespeare's Imagery* (ed. 1958), p. 316;
Knight, pp. 17, 32.

worlds' of a play, court *versus* country in *As You Like It*, nature and nur-
ture in *The Tempest*, Egypt and Rome in *Antony and Cleopatra*, or
Wittenberg face to face with the heroic past in *Hamlet*.[22] The overlap
in the five important studies of Hamlet which I have cited will be less
apparent in my all-too-brief summaries than is actually the case, but one
common feature must strike every reader: whether it goes under the
name of 'atmosphere' or 'mood' or 'imaginative environment' or
'values', nowadays we tend to consider the 'world of the play' principally as an ambience rather than as a 'reality' that is a 'system of things'.

Looked at as a system of things the world of *Hamlet* reveals a court
that differs in essentials from the English court (for example, in its dearth
of great noblemen), a constitution nowise resembling that of England,
a Christianity neither Roman Catholic nor Protestant, though the
imagined world shades into the 'real' one of Shakespeare's England,
more or less, in some of its social structures such as universities, burial
rites, dramatic entertainments. On a different level the system of things
in the play resolves itself into scene after scene of 'policy' or 'diplomacy'.[23] The king in council, in consultation with Polonius or Laertes,
and even at prayer, pursues the devious paths of policy, sifts, weighs,
bargains, glides over embarrassing obstacles; against him stands Hamlet,
whose 'crafty pollicy' and 'politike inventions' Belleforest lauded at
every opportunity[24]; against them both, as a foil, stands Polonius, the
politician gone to seed, whose brain

> Hunts not the trail of policy so sure
> As it hath used to do (II.ii.47)

so that before long 'a certain convocation of politic worms are e'en at
him' (IV.iii.21); and also those shallow vessels, Rosencrantz, Guildenstern and Osric, would-be politicians who 'did make love to this
employment'. The queen, too, tries her hand, wins Hamlet to her will
(I.ii.68 ff.), or briefs Rosencrantz and Guildenstern (II.ii.19 ff.), while
such innocents as Ophelia and Laertes become the tragic pawns of
policy. Three formal embassies enter upon the stage (to Norway; to

[22] Cf. P. Alexander, *Hamlet Father and Son* (1955), pp. 35, 169.
[23] Cf. Draper, p. 13: 'For the first time, in *Hamlet*, Shakespeare fully and
realistically portrays the political problems of a court: regicide, revolt, dynastic
succession, and all the accompanying policy and intrigue'; and Foakes, quoted
above, p. 144.
[24] Cf. pp. 199, 205, 217, etc.; in French, 'une grande et cauteleuse sagesse',
'Contre un desloial, il faut user de cautelle', etc.

K

England; from England), and diplomatic letters and messengers bustle in the background from the second scene to the last. Shakespeare also borrows from Belleforest the politic notions of the antic disposition, of the employment of Ophelia as a decoy, and so on, and throws in such further politic inventions as the play within the play entitled 'The Mouse-trap'. In private as in public life 'policy' and 'diplomacy' rule all: Polonius forgets his daughter's feelings, and the king has to hide behind 'painted words' (III.i.53) even with his closest allies, Polonius and Gertrude. When Hamlet throws aside 'policy' in the queen's closet (III.iv) and speaks daggers the result is a scene of such intensity that, atmospherically, we re-enter the 'world' of the soliloquies. No wonder, then, that Horatio's summary of the story of the play ends with an image inspired by 'the enginer Hoist with his own petar' (III.iv. 206), an image that reflects as in a raindrop the 'world' of policy and gives us Shakespeare's tersest formula for the play as a whole:

> And, in this upshot, *purposes mistook*
> *Fall'n on the inventors' heads:* all this can I
> Truly deliver. (V.ii.395)

Of course, the Danish court and constitution and the 'purposes' and 'policy' in *Hamlet* do not even add up to '*Hamlet* without the prince'. The legal and social and visible system of things in a play-world grows into an organism, but no simple formula really explains the life of that organism—partly because it cannot be removed from its medium, or 'ambience'. Unlike some of his modern critics, Bradley knew this: in his *Shakespearean Tragedy* he concentrated, as everyone remembers, on the system of things, and sometimes too hastily identified dramatic characters with 'real people'; nevertheless, he also wrote some splendid pages on the atmospheres of individual plays.[25]

The politics of Shakespeare's Denmark afford a useful example of the complex of elements in the 'world' of a play, and of their osmotic relationship. No one can tell whether Shakespeare planned from the start to make use of the distracted multitude and the elective constitution in the fourth and fifth acts, so that the unfolding of the political and general system of things helped to determine changes of 'imaginative environment'—or whether, at times, Shakespeare paid attention primarily to the moods of his play and fabricated correlatives such as

[25] Cf. pp. 303–4, 333–4.

the elective constitution (or a new character or location or the like) in response to the mood's requirements. The constitutional issue is laid before the audience at first vaguely, then more and more definitively, yet the mystifying indications and counter-suggestions of the first act serve an immediate purpose and in no sense commit Shakespeare in in advance to an elective Denmark. We *can* tell, however, that the 'mood' and the 'system' grow out of one another, or, perhaps, flash into existence simultaneously, and consequently we may guess that the principle of life in a play is intimately bound up with their organic unity.

VII

Character and Speech in 'Hamlet'

R. A. FOAKES

★

EVERYONE has a smack of Hamlet in himself, which is to say that he can find reflected in Hamlet something of his own feelings, aspirations and problems; but no such claim is made about Shakespeare's other tragic heroes. One reason may be that Hamlet stands apart from the other tragic heroes in his relative innocence. Othello out of the blindness of jealousy strangles his wife; Lear in the pride of his heart provokes civil war through an act of disastrous folly; and Macbeth out of envy and ambition kills a most sainted king; the prayer-book cries out against what they willingly and wilfully do,

> From all blindness of heart; from pride, vainglory, and hypocrisy; from envy, hatred and malice, and all uncharitableness, Good Lord deliver us.

Hamlet alone is shown in a situation where he is forced to act, and where, if the act could be accomplished simply in accordance with the moral laws of nature, of nations, and of the church, it would be an act of justice, not a deed of sin.

For Hamlet, as it appears, returns from abroad to Denmark almost as a stranger, ignorant of its history during his absence, to find all changed from what he once knew; and at once he is faced with an impossible moral dilemma. In its simplest terms, the problem is that the king, Claudius, the embodiment of justice in the state, has murdered Hamlet's father, the old king, and now sits in authority where no law can touch him, and where his influence seems to corrupt the whole state. Hamlet alone is told this, and is called upon, in a message from beyond the grave, to revenge his father. In order to obtain justice, he must kill, must revenge, must himself become a murderer; unless in carrying out the deed he can see himself as an agent of providence.

This is not enough to explain the special impact of *Hamlet*, but it points to a further characteristic that distinguishes this play from the other tragedies. The world Othello inhabits is readily comprehensible, limited, so that the play has been regarded as a domestic tragedy; the world of Lear opens out in vistas of bleak countryside, cliff and sea, but conceals nothing, unless it be what the thunder says; and the instruments of darkness in *Macbeth* finally leave no doubt about the nature of their equivocation. Only in *Hamlet* is there an overriding sense of mystery, a sense, as Maynard Mack has said, that 'uncertainties are of the essence' of what is 'easily the most various and brilliant, the most elusive' of the tragic 'worlds' created by Shakespeare. It is a world 'predominantly in the interrogative mood',[1] full of questions, which reflect or embody doubts and riddles, baffling difficulties. Much about Hamlet and his world seems to be finally unknowable; generations of actors and critics have not succeeded in plucking out the heart of his mystery.

This feature of the play is exemplified, as has often been noticed, in the continual clash between appearance and reality. More specifically, as Maynard Mack has illustrated, there runs through the play's language and action pervasive patterns of imagery relating to clothing as a disguise or cover, to the ideas of seeing and seeming, shows and painting, putting on and stripping bare. All these come together, he thinks, in the play's 'radical metaphor', the word 'act', which relates both to play-acting, and to the deed that must be done. Everyone in play could be acting a part in addition to his own; at least, it appears so to Hamlet, who feels he can rely only on Horatio; and one way of describing his problem is to say that he feels he must penetrate beneath the roles adopted by Claudius, Gertrude, Rosencrantz and Guildenstern, Ophelia and others, in order to expose the truth, to know his situation, and be able to act at all. To further his purpose he adopts various parts himself, as he is an actor, able to speak a speech 'with good accent and good discretion', and knowledgeable in the theory of acting; he puts on an antic disposition that can range from gaiety to

---

[1] 'The World of Hamlet', in ed. Cleanth Brooks *Tragic Themes in Western Literature* (1955), pp. 30–58; the quotations are from pp. 37, 32 and 33. The mysteriousness of the play has been much emphasised in recent criticism; see Honigmann above, pp. 139–41.

melancholy, and can stand on points with Osric, parody Polonius, and rank with Laertes.

Hamlet's range of roles is indeed much wider than those of the other characters, and if he has difficulty in finding out what lies beneath their shows, it is hardly surprising that he should leave critics still arguing about his own nature. There is always a final uncertainty about his behaviour in any scene, and the variety of Hamlets that have been seen on the stage, and described in print testify to this. Bold commentators claim to have discovered his secret, and unveil Hamlet the sensitive poet, Hamlet the prince marred by dishonest pride, Hamlet the delayer, Hamlet the man who could not make up his mind, Hamlet the revenger, Hamlet the young man obsessed with death, Hamlet the intellectual who can make no affirmation, and many more Hamlets,[2] but these portrayals do not convince, or convince only for a moment. The mystery remains, and partly accounts for the way in which Hamlet mirrors all men. Yet it is paradoxical that this character, who remains finally unknowable, should be, of all Shakespeare's creations, the most familiar, the one with whom we most readily identify ourselves.

Indeed, there is a familiar Hamlet, whose features are indicated in Ophelia's description:

> The courtier's, soldier's, scholar's eye, tongue, sword,
> Th'expectancy and rose of the fair state,
> The glass of fashion and the mould of form,
> Th'observed of all observers. (III.i.159)

The play shows him to have other abilities, as musician and actor, and he appears too as lover, as prince, and, in all his qualities, as young. Ophelia tells us rather more about him than is shown in action, but her words ring true as bringing together, in the first two lines, the wholeness of the character in his ideal aspects; he seems potentially to be a figure like Sir Philip Sidney, or Major Robert Gregory as Yeats saw him,

> Soldier, scholar, horseman, he,
> And all he did done perfectly
> As though he had but that one trade alone.

Perhaps the secret of Hamlet's appeal in this way is that he seems to

[2] For further comment, see Clifford Leech, 'Studies in *Hamlet*, 1901–1955', *Shakespeare Survey*, 9 (1956), 1–15.

combine the active and passive life as soldier and swordsman on the one hand, scholar, student and statesman on the other, and in both capacities he is, in the play, supreme. He defeats the expert, Laertes, in the swordfight, and his 'noble reason' readily outmanoeuvres the wiles of the court's elder-statesman, Polonius. His wit is too sharp for the skilful Claudius, his philosophy too deep for the scholar Horatio; he is supreme in all things, unless it be as a poet, and here he does not need to outshine others, for he is the only poet in the play, not so ill at his numbers that he cannot dash off a speech for the players,

> Soldier, scholar, horseman he,
> As 'twere all life's epitome.

A Hamlet so perfect would be far less interesting than the character shown in action; much of this ideal Hamlet, this golden young hero, is implied, or registered as potential. This rather generalised image has its power, and its reality in establishing a vast sense of tragic waste, but it offers nothing of Hamlet's special distinguishing features. The essential Hamlet is not grasped in such an account; nor is he found in any description of him which emphasises one of his attributes above all others, or adds to the qualities noted above those characteristics that emerge in action. Among these may be listed Hamlet's melancholy, his bursts of sudden, swift action and elation, his apparent cruelty at times, his self-searching. Sometimes a critical reading of the play is made to turn on one or more of these characteristics, but none of them pins the figure down. This is perhaps the more strange in that no character scrutinises himself so much as Hamlet, or confides in the audience at such length.

After all, as J. Dover Wilson said (N.C.S., p. lix) after years of work on the play, the mystery of Hamlet's character remains; and that 'elusive' quality of the world of this play resides in Hamlet himself finally. It is not a matter of general doubts, uncertainties, questioning, for, as a play, Macbeth can perhaps show more confusion, more questions, more uncertainties. And if the world of the play is more 'various and brilliant' than that of the other tragedies, it seems to most critics less richly significant, less profound, than that of King Lear. The mystery is not one of doubt, or one of profundity. Perhaps a clue to its nature may lie in the language and style of the play.

Discussion of these aspects does not seem to have proceeded very far, in spite of frequent tributes to their brilliance. Perhaps the vigour and scale of what first makes its impact felt have led critics to concentrate on one or two matters, notably imagery of disease, and word-play. The frequency with which we are told that the idea of corruption, associated with poison, ulcers, sickness, and decay, forms a 'leit motiv', or is 'dominant' or 'pervasive' in the play's imagery testifies sufficiently to the importance of this theme, but hardly reflects the variety and brilliance of the play's world noted by Maynard Mack. This imagery reflects the intensity of one mood of Hamlet the prince, but is not so prominent in performance, when the many other aspects of Elsinore, its order, formality, its warlike nature, its courtliness, are also apparent, and contribute to a total pattern that is rich and varied.[3] The intensity of one mood of Hamlet has diverted attention from the many moods of the play. So it is, too, with the quibbling, riddling wordplay of *Hamlet* which has been studied as revealing the prince's sense of 'ineradicable corruption'[4]; it has also been regarded as illustrating Hamlet's humour and nimbleness of mind, and, perceptively, as suggesting 'unfathomed and unfathomable depths'(Wilson, *N.C.S.*, p. xxxix) of associated meanings. It is true that Hamlet speaks much in puns, quibbles and riddles, which seem to be 'something very characteristic' of him. (Bradley, p. 124). However, they are less characteristic of him as personage, except to show his quick-wittedness, than of his state of mind. Shakespeare quibbles, puns and riddles in all his writings, vigorously in all the tragedies, and the associations of speeches in *Lear* or *Macbeth* are as unfathomable as those in *Hamlet*. The difference lies in the consciousness of the characters uttering them. For Hamlet, the pun and riddle are a means by which he consciously seeks to expose the truth of others or to conceal his own truth; they are as much his weapons as rapier and dagger.

Images of corruption, like puns and riddles, relate to Hamlet's perception of his world and it is proper to emphasise them because his voice and interpretation of events are so prominent in the play. But the play has much more in it than the prince; the imagery of corruption,

[3] Critics who have stressed imagery of disease, poison and corruption include C. F. E. Spurgeon, in her *Shakespeare's Imagery* (1935), W. Clemen, in his *The Development of Shakespeare's Imagery* (1951), and R. D. Altick, in his essay 'Hamlet and the Odor of Mortality', *Shakespeare Quarterly*, v (1954), 167–76. The more pleasant aspects of the imagery were noted by G. Wilson Knight in *The Wheel of Fire* (1930), and were studied in more detail in my essay, 'Hamlet and the Court of Elsinore', *Shakespeare Survey*, 9 (1956), 35–43.

[4] Molly Mahood, *Shakespeare's Wordplay* (1957), p. 112.

like much else in the play's language, needs to be seen as closely related to, and in some sense a part of it, a larger thematic structure concerned with seeming and being, with shows and the truths that they conceal, with fair appearance and ugly realities, and with the difficulties of interpreting what is seen. Gertrude looked on Claudius, and saw only a man she could live with as his mate, until Hamlet holds up for comparison portraits of him and the older Hamlet; but the recognition of this disparity can only come through a clearer inward vision; Gertrude's response shows this:

> O Hamlet, speak no more;
> Thou turn'st mine eyes into my very soul;
> And there I see such black and grained spots
> As will not leave their tint (III. iv.88)

Here Gertrude's eyes are opened, as the common phrase has it, meaning that she recognises her sin; here is acted out what Claudius described in his soliloquy just before this scene; Hamlet stands as mercy, confronts 'the visage of offence', and forces an exposure:

> There is no shuffling, there the action lies
> In his true nature. (III.iii.61)

The true nature of an action is not easily established in Hamlet's world however, where everyone may be playing a role, and even the most careful observation cannot often detect when 'our drift look through our bad performance' (IV.vii.152). Everyone watches and spies, from the opening scene; but though the ghost is most clearly seen, though Claudius and Polonius spy, 'seeing unseen', on Hamlet, though Reynaldo observes Laertes, Rosencrantz and Guildenstern study Hamlet's behaviour, and Hamlet and Horatio rivet their eyes on Claudius, it is difficult to interpret what is seen, or even to be sure that what lies there before the eyes is seen. If Hamlet needs to probe beneath the ordered surface of court-life, Claudius needs to discover, if he can, the reason for Hamlet's 'transformation'.

Claudius admits in an aside that he sugars over his evil 'with devotion's visage And pious action', but Hamlet's probing searches more deeply into his world and himself, reaching towards deeper perceptions, and deeper uncertainties, which remain unresolved, as when he sees the ghost and Gertrude does not:

HAMLET: Do you see nothing there?
QUEEN: Nothing at all; yet all that is I see. (III.iv.131)

Hamlet's puns and quibbles also relate to this larger structure of linguistic usage in the play, as they operate to reveal or conceal Hamlet's own motives and insights into the actions of others. For again, they are concerned with the true nature of action in a court marked by its 'formal ostentation' and attention to ceremony and stateliness of utterance. Except in moments of duress or urgency, matter tends to be dressed in art, and ordered in show. Claudius, Polonius, Rosencrantz and Guildenstern, Laertes and Osric, characters who belong to the Court of Elsinore, are all capable of fine sonorities, courtly flourishes, devious phrases; their indirections, their shows of formality, of proper behaviour, are marked by their language.[5] But where language may be an instrument of policy in the mouth of Claudius, or serve for the protestations of a hollow friendship in the flattery of Rosencrantz and Guildenstern, or consist of empty flourishes in the courtesies of Osric, the problem is to know when words ever represent the heart's truth. Words are another aspect of the play's shows, and it is as hard for others in the court to interpret them as for Hamlet. Where no language can be trusted, his expressions of love to Ophelia may seem no more than 'mere implorators of unholy suits' (I.iii.129), and Hamlet himself is capable of unpacking his heart with words that echo the court rhetoric, as when he jumps into the grave with Laertes. Where it is hard to distinguish between deed and 'painted word', everyone must doubt truth to be a liar.

Imagery of corruption and quibbling both represent a mode of Hamlet's own consciousness, for it is above all his sense of rottenness in the state of Denmark, and his intelligence in responding to others, that his disease images and riddling reflect. These features too may be added to the familiar picture of Hamlet outlined earlier; they complicate that picture but leave the sense of mystery unexplored and unaccounted for. A consideration of imagery and quibbling leads also out from the character of the prince to the overriding concern with seeing, seeming, shows and acting in the play, to general characteristics of language and style. Here another paradox seems to present itself; although the gen-

[5] This has been noticed by John Paterson, 'The Word in *Hamlet*', *Shakespeare Quarterly*, II (1951), 47–55, but I think he exaggerates the consciousness of their language on the part of characters other than Hamlet himself.

eral characteristics of the play's style can be described, it is hard to point to the special stylistic attributes of Hamlet himself. The other tragic heroes have their distinguishing marks of speech, Othello perhaps most plainly, with sonorous gravity; only he would address a council as

> Most potent, grave and reverend signiors, (I.iii.76)

speak of 'antres vast and deserts idle', or use the exotic language of an Atlas, the ringing sound of

> To the Propontic and the Hellespont. (III.iii.456)

Lear's rashness and absolute conviction of his right are also marked in his utterance, the virulence of his curses, his sudden explosions, which begin in the first scene with his

> Come not between the dragon and his wrath,

and his oath in discarding Cordelia. Macbeth speaks at first in a troubled syntax as his ambition strives with his duty and conscience,

> If it were done when 'tis done, then 'twere well
> It were done quickly.

Othello's dignified and proud assurance of his power and worth, Lear's explosive arrogance and selfishness, Macbeth's overweening ambition in struggle to overcome his human kindness, are reflected in the manner in which these characters speak. Each has his own resonance, marking what is central in his personality, his desires and passions. The one feature of Hamlet's style that is generally remarked, his addiction to word-play, does not illustrate his personality in this way; it is a sign of his intelligence.[6]

[6] Bradley, pp. 123–4, noted as 'unmistakably individual' repetitions of words in speeches by Hamlet, as in 'I humbly thank you, well, well, well' (III.i.92), and other critics have followed suit. Harold Jenkins has convincingly argued, however, that many repetitions can be explained as actors' interpolations in the Folio text, and those in Q 'are closely related to the moment and the mood and it is doubtful whether from Q alone one could reasonably infer that they are an idiosyncrasy of Hamlet's speech' ('Playhouse Interpolations in the Folio Text of *Hamlet*', *Studies in Bibliography*, XIII (1960), p. 39). The wide acceptance of Bradley's belief is marked in the edition of the Good Quarto by T. M. Parrott and Hardin Craig (1938), in which they emend the line cited above as it appears in Q2, 'I humbly thanke you well', to include the Folio repetitions, as 'characteristic' of Hamlet.

Perhaps the 'unusual variety'[7] of styles in the play is most striking, ranging from the earthy prose of the gravediggers to the flourishes of Osric, from the set description of Ophelia's death to the passion of Hamlet's exchange with his mother, from the simplicity of Horatio to the rhetorical amplification of the First Player. Some of these styles relate more to the occasion than the character, as, for example, the passages of descriptive poetry spoken by Marcellus and Horatio in the opening scene, or Gertrude's description of Ophelia's drowning in IV. vii. It seems that in such a lyrical flight as Horatio's

> But look, the morn in russet mantle clad
> Walks o'er the dew of yon high eastward hill,

the character is drawing on a 'common "pool" of blank verse',[8] in order to bring a scene of some excitement to a quiet close. There is also a general contrast between the use of prose in the easy interchanges, for instance, of Hamlet, Rosencrantz and Guildenstern in II.ii, or Hamlet and the gravediggers in V.i, and the use of verse to mark more formal or serious interchanges, such as Hamlet's attack on Gertrude in IV.iii, or the plotting of Claudius and Laertes in IV.vii. A further general distinction can be made between modes of blank verse in the play; the stately, official diction of the court, which has links with the verse of the play within the play, contrasts with the more flexible and familiar manner of the private interview or soliloquy.

The particular distinguishing modes of utterance of the characters are to be sought within these general distinctions relating to occasion, or to the mood or tone of a scene. Some are readily located; the empty elaborations of Osric's 'golden words' sum up the character of this silly courtier, just as the First Gravedigger's speaking by the card marks his shrewd and earthy humour. In the spectrum of the play's language, they represent opposite extremes, one of a hollow rhetoric, with which Osric knows only how to flatter and comply; the other of a literal-minded sticking over the meanings of common words, with which the gravedigger has his petty and elementary, but telling, jest over Hamlet:

> HAMLET: What man dost thou dig it for?
> 1 CLOWN: For no man, sir.

[7] Bradley, p. 96.
[8] B. Ifor Evans, *The Language of Shakespeare's Plays* (1952), p. 94.

> HAMLET: What woman then?
> 1 CLOWN: For none neither.
> HAMLET: Who is to be buried in't?
> 1 CLOWN: One that was a woman, sir; but, rest her soul, she's
> dead. (V.i.141)

The jest is telling because it reflects Hamlet's problem in so far as he continually strives to probe beneath exterior shows, to separate matter from art, and because it reveals the difficulty of communicating a straightforward meaning in the simplest words; here Hamlet is the courtier, and might say to the gravedigger, as Pandarus does to the servant at Priam's palace, 'I am too courtly, and thou art too cunning'.

Other characters range between these extremes. In some ways the most interesting in respect of their style of speech are Claudius and Gertrude. The important fact about their utterance is that in a play which has much prose, they speak verse, Gertrude invariably, Claudius almost always. That rather dignified, ceremonious and unimpassioned utterance, which seems appropriate to them as public figures, is especially marked in I.ii, the first scene in which they appear; here the balanced orotundity of Claudius suggests at once a proper order in the court, and a certain hollowness; it justifies the common reaction to Claudius, on the part of audience or readers, as 'courteous and never undignified', an efficient and respectable monarch, and excites Hamlet's suspicion. [9] There is much art in the King's manner of speaking, and in II.ii he indulges in an amplification of a kind which, in the mouth of Polonius, earns a rebuke from the Queen:

> KING: Something have you heard
> Of Hamlet's transformation; so I call it,
> Sith nor th'exterior nor the inward man
> Resembles that it was. (II.ii.4)

> POLONIUS: Your noble son is mad.
> Mad call I it; for, to define true madness,
> What is't but to be nothing else but mad?
> But let that go.
> QUEEN: More matter with less art. (II.ii.92)

[9] Bradley, p. 138, and cf. Honigmann, above, p. 140. Knights, pp. 41–2, finds Claudius 'repulsive', a 'slimy beast', on his first appearance, but the text simply does not warrant this response.

This does not mean that Claudius is simply artful or hollow, but that his characteristic mode of speech is elaborate and dignified; even when he reveals his guilt in an aside in III.i, or attempts to pray, or plots murder with Laertes, he maintains a commanding tone, and speaks in verse. The Queen initiates nothing, and has much less to say; she seems morally shallow, and if the 'thorns that in her bosom lodge' prick her, they do so only on occasion, and she quickly forgets; but this is all that can be held against her as she is shown in action, and her language throughout has dignity. Hamlet's attack in the closet scene proceeds more from his imagination than from anything the audience has seen or heard, so that if her election in marrying Claudius reveals her inadequacies, it would have been a good question to ask of Hamlet's father why his choice fell on her.

Laertes and Ophelia have much of their father in them. Laertes inherits the assurance of his father's commonplaces, as well as his lack of scruple, while Ophelia takes over something of his simplicity, a simplicity close to foolishness. Laertes is always positive, inclined to burst out in a 'speech o'fire', and although his language is more impassioned and less stately than that of Claudius, he is given a certain dignity as speaking, like the King and Queen, almost always in blank verse. Ophelia says little, and much of that little is negative; unlike Laertes, she is pliant to the will of others, and admits to her father,

> I do not know, my lord, what I should think.

Her mode of speaking is neutral or cool, and when she runs mad, she does so not in rage or passion, but turning all 'to favour and to prettiness', before dying in water, as one 'native and indued unto that element'.

These characters may borrow at times, especially Ophelia and Gertrude when describing an event, from the 'common pool' of verse, but generally they each have an individual manner, which remains consistent, and seems natural, not affected. Polonius, Rosencrantz and Guildenstern can speak with appropriate formality in the King's presence, but for them it is clearly a politic, not a natural style; they adapt their speech to suit the occasion. The cunning of Polonius is limited by his stupidity, and he is liable to fall into a series of foolish figures, to elaborate what he has to say, for the sake of his self-importance. The greatest insights of his policy emerge in rhetorical flourishes, or the commonplaces of his advice to Laertes. If Polonius is smugly unaware of the deficiencies of his conscious craft, Rosencrantz and Guildenstern give themselves up to the service of the King, and become his instruments, adapting themselves, like Osric, to the 'tune of the time'; they are jocular with Hamlet, formal at court, and flatter the King in private, as in their acceptance of the commission to England in III.iii. They are sponges, to use Hamlet's word, soaking up not only 'the King's countenance', but his style of speaking, or Hamlet's, as occasion demands.

These figures, like Osric, are limited and defined by their inadequacies, Polonius by his stupidity, Rosencrantz and Guildenstern by their surrender of themselves as the King's instruments; these two cannot even be distinguished one from the other. Polonius has a special function as a critic of language; he once acted, and still feels qualified to judge an actor, as also to comment on words, to damn 'beautified' and praise 'mobled'. In his insensitivity, his lack of true feeling for language, he acts as a foil to Hamlet, whose skill, intelligence and sensitivity show the brighter by contrast. There is another critic in the play, Horatio, who, after reporting the history of Denmark in the opening scene in verse which belongs to the 'common pool', rather than the character, becomes himself in speeches marked by their brevity and directness. A certain irony or self-depreciation appears in characteristic phrases, 'A piece of him', 'A truant disposition', 'Half a share', 'You might have rhymed', and elsewhere he goes straight to the point, clear-sighted and honest. No flatterer, certainly not 'passion's slave', he seems, more than any other character, to know himself, and hence affords a point of rest, as the one personage about whom there is no doubt, who speaks his mind, and who criticises the excesses of Hamlet, with his 'these are but wild and whirling words, my lord', or his ' 'Twere to consider too curiously, to consider so'.

As the companion of Hamlet, Horatio exposes, by simple contrast, as well as in his occasional criticism, the Prince's wordiness, his habit of considering too curiously, of pursuing a quibble or an image into wild speculation or generalisation. While Horatio contracts his sayings into bare phrases, Hamlet expands a comment into a paragraph, as if unable to resist adding another word or two. He is a born actor, continually improvising, and the only figures who match him are the players, his 'good friends'; he knows them well, and shares a speech with the First Player, delivering it with good accent; he instructs them in acting, and writes a passage for a play. He is never so confident and full of humour as when he hears of them or is in their company; if he were not a prince, here he would be at home.

When he first appears, Hamlet is in a solemn suit of black; it is a costume fitting the role of continual mourner in which he has cast himself, as he acknowledges in his first lines,

> These indeed seem,
> For they are actions that a man might play,
> But I have that within which passeth show,
> These but the trappings and the suits of woe. (I.ii.83)

He soon frees himself for other roles by putting on an 'antic disposition', which allows him to play any part. Usually this is planned, as in his teasing of Polonius, or of Rosencrantz and Guildenstern or of Osric, but sometimes he seems almost unconsciously to adopt a role, as when he jumps into Ophelia's grave to rant with Laertes; his visit to Ophelia, as she describes it, seems of a piece with this, as does his behaviour in the nunnery-scene, or his outburst against his mother. On these occasions, as devoted lover, scorned and bitter suitor, or shocked and scornful son, he plainly overacts; the feeling exceeds its object, but is not to be explained simply as a form of 'emotional relief'.[10] Only by a degree of overacting can Hamlet convince others that his reason is tainted, as when he acts the fool outrageously with Polonius, or with Claudius in IV.ii; and it is difficult to know the borderline between what he does deliberately and what is involuntary, when he can so catch the accent of any role.

For a moment in V.ii, Hamlet most fulsomely plays the courtier, and, in a speech that echoes the hollowest court rhetoric, apologises to Laertes:

> Was't Hamlet wrong'd Laertes? Never Hamlet.
> If Hamlet from himself be ta'aen away
> And when he's not himself does wrong Laertes,
> Then Hamlet does it not, Hamlet denies it.
> Who does it then? His madness. If't be so,
> Hamlet is of the faction that is wrong'd. (V.ii.244)

Hamlet is hardly himself in this speech, or in the many parts he plays. Apart from some neutral exchanges with Horatio, there remain the soliloquies, where, if anywhere, the style of the real Hamlet might be

[10] T. S. Eliot, *Selected Essays* (1951 edition), p. 146.

expected to appear. In fact, two of the major soliloquies present a gloomily introspective figure half in love with easeful death, and two others show an aggressive, self-critical revenger. The accents of both Hamlets are familiar, the drooping, and the vigorous:

> O, that this too too sullied flesh would melt;

> O, what a rogue and peasant slave am I.

Hamlet passive and active, wan with the pale cast of thought and Hamlet firm in the native hue of resolution are both real and the same person. Here, when Hamlet is alone, and can divest himself of his roles, he appears in contradictory aspects, and speaking in different rhythms.

He has no characteristic resonance, but a multitude of voices, among which those represented in the soliloquies seem most nearly to suggest certain certainties about him; it was perhaps necessary to give him soliloquies to provide some centre of focus for a character of so many shapes and voices, but the certainties these offer are contradictory. Hamlet seems the master of all styles, but has no distinctive utterance of his own; like the actors to whom he is devoted, he can suit the action to the word, the word to the action, and is able

> to show virtue her own feature, scorn her own image, and the very age and body of the time his form and pressure; (III.ii.26)

but, still like the actors, his personality lies in the roles he plays; then he can mirror nature and act the part to the life, or better. When he is himself, he reveals a mass of contradictions, which he escapes from, or resolves temporarily, in taking on another's personality. By doing this, he can conceal his aims, and unmask those of others, who are confined within their given modes of utterance; but he eludes definition himself, and his mystery remains, the mystery of the supreme actor, who never reveals himself, but can explain

> any show that you will show him. Be not you asham'd to show, he'll not shame to tell you what it means. (III.ii.154)

Hamlet's consciousness dominates the play, and it is largely because of his play-acting, and because he feels unable to trust any appearance, that we are made to sense the excitement of craft meeting craft. Though others may, as he says, fool him to the top of his bent, that is, make him play the fool, he is never taken in by them, and he seems to credit

L

Polonius, and his aunt-mother and uncle-father, with far more sublety in intrigue against him than they display. They are more stupid, and more straightforward than he would have them be. All his manoeuvres seem directed more towards resolving or escaping from the clashes between the active and passive elements in himself than towards ex- posing other characters; and there is no final resolution or escape, only a trusting to providence, or chance, in 'The readiness is all', before he dies, addressing his 'audience to this act', in his last and best role, that of hero.

VIII

The Setting for Hamlet

JOHN RUSSELL BROWN

★

Let me tell you at the commencement that it is the large and sweeping impression produced by means of scene and the movement of the figures which is undoubtedly the most valuable means at your disposal. I say this only after very many doubts and after much experience.[1]

THIS is Gordon Craig instructing a theatre director in the art of producing Shakespeare's tragedies. It is not the usual language for a discussion of *Hamlet:* instead of fine distinctions and discriminations, here is talk of a 'large and sweeping impression'; and nothing is said about words, poetry, style, levels or ambiguities of meaning, moral problems, politics, religious concepts, structure, characters. His 'impression' might be quite abstract, existing only in space and time, requiring the actor to be a 'figure' rather than a voice or a human being. Yet in performance *Hamlet* has a full and extraordinary life which is so difficult to describe in customary terms that Gordon Craig might possibly be right in thinking that it is controlled by the general effects of scene and movement. He is at least a conscientious witness: he had many doubts and much experience; he thought so highly of Shakespeare's plays that he later came to believe that they should never be performed, not that the theatre was too crude for them but that actors and directors did not have sufficient skill to match Shakespeare.

In this chapter I propose to follow Gordon Craig's lead, and neglect hero and themes in order to discuss the setting, movements and tempos of *The Tragedy of Hamlet* in performance. If this approach seems too insubstantial, or incapable of sufficient precision, remember that the most abstract forms of art have their own kinds of discipline and refine-

[1] G. Craig, *On the Art of the Theatre* (ed. 1957), p. 21.

ment. A lifetime's experience lies behind the creation and appreciation of a painting by Jackson Pollock or Ben Nicholson. And no one could doubt the subtleties of music with many centuries of evolvement and experiment. Moreover, if a 'large and sweeping impression' seems unable to embody Shakespeare's *Hamlet*, consider that this must co-exist with the words of the play: it will certainly be modified by them and, if Craig is only partly right, the text may be affected in return by the manipulation of objects, figures and time. Theatrical art is one of the most complex of human activities; let us start this approach to one example of it by taking the way which a theatrical artist suggests.

★   ★   ★

Of course, Craig's notion of 'scene' was not Shakespeare's: no Elizabethan would think of constructing a series of 'sets' to imitate or suggest the appropriate locale and mood for each scene. But the setting of a play was just as important. Perhaps the main difference was that Elizabethan actors could never forget it, never construct an ingenious piece of scenery and then perform in front of it with no further regard for its mood or form. Setting and acting were necessarily in accord, because the most common means of changing the stage-picture were the actors' costumes, properties, bearing and behaviour. In addition, there were a few larger properties and sound effects that could be used, and music. But actors, by their very presences, could completely change the picture, its mood, line, colour, form. Many effects were obviously beyond them—the suggestion of a particular house or a particular landscape—but we should not underestimate the range or effectiveness of their settings.

Consider the change from an interior to the open air. Fine clothes would be cloaked as for a journey, or light clothes exchanged for more durable ones. Distances would seem to be greater, as the actors call instead of speak, or crowd together to hear a confidence that would have been exchanged at ease within doors. In the open they would perhaps look further off, and leave the stage with a greater sense of resolution and purpose. If this change took place during winter or at night, all these effects would be greatly accentuated; the relaxed behaviour of a sheltered interior would contrast with the quick movements and huddled forms appropriate to the cold air, the apparent openness of a well-lit interior with the difficult recognitions of the dark.

The fact that snow was not represented on the stage, nor darkness, great height or distance, would only serve to accentuate the means whereby the 'scene' was suggested: long, heavy and dull-coloured cloaks, close groupings, the alternating stillness and rapidity, whispers, sudden calls. Some changes of setting were even more impressive: from a court scene with costly, crowded costumes and formal groupings to the low-pitched colours and relaxation of servants' quarters, or the countryside; from a public room to a private, from a domestic scene to a military, or to a religious. These are some of the settings which Shakespeare used in *Hamlet* and which any staging of the play should try to represent, no matter how complicated or simple the scenery may be. To consider these changes in due order is to view an element of the play which Shakespeare controlled with care.

It begins high up in the open during a bitterly cold night, with only a few cloaked figures and a silent, questing ghost: and the ghost alone does not feel the cold nor, until the end, move with any neglect of formal majesty. Then, with a great and unheralded change, there is a crowded court interior, ample in words and gesture, formal and colourful for a royal celebration. Soon the stage almost empties, but remains an interior until a return to the battlements, night and the ghost. Then it is the court again, and will remain so for more than two consecutive acts. But now there is less formality and much coming and going, hearing and overhearing; and Hamlet is for a time alone, and for at least a few moments, silent and defeated. Within the interior, the action moves forward but the stage twice empties completely, once after Hamlet's new resolve to watch the king and once after Claudius' to watch Hamlet; and then it fills steadily towards a second formal scene, the crowded play-scene. This time there is a double formality, that of Elsinore and that of the world of the play. It ends suddenly in disorder and, as lights are called for off-stage, with a new impression of darkness, the more alert for being indoors where entrances can be made in an instant. Short, broken episodes follow, still in the interior and at night, and with one long emotional scene played intimately as in the queen's private chamber; and there the ghost reappears to be seen only by Hamlet. It is still night when, after a brief pursuit, Hamlet appears guarded before Claudius, and is ordered to leave the court under escort. Then, after this long sequence in the interior, the stage is again the open air, the change accentuated by the introduction of the new marching figures of Fortinbras and his army; they belong to a different nation, as

well as introducing a full military setting. Just as they are going, Hamlet
enters attended and dressed for travel. He is soon alone again but now
as if in a vast stretch of open country; and then he walks off-stage. The
release to the wider, relaxed setting was brief, for at once the scene
returns to an interior for further action at court. But now Hamlet is
no longer there, and no more than three or four people are on the stage
at any one time; and they repeatedly move apart from each other. The
wider setting is, however, suggested by the freedom of Ophelia's madness which disregards court and domestic proprieties, by the entry of a
sailor and, most strongly, by the noise and shouts of an angry crowd
twice heard off-stage when Laertes returns as if from France. Then there
is a fourth move to the open, for the gravedigger, Hamlet's return to
Denmark and the funeral of Ophelia. This ceremony with procession,
bell and priest is the only elaborate religious setting in the play, but in
the shrouded presence of the king and queen it also echoes the formalities of Elsinore. And, like the large court scenes, this also breaks into disorder as Hamlet and Laertes have to be parted from each other by
force. Then the stage rapidly empties and the scene is once more the
interior with Hamlet and Horatio alone, and twice visited by single
messengers. The stage fills for the duel and this new formality, with the
king and queen enthroned, leads like the previous two, to an uproar;
but this time it leads on, not to hurried partings and an empty stage, but
to the stillness and quietness of death. At once drums are heard in the
distance and Fortinbras enters the scene, its splendour now in ruin at his
feet. He is attended by his soldiers and dressed as for his earlier appearance outside Elsinore in the country, and he is accompanied by the
English Ambassadors, entirely new figures who also come as from a
journey. This entry from the world outside brings a last formality, so
that in procession the bodies of Hamlet, the king, the queen and Laertes
are taken out of sight, borne aloft to be placed 'high on a stage' in view
of the 'yet unknowing world'.

     If we borrow terms from the criticism of the visual arts, we may say
of the changing impression of the 'scene' that the stage-picture is
alternately an 'open' and a 'closed' composition: sometimes it is a self-
contained whole, bounded by apparent limits; at other times it is
limitless and flowing, suggesting continuations beyond the bounds of
the stage. And in these changes, the picture is eloquent: the court is a
prison from which escape can be made, an established pattern that is
broken, an arrangement, with a clear centre and interdependent ele-

ments, which gives place to one isolated figure within its emptied frame, and later to disorder and forced actions at night, and finally to carnage and a new central authority. Or in its open form, with distant views obscured at first by darkness, it is a place free for visitations and for movement.

(This contrast between open and closed compositions was accentuated by the form of Elizabethan playhouses. If an actor stood close to the tiring-house façade he was viewed by all the audience in relation to an architectural background with a regular, centralised composition. But if he stood near the outermost edge of the platform-stage a large proportion of the audience would see no background to his figure except an anonymous audience and the horizontal lines of the galleries at some distance from the stage. These two extremes were modified in many ways, particularly when a crowd of actors or large properties were introduced to remove the sense of isolation natural to the extreme edge of the stage; but the eloquent contrast between them is probably why so many Elizabethan plays, besides *Hamlet*, use an alternation between interiors and open country so frequently and so confidently).

The *dramatis personae* are meaningful as soon as they appear in these varied settings, before they have spoken a single word. Hamlet himself starts with a long silence in a formal set scene, watched and watching; he is drawn into the pattern and then moves apart and is left alone; he leaves on talk of the ghost, and subsequently waits for the ghost on the battlements, and then follows it; returning to the interior, he plans his own formal scene and then in darkness and rapid movement seeks his mother; he is pursued and escapes to the open; he is absent from the court to return, at first unrecognised, for the funeral; then after some preparation he takes another formal position, stripping himself of his doublet and signs of rank for the duel; in the last rapid and extended disorder he assumes control and dies in silence; and then his body is honoured as it is carried off-stage. Or, for example, Laertes: dutifully taking his time and place in the formal picture and then dressed and ready for a journey from court; returning to an emptier court with an insurgent, disordered crowd off-stage; the King and Queen following him outside in mourning; taking part in the duel and helplessly dying in the final static picture. Or, Claudius and Gertrude leaving Elsinore for the funeral. Or, Ophelia moving with circumspection, until she is the only person to act within the court as if she were anywhere, or nowhere, free from all restraint. Or Horatio who goes to the court from the battlements, who greets the sailor and then appears at the graveyard, who is never at the centre of a formal grouping until at the end when he is with the dying Hamlet.

The story, or sequence of events, also gains relevance from the settings. This is chiefly effected by the device of repetition, so that each return to Elsinore catches reflections of its earlier manifestations and is given significance by them. The last formal grouping, for instance, contains memories of earlier ones: the first apparently for Claudius to express his purposes unopposed, until he is disturbed by the black figure of Hamlet; the second to watch an acted intimacy and then an acted murder; the third to reverence Ophelia's corpse; the fourth for a duel. And 'atmospheric' effects are repeated too: the impression of darkness in Elsinore after the play-scene recalls that of the battlements, so that the ghost's return may be almost expected. For the repetitions also tie the various elements of the action together and, in the last scene, give a clear sense of completion, a strength very necessary in so episodic a narrative with ambiguous characterisation and almost continual verbal elaboration. When Hamlet finally controls the disordered formality the audience will sense through the setting that a new pattern has been established from the old. This may even be the first and most powerful impression of the last scene, for it is visual and, therefore, rapid, complete and unquestioned. And, when Fortinbras and the Ambassador enter, the audience will know that Elsinore is no longer a restricted and threatened enclosure; the scene is open, if not freed.

Gordon Craig was right: the changing setting is a 'valuable means' of expressing story, themes and characters, and of giving coherence to many elements. Its impressions are not conveyed by words, but visually, by objects and behaviour, and by sounds and modes of speaking. Because of this, they affect an audience without it realising what is happening, and swiftly and largely; in performance they can carry and shape the play in spite of predisposition or conscious reaction or in-attention.

*　　　*　　　*

For all its broad effectiveness, the setting contributes to the subtlety of the play in performance, by the interaction of closed and open stage-pictures, and by repetitions. And subtleties within a robust eloquence are found again in 'the movement of the figures' within the 'scene'.

1 The duel, V.ii., at the Shakespeare Memorial Theatre, Stratford-upon-Avon, 1961

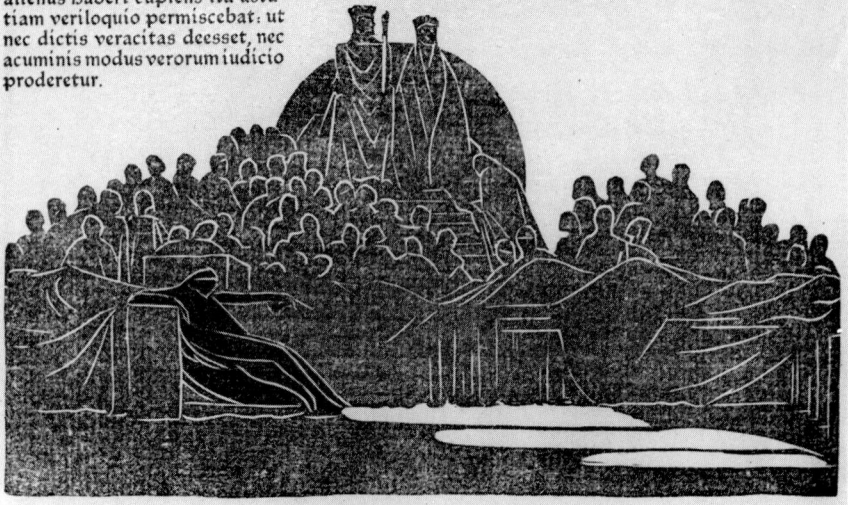

alienus haberi cupiens ita astu-
tiam veriloquio permiscebat: ut
nec dictis veracitas deesset, nec
acuminis modus verorum iudicio
proderetur.

2a I.ii: The first Court scene

ACT I SCENE III
LINES 1-10
THE TRAGICALL HISTORIE OF

2b I.iii: Ophelia, Polonius and Laertes

(Illustrations by Gordon Craig from the Cranach Press 'Hamlet')

3a III.i: Hamlet's soliloquy, 'To be, or not to be'

3b III.ii: 'The Mousetrap'

(Illustrations by Gordon Craig from the Cranach Press 'Hamlet')

4 The arrival of Fortinbras, V.ii. Forbes-Robertson as Hamlet

The most unquestioned effect when we start to consider movement is the dominance and unusual independence of the hero. Sir Tyrone Guthrie has said that:

> *Hamlet*, oddly enough, is a play which can be rehearsed very quickly . . . If the producer and the actor who plays Hamlet are well prepared and in full agreement, the production can, in my opinion, be put together in two weeks. The reason for this is that none of Hamlet's scenes demand a very close *rapport* between the partici- pants. Most of the psychological material is conveyed in soliloquy; to a unique degree the *rapport* is not between actor and actor, but between Hamlet and the audience.[2]

Hamlet is alone for his soliloquies of course, and throughout the play he voices thoughts which are almost soliloquies within the dialogue; he first speaks in an aside; he watches and is watched. He repeatedly moves apart from the other figures, and they must 'seek my Lord Hamlet'—the ghost, Horatio and the soldiers, Rosencrantz and Guilden- stern, Polonius, the 'tragedians of the city', Claudius, Laertes, Osric and the second messenger who follows him. Once Claudius and Ger- trude avoid an encounter with him, but Ophelia is 'loosed' to him and later his 'mother stays' for him. Hamlet does not need to seek other characters, but Horatio, the actors, the musicians and the Norwegian Captain come when he calls. Only the gravedigger, the memory of Yorick and Ophelia's funeral procession are encountered by Hamlet without being summoned or seeming to wait for him. Many scenes conclude with movements directing attention towards Hamlet: the stage first empties so that Horatio may seek him and, despite many new characters and interests, it does not empty again until Hamlet is shown alone preparing to see his father's spirit. Every one of his exit-lines arouses strong expectation for his subsequent action: he has to follow the ghost, return to court with a new and compelling duty, prepare *The Mousetrap*, fight apparent madness, confront his mother, the king, treacherous friends, his own apparent lack of resolution. In the last scene but one, after a general climax, he walks off-stage before its conclusion; but here he speaks a riddle-like defiance and afterwards there is a marked hiatus in dramatic development in which Claudius speaks briefly, sending Horatio and Gertrude to attend on Hamlet and strengthening his own and Laertes' purposes. Even on this occasion, when he leaves

[2] *A Life in the Theatre* (1960), pp. 58–9.

the stage for no expressed purpose, the groupings are disturbed and rapidly displaced.

Hamlet dominates so obviously that the figures among whom he appears are often underestimated, not least by those who have to produce and perform the play without sufficient time or patience to discover the qualities inherent in the text. (Shakespeare often exceeds ordinary assumptions, and contrives more than can be easily appreciated.) This hero he has placed among characters who are subtly strong, and subtly related to each other. And this achievement is not revealed until the play is allowed to grow and establish itself in production on the stage. First, there is a concerted effect, the impression of Elsinore as a dangerous and involved society. In the simulated court and family, sudden arrivals are discovered to be foreknown; even casual re-entries are often expected. Other figures, besides Hamlet, are watched or shadowed—Ophelia, Laertes, the players, Claudius, Gertrude. Public pronouncements and general celebrations have private implications; what seems leisurely is truly hurried, and sudden orders have been long deliberated. At the very beginning, a spirit visits Elsinore who is unconfined by darkness and bitter cold, and who fades on the 'crowing of the cock' and the tender light of matin. And throughout the play there are moments, without movement, when characters remember 'our Saviour's birth', 'the burning eyes of heaven' or 'heavenly powers'; when Claudius begs help of 'angels'. The figures on stage move carecarefully, with hidden urgency or reluctance, with interdependence and with an awareness of another, spiritual reality.

Secondly, the strength of individual movements or gestures cannot be judged from the text alone; their eloquence is often achieved without words or where words seem unimportant. Here indeed is their unique contribution, for movements can represent reactions which are consciously hidden or beyond the conscious grasp of the characters. This may be seen in Claudius and Gertrude. Their first appearance together for a public celebration of marriage is a large and simple visual effect, and Gertrude's close concern for her son a simple and, perhaps, unremarkable modification. The only movement which is strange here is the speed with which Claudius leads her off to celebrate a reconciliation with Hamlet and at the same time leaves him, apparently unnoticed, behind. From this point until after the play-scene Claudius and Gertrude always enter together, and remain together except when the king wishes to spy on Hamlet. Their movements seem to represent a comparatively single-minded relationship. But Claudius enters without Gertrude for his 'prayer-scene' (III,iii) and, for the first time, Gertrude enters without him for the 'closet-scene' (III.iv) and is left alone, again for the first time, when Polonius hides behind the arras. Thereafter earlier accord is revalued by an increasing separation, often poignantly silent, and unexpected. When Claudius calls Gertrude to leave with him after Hamlet has dragged off Polonius' body, she makes no reply; twice more he urges her and she is still silent. But he does not remonstrate or question; rather he speaks of his own immediate concerns and, far from supporting her with assurances, becomes more aware of his own fears:

> O, come away;
> My soul is full of discord and dismay. (IV.i.44)

Emotion has been heightened, but they leave together without further words. The audience has been made aware of a new distance between Gertrude and Claudius, of her immobility and silence, and of his self-concern, haste and insistence. From this moment onwards their movements on leaving the stage become increasingly eloquent. When Claudius has set a watch on Ophelia, he appeals to Gertrude for sympathy, telling what he can of the dangers that threaten; but she says nothing and, if Claudius pauses, will draw attention away from him to her physical withdrawal. When Laertes enters, supported by insurgents, Gertrude instinctively tries to hold him back and protect Claudius; but he, in contrast, faces Laertes' sword, assumes command, and after curt assurances, forgets his queen in immediate concerns. At the end of the scene, after Ophelia's second appearance, Gertrude has to leave the stage without a word from Claudius, or to him. Danger had brought them together for a moment, but the spectacle of Ophelia's suffering separates them further than before: this is the first time that the queen must leave entirely alone. The point will not be lost in performance, for as the king moves with urgent purpose, she will leave slowly with silent grief and helplessness; there will be a contrast of tempo and, quite simply, her exit will take much longer to complete, so that she must be seen alone on the empty stage. (An actress will be tempted to wait and then make a separate exit expressing her own unappeased grief.)

When Claudius returns with Laertes, he momentarily departs from duologue for a kind of soliloquy:

> Not that I think you did not love your father;
> But that I know love is begun by time;
> And that I see, in passages of proof,
> Time qualifies the spark and fire of it.
> *There lives within the very flame of love,*
> *A kind of wick or snuff that will abate;*
> *And nothing is at a like goodness still* . . . .(IV.vii.110)

His new isolation from Gertrude supplies a motive for this digression from immediate and dangerous concerns; and will strengthen its effect. If Claudius moves apart, or merely breaks his contact with Laertes, the stage-picture will lose definite focus, judder or stall with the absence of explicit motive, and the audience's sense of time, relevance and perspective will become insecure. It may hear echoes of the Player King:

> What to ourselves in passion we propose,
> The passion ending, doth the purpose lose;
> This world is not for aye, nor 'tis not strange
> That even our loves should with our fortunes change. . .
> (III.ii.204)

and even of the ghost himself:

> O Hamlet, what a falling-off was there!
>   . . . to decline
> Upon a wretch whose natural gifts were poor
> To those of mine! (I.v.47)

These are refinements which may not be realised in performance, but because of the movements of the figures in the later passages of the play, Claudius can at least seem far removed from the immediate context of persuading Laertes and appear to consider, momentarily, his new isolation. The audience will note an effort as he recalls himself with 'But, to the quick of the ulcer', and once more seeks 'desperate appliance'.

Nothing stops the physical and emotional separation of the king and queen, and some movements express it more sharply. After Gertrude has told of Ophelia's death, Laertes leaves precipitously and it is of him that Claudius is thinking as he follows, not at all of Gertrude still rapt in her evocation of Ophelia's death and her helpless admission of 'Drown'd, drown'd'. When Hamlet has left the graveyard, Gertrude is ordered in a single line to 'set some watch' over her son; now Claudius can easily dismiss her and be free to ensure an immediate attempt on Hamlet's life and take a kind of pleasure in the prospect. At no point has Shakespeare caused either of them to comment directly on their progressive separation, yet the audience's awareness of it develops; and so strongly can this be fostered in performance that it may seem at last that, in failing either to speak or to make a complete break, these characters are unable to understand all that is happening, and powerless to help themselves. The audience is encouraged to observe more deeply than either of the *dramatis personae*. Their dying cries gain ironic force and clarity from this long preparation: Gertrude calls on her 'dear' son and implicates her husband in murder; Claudius, with 'O yet defend me, friends; I am but hurt', appeals for a response he has never considered and tries a desperate lie. The audience may sense, without further information, that these few words express what has been progressively implied by movement and gesture, and that the subsequent immobility of death marks a true termination.

Shakespeare has ensured that the audience of *Hamlet* views its characters in depth. Yet this metaphor is hardly adequate; for what he has added to the stage-picture is a fourth, or psychological, dimension in which the hidden and subconscious reactions of each character can be presented, by movement as well as words. And there is even a fifth dimension in which consequence and providence, or fate, play out their parts: so Claudius and Gertrude take their various places on the stage according to their unspoken thoughts and feelings, but also impelled by the pressure of their earlier actions and by uncontrollable events. Like other characters they seem in part helpless, their final positions inevitable. Despite the energy of words in *Hamlet* there are manifestations of character and of situation which are expressed by movement rather than speech. The mirror of the stage gains a clearer attention than life because its dimensions can represent the deeper reality of individual consciousness—as contrasted with the realism of outward behaviour and speech—and suggest another reality in which some fate or process of cause-and-effect leads individuals towards an expression of their inward truth and their true inter-relationships.

These silent stage-realities are less immediately apparent than sharp exchanges of dialogue, resonant or poetic sayings, or constructed rhetoric, and less easily studied than repetitious images of corruption verbal distinctions between appearance and reality, or affirmations of an ideal world behind that of imperfect action. But again Gordon

Craig was right: movements play a significant part in the audience's concerted and developing reaction to the tragedy.

Although the strong and subtle eloquence of movement should be viewed in its large impressions, it can best be identified by following individual figures through the play. By making Rosencrantz and Guildenstern move together at Claudius' command, Shakespeare ensured that their minds seem mechanical and undistinguished: so much so, that theatre directors often assume that the two characters are indistinguishable.[3] Their unspoken thoughts are first clearly indicated after Hamlet's direct questions, when their mutual silence and then the whispered 'What say you?' draw close attention to their instinctive need to keep together. Their eagerness to play safe is also manifested when Hamlet dismisses them with brief courtesy on three successive occasions, for as they murmur quick civilities, bow or exchange looks, the audience will see an unspoken embarrassment and, as they go out, a drawing together. When Claudius calls Guildenstern after the closet-scene, both of them enter at once, silently. Guildenstern has the smarter mind, smoothing over awkward moments and being quick to question, with 'Prison, my lord? . . . In what, my dear lord? . . . A thing, my lord?' Yet when action is needed for pursuing and guarding Hamlet it is Rosencrantz who assumes the lead without discussion. They at last drop all pretence of friendship and appear with the 'guard' as Hamlet's captors and warders: they leave that scene at one with the silent soldiers who move impersonally, under orders. Their natures are progressively revealed, one brusque and one watchful, and the consequences of having become the tools of Claudius are progressively manifested, without their choice or knowledge.

The audience's view of Horatio changes less, but deepens in the same way and widens. In the first scene, although he 'trembles and looks pale', he holds back his judgement until he can speak in an ordered way:

> Before my God, I might not this believe
> Without the sensible and true avouch
> Of mine own eyes. (I.i.56)

And in the course of the play he has no sudden movement or impulse, or immediacy of speech, to draw attention to him. Yet he is often on stage silent and watchful, and ready with a brief reply when such is

[3] Cf. A. C. Sprague, *Shakespeare and the Actors* (1944), pp. 147–8.

required by Hamlet. Before the play-scene, he enters with an unasser-
tive promptness when Hamlet calls. Perhaps the audience's view of him
is more ambiguous when he proves unable to keep 'good watch' over
Ophelia; but this is not made an issue in the dialogue nor emphasised
by a return to the stage. It could be sensed only as an unspecific uneasiness, and it would not prevent 'Now cracks a noble heart. Good
night, sweet prince. . . .' from sounding with a steady, deeply felt
assurance. It is for such moments that his static and always unembarrassed
physical presentation was chosen. This figure has been made remarkable
and strong by lack of movement and by silent attentiveness, as well as
by brief speeches.

The comic aspects of Polonius' speech and behaviour ensure that the
audience views him with a measure of detachment; yet Shakespeare
also presented him as an isolated figure and this can draw sympathy.
He grows as a comic butt when he becomes certain that Hamlet is mad
for love, yet having claimed:

> I will find
> Where truth is hid, though it were hid indeed
> Within the centre (II.ii.157)

he rapidly leaves the private encounter he has sought with only an
artless and simple courtesy to withstand the prince's satire and his
comment, perhaps overheard, 'These tedious old fools': his movements
may now seem ignominious. After *The Mousetrap* has manifested something like the full danger of the situation, Polonius comes to Claudius
and his busy insistence on his original plan for trapping Hamlet is
neither welcomed nor heeded by his master whose thoughts are elsewhere; the eager Polonius must pause and then leave without any
response commensurate with his purposes. His urgent words to Gertrude meet with an almost equally slack reply, as though she too has
other thoughts than his. By movements and contrasts of tempo the
audience will view Polonius less simply than at first. After it has been
shocked by disregard for his daughter's feelings and has laughed at
misplaced confidence in his own intelligence and petty cunning, it
may recognise in hurried, surreptitious, isolated movements the limitations of a self-centred mind; there may be a quickening of sympathy
for his blindness and clumsiness. His death, fussing helplessly in the
toils of an arras, seems an unalterable conclusion.

On his return to the play in Act IV, Laertes is an important contrast with Hamlet, not only in his reckless and outspoken attitude to revenge, but also in the way that his independent action yields to movements alongside Claudius, even at his sister's funeral and between the bouts of the duel. Ophelia, on the other hand, has an effective isolation. She is presented as of key importance to Hamlet, but is not shown with him until she stands as a speechless decoy during the 'To be, or not to be' soliloquy. When she has to make a decision, her brief speeches—'no more but so? . . . I shall obey, my lord . . . . My lord, I do not know . . . No, my lord. . . . Ay, my Lord . . . I think nothing, my lord'—cannot answer the audience's curiosity: she might evade or misrepresent; she may seem to have considered deeply, or to live only for the moment, lightly. The audience will intently view her young, untried body for some further sign: her silences and brevity of speech, contrasting with the volubility of her brother and father, and her passive waiting for Hamlet to 'affront' her, ensure that, if she speaks her lines with the studied care their versification, syntax and vocabulary seem to suggest, she will appear to have a painfully private, uncommunicable conscious-ness; when she exposes herself to Hamlet's scorn ('you made me believe so, . . . I was the more deceived') and then lies to him about her father, a strong and hidden conflict of sensations will be keenly felt. She sits at *The Mousetrap* taunted by Hamlet and then trying to enter the world of the play he has prepared; but he does not notice her depar-ture and probably the audience does not either. She returns for the two mad-scenes in which both words and movements express her helpless thoughts at last, in all their range: sexual, pitiful and wilful. She leaves the first scene in patient pride and the second with remembrance of her father and of 'all Christian souls'. But her isolation is greater than before, for no one can contact her or restrain her, not even Laertes. Her in-fluence upon the play continues without her actual presence, as Ger-trude reports she died making a wreath for the dead, supported and then lost in flowing water. The movements of this slight figure express the limits of her being and add to the impression of the effects of time and accident in the play. Most characters move towards a single-minded utterance and gesture, but the spirit of the young and beautiful Ophelia is expended wastefully and, until she has become a corpse, out of reach of others.

Hamlet is often seen as a hero who through uncertainty seeks to 'end his part in peace' like a perfected actor, with his cause 'rightly' known, to accept his role of 'scourge and minister', to be 'ready' for his 'end' and accept heaven's 'ordinance' in its timing and planning. But he does all this in a world which is also progressively known and progressively caught by processes which are not controlled by the characters' conscious thought. The direction of Hamlet's passage through the play differs most significantly in his attempt to understand this process. He has not won a 'special providence' for his particular cause; he has won a thoughtful and difficult confidence in that providence. While his courage, affection and deliberation are revealed, and his anger, pain and despair for the 'harsh world', the others move with equal certainty towards an unwilled revelation of their deepest natures. The end of *Hamlet* is the end of a world, of Elsinore as well as its prince. It is a general doom, like the last scene of *Lear;* perhaps more thoroughly, for the dead bodies must be removed by foreign captains at the command of a foreign inheritor.

Hamlet's own reality in the fourth and fifth dimensions of the stage-picture will be readily acknowledged. Here it is more important to show how his movements towards the end are concerted with a general realignment and a resolution of the tensions and interrelationships of Elsinore. First, there is the unsought encounter with the gravedigger, in which Hamlet's movements reveal a series of coincidences. He does not say why he visits the grave and does not know whose it is, yet the audience knows it is Ophelia's. He is held in talk and attention before being told that this nameless man started to dig graves on the 'very day' that he himself was born; and this time the audience could not foresee the coincidence either. When Yorick's skull is put into Hamlet's hand, his past enjoyment comes unsummoned to his memory. This situation seems designed for him without his knowledge, and he may well pause several times; certainly when the funeral procession enters he holds back until, as he explains later, he 'forgets himself' (V.ii.76). Such hesitation is an important indication of his mind, for, now that he has returned from England, Hamlet is not given any soliloquy to speak his thoughts. He is closest to this in the dialogue with Horatio at the beginning of the following (and last) scene. Now Hamlet is fully prepared for action ('is't not perfect conscience To quit him with this arm . . . . The interim is mine'), and Horatio seems apprehensive for his safety; but he is content to wait for the encounter, this one seeming to be arranged by his enemy rather than by coincidence or providence. In a gathering complexity of action, he now accepts the circumscribed actions of the duel. The audience has been trained to expect a final

M

resolution and a controlled alignment, and Hamlet seems to expect the same:

> there's a special providence in the fall of a sparrow. If it be now, 'tis not to come; if it be not to come, it will be now; if it not be now, yet it will come: the readiness is all . . .

So Hamlet takes his place in the full court of Elsinore.

The staging of the last scene requires careful and complicated direction, and this is an indication of the eloquence of its movements. King and Queen must enter together, with spectators and assistants for the duel; Laertes must choose the poisoned rapier so that the audience may see, but not Hamlet; a cup must be taken to Hamlet, and 'set aside'; Gertrude must be able to cross to Hamlet, give him a napkin, drink from his cup and wipe his brow, and the cup must again be put aside so that it is not spilt in the uproar that is soon to follow, and can be found quickly by the wounded Hamlet; Laertes must be able to speak aside to Claudius and then, on his return to the combat, to himself; the duel must become an 'incensed' fight; Gertrude must swoon and be attended out of reach of Claudius; Hamlet must be able, rapidly, to take command of the whole scene, order doors to be locked, kill Claudius with his rapier, reach for the cup, force him to drink from it, and put it down again so that Horatio may find it later; many voices must shout 'Treason', yet Claudius must be helpless during Laertes' eight lines of explanation. In all this, movement and positioning must be clearly fixed, or 'shaped', by the stage-director during rehearsals, so that 'rashness' and 'indiscretion' as well as considered 'plots' all work together on the crowded stage towards a certain end. The actors could not perform the scene, simulating the various passions called for by the text, without this hidden control and co-ordination. But after the coincidences of the previous scene and Hamlet's duologue with Horatio, we may judge that Shakespeare knew this, and calculated upon its effect: the complicated difficulties of stage-direction will mean that a plan can be sensed behind the most hurried and unconsidered movements; and this, in turn, adds to the impression in performance of fate or 'divinity' controlling the interrelated movements of the characters, an inevitability something like that of the last stage in a game of chess, without any speech to direct attention to it.[4] The attentive presence of

---

[4] See plates 1 and 4, for examples of controlled grouping in this last scene.

Horatio and the entry of Fortinbras are further movements which place Hamlet, Elsinore, Denmark and the world outside, in a theatrical reality with a large and sweeping impression of men motivated from deep within themselves and drawn to their final positions by an unseen, unheard control or providence, a reality that reveals at last men's inward truth, through accident and intention, falsehood and truth, villainy and virtue.

* * *

Implied in Craig's description of a '*sweeping* impression' is the tempo of the play in performance. This element, which I now want to consider, is at once a pervasive influence and an intangible. Anyone who has acted or directed will know that a change of tempo can affect character, mood, clarity, size, force and even meaning, and that an acceptable, workable tempo is often the most elusive element in a production, the one that must wait for the latest rehearsal for proper adjustment. With tempo is rhythm, and both are at once general to each scene, act and play and particular to each incident and character. A single character may have one timing for his outward behaviour and others for his inward thoughts and feelings. Stanislavski felt the need for a conductor to give the beat to actors during a performance as if they were a complicated kind of orchestra. For some acting exercises, he introduced numerous metronomes, all ticking at different but related speeds. He relegated these matters to the end of his course of instruction, because of their importance and their difficulty.[5]

Tempo is, then, a continual concern of all responsible for a performance and is capable, at all times, of affecting the audience's reaction. But to consider its 'large' effects that present the play forcibly to an audience, it is necessary to pass beyond subtle adjustments and minute services to text and movement: striking contrasts, which are frequent in *Hamlet*, are the most important features here.

The slowest tempos are in reflective passages, where feeling and thought are not related to purposeful action. Among these are parts of the longer soliloquies, the disquisition on a 'sterile promontory' and 'brave o'erhanging firmament', the instructions to the players and the following talk of a man that 'is not passion's slave'. All these passages are centred on Hamlet himself; while he is absent from the stage only Gertrude's account of Ophelia's death, evoking a regard for suffering

[5] Cf. *Building a Character* (tr. 1949), Chapters XI and XII.

and helplessness, has anything like the same restrained tempo and self-contained rhythms. Later there are passages between Hamlet and the gravedigger, allowing the prince to consider the 'noble dust' of an emperor with a curiosity which looks before and after the dramatic event. These moments introduce and wholly sustain a slow tempo, but with them should be linked others in which this co-exists with a more urgent tempo beneath words or outward behaviour: in such passages the state of Denmark is considered deliberately while waiting for the ghost, or the formalities of Elsinore, the dumb-show, the funeral procession and preparations for the duel are presented as a cover to thoughts and inclinations which are more alert. Their main effect is the same: to encourage the audience to deliberate, as Hamlet does, in preparation for some other action; often they ensure a fully elaborate involvement before some of the most rapid passages of the play.

Rapid tempo, as far as Hamlet is concerned, usually comes with action after some new realisation: such are his 'wild and whirling words', his strange jests and behaviour to his friends after seeing the ghost, the 'rogue and peasant slave' soliloquy as soon as he is alone after the player has wept for a 'mobled queen', his elation after *The Mouse-trap* has caught the conscience of the king, his conflict with Laertes at Ophelia's grave in which he 'forgets himself' and reveals 'something . . . that is dangerous' from deep within (V.i.285). There are a few brief passages of swift words and action when Claudius or his servants move with 'deliberate' suddenness (IV.iii.8–9), but as a slow tempo was mainly used to show Hamlet's deliberations, so a rapid tempo shows the flame, or as one might say 'the whirlwind' (III.ii.708), of Hamlet's passion. It marks his instinctive involvements: first with his mother's marriage and Claudius' succession, then with his father, his mother, Ophelia, and, in his rapid jesting when Claudius pursues him after the killing of Polonius, with death and a sense of heaven's judgement. Slow tempo for Hamlet's deliberate involvement with himself and an ideal world; rapid for his instinctive and passionate response to others: so tempo impresses an important polarity within Hamlet and within the play.

This is a simplification, a first view of the most obvious extremes. In performance large impressions may also derive from a less obvious device which brings strong and contrasting tempos into conflict. This is surprising, rhythmic and sustained, and is mainly used for the presentation of Hamlet's response to women, Ophelia and Gertrude.

Other stage-techniques, like the exceptional use of a sustained and simple slow tempo for the account of her death, suggest that Shakespeare was more concerned with the presentation of Ophelia than her words alone can imply, and tempos in Hamlet's main scene with her supports this notion. First, the encounter is delayed until Act III, so that the audience is particularly attentive. In soliloquy Hamlet has considered 'enterprises of great pitch and moment', but seeing Ophelia he is drawn away, simply and immediately, and then envy for her apparent purity—or a pained irony—follows rapidly:

> Soft you now!
> The fair Ophelia! Nymph, in thy orisons
> Be all my sins remember'd.

As she acts an anonymous courtesy, he gives a similar stumbling performance:

OPHELIA: Good my lord,
How does your honour for this many a day?
HAMLET: I humbly thank you; well. . . .

There is no need to suppose that Hamlet knows Polonius and Claudius are overhearing: the tempo of this meeting is both slow *and* watchful. As he is drawn towards her, they both deceive each other, or try to do so, and, searching her eyes with 'are you honest? . . . Are you fair?', Hamlet could sense the prevarications. From this intimacy he is stung to abuse her, himself, man, woman: he loved her, and then, rapidly, he loved her not; she is fair and honest to him, yet she is no longer so; this is and is not Ophelia. His mother had left 'Hyperion' for a 'satyr' and now Ophelia becomes associated in his imagination with this betrayal, and now he is passionate in *rapid* denunciation. The suddenly direct 'where's your father?' probably brings a break in the scene, and then the direct lie. But even in his mounting anger there is conflict: as he attacks her, he leaves her; as he abuses her as whore and enemy, he repeats the one escape he can offer:

Get thee to a nunnery: why wouldst thou be a breeder of sinners?

Thoughts of great enterprise have not been 'turned awry' by fear of death as he had thought, but by hatred and love, by unappeased frustrations and desires. And in the whirlwind of abuse he impulsively repeats 'To a nunnery, go' five times, until he rushes from the stage: in the new rapid tempo, a more deliberate, lingering reaction, the slower one of care or irony—whichever way the actor takes the words it will be slower—is still maintained as a rock among currents, an under-surface tempo emphasised by its rhythmic repetition. The stillness within the tempest is made more apparent on Hamlet's exit, for Claudius and Polonius still hold back and Ophelia is able to speak her controlled and elaborate regret for the 'courtier's, soldier's, scholar's, eye, tongue, sword; The expectancy and rose of the fair state', in a following calm.

The closet-scene, between Hamlet and his mother, has something like the same handling of tempo and rhythm. It is the most sustained scene in the play and, from the first passionate interchange which makes Gertrude suppose that he will murder her, its development is both close and overcharged. But there are at least three moments of contrasting calm, following the death of Polonius, on the ghost's entry and then on Gertrude's response as Hamlet drives his meaning home. At first his compulsive denunciation of his mother's 'compulsive ardour' cannot be halted by her admission of guilt and three calls for 'no more'; but when the ghost has deflected the course of the scene so that he 'temperately' proceeds (l. 140) and she forgets her own defence in concern for his apparent madness, then there is a certain calm: she can speak slowly and with the impression of a deep-seated truth: 'O Hamlet, thou hast cleft my heart in twain.' This is, indeed, the heart of the scene: assured in his relationship with his mother, Hamlet now looks forward and outward, seeing himself with settled deliberation as 'heaven's scourge and minister' (III.iv.175). From this point tempo once more increases; for now he mocks the 'bloat king', his schoolfellows and politicians; he mocks at death, too, and 'lugs' Polonius from the room. But in the rising tempo and more savage involvement of the end of this scene, Hamlet retains a contact with its calm centre; this is made apparent in his intimate, five-times repeated, 'Good night' to his mother. Like Ophelia, Gertrude remains in the slower tempo. She is left alone and speechless: when Claudius finds her, she is still rapt in silence. Twice a rapid involvement is held, or harnessed, by a fixed, slower response which is also passionate.

Tempo in the last two scenes indicates a new control. When the memory of Yorick brings a flash of earlier denunciations of women, this is subdued at once. Hamlet cuts short the struggle with Laertes after his mother's final intervention, reasonably asking for understanding; but control is still precarious and Hamlet immediately leaves the stage. The last scene begins with sustained deliberation, easily rising to the rapidity and finesse of the water-fly Osric and then changing for answering his more weighty seconder. Immediately before the court enters for the duel the tempo is slow, but with an inward excitement. Then the duel gives a new mixture of tempos, both alert and slow, and sometimes rapid; timing follows a regular pattern in the formalities and intermissions; it quickens as either combatant makes a thrust and is held back with their wariness; it is at once circumscribed by the rules of the art and surprising in its precise movements and sequences. And inevitably the actor of Hamlet will be tired from the demands his long performance has made upon him, so that there will be another, strong inner-tempo of determination and doggedness. Speed and forcefulness increase as the fight becomes 'incensed' (l. 314); and suddenly, with blood, all is still. Disorder at once follows, with sharp moments of recognition; then Hamlet with passionate involvement is the central, dominating figure; and once more stillness follows, weighty with both pain and consideration. Yet, even now, the tempo is quickened once more, by affection and responsibility, in an interchange between Hamlet and Horatio. Then, from a distance, is heard a soldiers' march and the reverberations of a 'warlike volley'. This is to be the tempo and rhythm of the conclusion: regular and impersonal.

The duel and concluding moments of Hamlet's role provide both stillness *and* excitement; the extremes of deliberation and passion are expressed, and the more gentle quickening of affection. To an audience who did not understand a word of the language of the play, this complicated mingling of tempos would, alone, bring a true conclusion, a discovery of a new comprehensive control and a resolution of contrasts and conflicts and suggestions from the earlier tempos of the performance.

*   *   *

As I said at the beginning, an attempt to discuss the setting, movements and tempos of *Hamlet* will seem imprecise compared with more literary investigations. It will also be less sure-footed, a less-practised criticism with a smaller vocabulary and many opportunities for misreading Shakespeare's text. But it directs attention to a part of Shakespeare's achievement and so we must tackle the imprecise task.

It is chiefly valuable as a means of describing more fully the effect of the play in performance. Variations of tempo, for example, can reveal the large impression that Hamlet's meeting with Ophelia can make, and how the conclusion manifests not only Hamlet's moral and intellectual state of mind, but also the continuing energy of his passions and the power of his affection for others to motivate him—as it motivates Lear—to the very end of his complex engagement. A study of theatrical techniques of presentation provides an opportunity for describing the effect of the whole play. We may say, perhaps, that Shakespeare has ensured a threefold reception. First, he has presented a man in relation to society, his family and time; the setting and movements of the last scene ensure that the audience views every character on the stage, separately and together, judging their responsibilities and fulfilments, and the future of those that remain. Secondly, to a deeper view, there is the completed drama of human consciousness, seen in all the characters but in Hamlet pre-eminently; having followed the hero through the play, the audience will hear and see him in the last scene as a man, not miraculously redeemed or purified, not executing an elaborately prepared revenge or process of justice, not suffering hopelessly, but acting with deliberation and passion, fully known according to his conscious, subconscious and physical being. Thirdly, there is a final simplicity and weight of utterance, an inevitable process. So the play can be received as a public ritual: the hero, who has made a solitary journey through hardship and across the sea, returns to single combat, death and acceptance; and in all, in the final presentation of all the characters according to their inward truth, the heavens seem 'ordinant'. These conclusions might be deduced from various literary discussions; the prime advantage of the theatrical view is that it can show us how the play is able to be *all* this, in the brief time of its lengthy performance, and how it involves the audience in many ways: *Hamlet* is an intellectual, sensuous, passionate and instinctive experience.

IX

The Decline of Hamlet

T. J. B. SPENCER

★

'IN the twentieth century,' L. C. Knights has told us, 'Hamlet has yielded to King Lear the distinction of being the play in which the age most finds itself.'[1] Perhaps it is a vice of criticism that an age 'finds itself' in one of Shakespeare's plays; or perhaps the identification of Shakespeare with the intellectual and emotional preoccupations of an age is what gives vitality to its Shakespeare criticism.

But how much has the character of Hamlet sunk in esteem, if we were to judge from Knights and some of his contemporaries! The sensitive Romantic hero, the glass of Fashion and the mould of Form is quite, quite down. Salvador de Madariaga once explained to us that Hamlet was a typical Renaissance personality, Borgia-like, selfish, sensual, ambitious, and (whenever his interests were at stake) murderous. But it was still possible to retain a certain grudging admiration for that vigorous and brilliant figure. Knights is more meanly derogatory. Hamlet is not a good man suffering; he is corrupted by the very corruption that he combats. He is one whose judgement has been vitiated by his association with evil. Consider (unless 'twere to consider too curiously, to consider so) his encounter with the ghost, who 'is tempting Hamlet to gaze with fascinated horror at an abyss of evil'; and when he swears to avenge his murdered father, 'he commits himself to a passion that has all the exclusiveness of an infatuation'. Revenge is a bad thing. So Shakespeare must have shown that it was a bad thing in a play about revenge. 'I cannot believe,' Knights gravely tells us, 'that such a poet could temporarily waive his deepest ethical convictions for the sake of an exciting dramatic effect.'

---

[1] An Approach to 'Hamlet' (1960), p. 11. Also pp. 46, 47, 51.

That sort of remark pulls us up with a jolt and reminds us of the moral ambiguities and irrelevancies that must exist in a play of which the main theme is vengeance taken upon a criminal. The rights and wrongs of revenge were much discussed in Elizabethan times. The preachers and moralists (like the gentle critics of Shakespeare in our own century) were against it. But there were plenty of examples of private vengeance; for mankind has commonly held the belief that 'revenge is a kind of wild justice'; and still today the justicers (if not the law) take a lenient view of a murderer who has been provoked by severe wrongs. Revenge is, of course, an excellent subject in the theatre; there are similarities in the dramatic situations in three of the most famous and successful plays in the Elizabethan theatre, *The Spanish Tragedy*, *Titus Andronicus*, and *Hamlet*. The wrongdoer is powerful, and the wronged man cannot obtain ordinary justice; we watch in suspense while the wronged man devises methods of achieving his revenge and while his victim attempts to evade him. What are we to reply to Knights when he tells us that he cannot believe that Shakespeare 'could temporarily waive his deepest ethical convictions for the sake of an exciting dramatic effect'?

The best Shakespeare critics, from Rowe to Bernard Shaw and beyond, have—with few exceptions—been practising playwrights, failed playwrights, the associates of actors, professional theatre-critics, or (at the very least) assiduous devotees of the theatre: Dryden, Rowe, Dr Johnson, Lessing, Goethe, Coleridge, Lamb, Hazlitt. . . . Only with Dowden and Bradley does worth-while criticism begin to come from a wholly untheatrical environment. For most of those who wrote about *Hamlet*, frequent experiences in the theatre were an important guide, and control, of the judgement. The *Hamlet* that has been played during the last three and a half centuries is, of course, (with rare exceptions in the twentieth century) not the leisurely work of nearly 4,000 lines which editors have made by conflating the texts of the second Quarto and the Folio. When drastically cut for performance, the play loses a good deal of its ruminative quality; the action is more frequent and abrupt.

It is clear that the early critics of the play are really talking about the theatrical performances. *Hamlet*, said Farquhar in his *Discourse upon Comedy* (1702), is 'long the Darling of the English Audience, and like to continue with the same Applause.' And Shaftesbury—perhaps a little unexpectedly—gives a testimonial to the play in his *Characteristics*:

That Piece of his, The Tragedy of *Hamlet*, which appears to have most affected *English* Hearts and has perhaps been oftenest acted of any which have come upon our Stage, is almost one continu'd Moral; a Series of deep Reflections, drawn from *one* Mouth, upon the Subject of *one* single Accident and Calamity, naturally fitted to move Horror and Compassion. (*Advice to an Author* (1711), II.iii)

Dr Johnson, in accordance with his customary view that Shakespeare 'sacrifices virtue to convenience, and is so much more careful to please than to instruct, that he seems to write without any moral purpose', found defects in the morality of *Hamlet*. But he did not doubt the worth of the Prince, who has been 'injured in the most enormous and atrocious degree' and has 'no means of redress, but such as must expose him to the extremity of hazard' (note on III.ii (III.i.56)). Only Steevens offered a contradictory view:

Hamlet cannot be said to have pursued his ends by very warrantable means; and if the poet, when he sacrificed him at last, meant to have enforced such a moral, it is not the worst that can be deduced from the play. . . . Hamlet seems to have been hitherto regarded as a hero not undeserving the pity of the audience; and . . . no writer on Shakespeare has taken the pains to point out the immoral tendency of his character. (1773 edition)

But Steevens's hostility was in this respect paradoxical, and probably merely provocative. And soon a new interpretation was to be offered by one of the experienced and original novelists of that generation. Henry Mackenzie had published *The Man of Feeling* in 1771, followed by other stories in the same vein; and in 1780 wrote two remarkable papers on *Hamlet* in *The Mirror* (Nos. 99 and 100) which can be seen to derive from the same kind of exploration of sensibility as his novels. Mackenzie explained that Hamlet was one 'the delicacy of whose feelings a milder planet should have ruled, whose gentle virtues should have bloomed through a life of felicity and usefulness'. The basis of his character was 'an extreme sensibility of mind, apt to be strongly impressed by its situation, and overpowered by the feelings which that situation excites'. He was naturally of the most virtuous and amiable disposition; amidst the gloom of melancholy and the agitation of passion, we perceive a mind richly endowed by nature and cultivated by education; 'we perceive gentleness in his demeanour, wit in his conversation, taste in his amusements, and wisdom in his reflections.'

He is a person endowed with feelings so delicate as to border on weakness, with sensibility too exquisite to allow of determined action. 'Shakespeare, wishing to elevate the hero of his tragedy, and at the same time to interest the audience in his behalf, throws around him, from the beginning, the majesty of melancholy, along with that sort of weakness and irresolution which frequently attends it.' And what is the consequence? 'We feel not only the virtues, but the weaknesses of Hamlet as our own.' The deeper analyses of the character, especially in terms of sensibility, involved a new sympathy with Hamlet. Even his weaknesses are 'amiable weaknesses'. Sympathy, rather than judgment, guides the interpreter; and this has little to do with experiences in the theatre.

Johnson and his English followers had tried, with considerable success, to describe what a character *is*. The new criticism began to analyse how the character had *become* what he is, how this character 'in progress' affects the situation of the play. Most of the English character-writers before the nineteenth century are Theophrastan in their way of thinking about a dramatic personage; Johnson's sketches of Polonius and Falstaff might almost have come from Earle's *Microcosmographia*. But from the time of Lessing onwards, the Germans approached the praises and problems of Shakespeare's persons with new intuitions. Shakespeare's characters, Goethe's Wilhelm Meister says, are like watches with dial-plates and cases of transparent glass; they show you the hour like others, and meanwhile the inward mechanism, the combination of wheels and springs, is also all visible (*Wilhelm Meisters Lehrjahre*, III.xi.). Shakespeare gives us *the history of minds*, said Schlegel (and the remark was quoted with approval by Hazlitt). He lays open to us a whole series of their anterior states.

It was no accident that Goethe's great character-analysis of Hamlet (published 1795–6, but written before about 1783[2]) appeared in a work of fiction, not in a work of criticism. The growth of what can be called the 'psychological novel' (that is, the kind of fiction which describes in great detail the states of mind of its characters) profoundly influenced the interpretation of Shakespeare's powers of characterisation. Since the effect of Shakespeare's characters on the reader or audience was one of intense reality, comparable to that of Pamela, Clarissa, or Wilhelm Meister himself, it was natural to suppose that his techniques of characterisation must be similar to the novel of manners. Schlegel approvingly

[2] Roy Pascal, *Shakespeare in Germany, 1740–1815* (1937), p. 17.

quoted Lessing's praise of the way Shakespeare exhibits the gradual progress of passion from its origins. 'He gives a living picture of all the slight and secret artifices by which a feeling steals into our souls, of all the imperceptible advantages which it there gains, of all the stratagems by which it makes every other passion subservient to itself, till it becomes the sole tyrant of our desires and our aversions.' This was how things really happened. This was natural. This was 'nature'. Shakespeare's art was not artifice. The notion that he decided to insert various indications of character at points of the play, and gained his effects by such crude and casual trickery, was abhorrent. No, Shakespeare held the complete characters in his mind. He knew how they would speak on every occasion and how they would act in any circumstances. Just as Shakespeare himself held a character complete in his mind, so the reader (or the actor wishing to interpret the role) can, by noticing every indication the author gives, also hold the character complete in his mind. There may be differences of opinion about what one of Shakespeare's characters is really like; there may be rival interpretations. But that is only natural. Indeed, it is just like life.

Goethe's theory that the tragedy of *Hamlet* proceeds from irresolution and weakness in the soft, calm-tempered, cultivated prince is novelistic rather than theatrical. When Goethe thought in terms of the drama his views were astonishingly at variance with his psychological interpretations. In 1791 he took over the theatre at Weimar and his productions were by no means free from the old theatrical improvements, nor from new ones. Although the struggle to have Shakespeare's plays presented on the stage in a reasonably authentic form began earlier, and with more success, in Germany than in England, the old theatrical falsifications lingered on. In the *Hamlet* produced by the famous actor Friedrich Ludwig Schröder at Hamburg in 1776, the prince was left alive and well at the end of the play, and, as the reward of merit and in recognition of the noble way in which he had performed his duty, acceded to the constitutional throne of Denmark. Garrick had already shown the way to make Hamlet's heroism unambiguous in his 1772 adaptation, where he 'rescued the noble play from all the rubbish of the fifth act'. He cut out the voyage to England, the execution of Rosencrantz and Guildenstern, the funeral of Ophelia, and the gravediggers; and the concluding scenes were skilfully condensed: Hamlet is made to burst in upon the King and the Court, where Laertes reproaches him for his father's and his sister's death. While they are both exasperated, the King interposes and declares his wrath at Hamlet's rebellious spirit in not departing for England. 'First feel mine!', cries Hamlet, and stabs him to death.[3]

Goethe, however, eventually allowed Hamlet to be killed, and reintroduced the gravediggers and Laertes. But his opinions were consistent; for even in *Wilhelm Meister's Apprenticeship*, the hero, after all his excited praises of the play and his analyses of its principal characters, practically rewrites it for his production. Shakespeare, although of abounding poetry and subtle characterisation, was not sufficiently dramatic. Perhaps he was misled by the novels which furnished him with his materials. Indeed, in their analysis of the nature of the novel and the drama, Wilhelm and Serlo agree that *Hamlet* had, to some extent, the method of development characteristic of the novel (V.vii). Shakespeare wrote dramas for the study; some revision was required to make them acting dramas, fit for the stage. In *Hamlet* the interest of the play flagged after the end of the third act, and its unity was marred by the introduction of too much extraneous material—Fortinbras, the envoys to Norway, the expedition to Poland, Horatio and Wittenberg, Laertes and Paris, the pirates, the death of Rosencrantz and Guildenstern. All these circumstances would have been very suitable for expanding and lengthening a novel, but in the play they were entirely out of place. Wilhelm, therefore, with the full approbation of his friend Serlo, proposed to add one single great external circumstance to prop the action of the play, to replace the multifarious and mutually irrelevant events which Shakespeare had introduced. The plan was very ingenious; moreover, it was based upon something already in the play, the disturbances in Norway. After the death of Hamlet the king, the Norwegians (who as we know have recently been conquered) grow unruly. The Danish viceroy of the country sends his son Horatio, an old school friend of young Hamlet, to Denmark to press forward the equipment of the fleet, which under the new luxurious King Claudius has been proceeding but slowly. Horatio has known the former king, having fought in his battles and stood in high favour with him—this circumstance improves the first scene with the ghost. King Claudius gives Horatio audience and sends Laertes into Norway with news that the fleet will soon arrive. Queen Gertrude will not consent that Hamlet, as he wishes, should go along with him. (We thus felicitously get rid of Wittenberg and its University.) The rest of the play now follows easily and consistently. When Hamlet tells Horatio of his uncle's crime,

[3] Cf. G. W. Stone in *P.M.L.A.* (1934), 890–921.

Horatio counsels him to go, as his companion, to Norway with the fleet, to secure the affections of the army and to return to Denmark in warlike force to unseat the fratricide. Hamlet has now become dangerous to the king, who can find no readier method of delivering himself from his unwelcome presence than to send him in the fleet to Norway, with Rosencrantz and Guildenstern as spies upon him; and Laertes, who has now returned exasperated to murder by his father's death, shall go after Hamlet. Unfavourable winds, however, detain the fleet. Hamlet temporarily returns. The king resolves to get quit of Hamlet forthwith, and arranges some knightly sports as a festival of his departure and as a celebration of his pretended reconciliation with Laertes. The rest follows as we all know—except that, at the end, when the elective throne of Denmark is vacant, it is Horatio who has Hamlet's dying voice.

'Quick! quick!' said Serlo to Wilhelm, 'sit down and work the piece: your plan has my entire approbation' (V.iv).

This is the reinforced theatrical Hamlet. But it has little to do with the closely analysed character in Shakespeare's play, the typical *homme de sensibilité* or *Gefühlmensch* of the later eighteenth and early nineteenth centuries. It is certainly impressive how many European writers felt able to identify themselves, for better or for worse, with Hamlet, perceiving the character each in his own image. With a sure instinct Keats saw himself as Hamlet, and Fanny Brawne as Ophelia, when he wrote his terrible last letter to the girl in 1820:

> Shakespeare always sums up matters in the most sovereign manner. Hamlet's heart was full of such Misery as mine is when he said to Ophelia: 'Go to a Nunnery, go, go!' Indeed I should like to give up the matter at once—I should like to die. I am sickened at the brute world which you are smiling with. (*Letters*, ed. Forman, p. 503.)

Hamlet's speeches and sayings (wrote Hazlitt in his *Characters*)

> are as real as our own thoughts. Their reality is in the reader's mind. It is *we* who are Hamlet. This play has a prophetic truth, which is above that of history. Whoever has become thoughtful and melancholy through his own mishaps or those of others; whoever has borne about with him the clouded brow of reflection, and thought himself 'too much i'th'sun'; whoever has seen the golden lamp of day dimmed by envious mists rising in his own breast, and could find in the world before him only a dull blank with nothing left remarkable in it; whoever has known 'the pangs of despised love,

the insolence of office, or the spurns which patient merit of the unworthy takes'; he who has felt his mind sink within him, and sadness
cling to his heart like a malady, who has had his hopes blighted and
his youth staggered by the apparitions of strange things; who cannot
be well at ease, while he sees evil hovering near him like a spectre;
whose powers of action have been eaten up by thought, he to whom
the universe seems infinite, and himself nothing; whose bitterness of
soul makes him careless of consequences, and who goes to a play as
his best resource to shove off, to a second remove, the evils of life by
a mock representation of them—this is the true Hamlet.

Coleridge's friends pointed out at the time that when he was analysing
Hamlet he was actually describing himself. If we are to believe the
account of his conversation in the *Table-Talk*, he saw Hamlet as exhibi-
ting 'the prevalence of the abstracting and generalising habit over the
practical. He does not want courage, skill, will, or opportunity',
Coleridge explained; 'But every incident sets him thinking; and it is
curious, and at the same time strictly natural, that Hamlet, who all the
play seems reason itself, should be impelled, at last, by mere accident
to effect his object.' A great man's post-prandial vagaries and quips are
not to be taken in a ponderous, humourless way. One can easily imagine
the context in which (as is alleged) Coleridge uttered his notorious
remark: 'I have a smack of Hamlet myself, if I may say so.' (15
June, 1827.)

It was not merely in England and Germany that Hamlet was seen to
be the type of the modern intellectual, but also in France, once Shakespeare had established himself and the controversies of the eighteen-
thirties had subsided. The success of Macready and Helena Faucit, when
they took a theatrical company to Paris in 1844 and 1845 and played
before Louis-Philippe at the Tuileries, gave several of the French
critics a new opportunity for assessing the merits of Shakespeare. A
writer in the *Journal des Débats* gave a careful and revealing analysis of
Hamlet. Whence is the appeal, he asks, of this play—a tragedy without
form or rule, without action, without love? It is because the voice of
Hamlet awakens thoughts which have pervaded the heads and hearts of
this age of ours. In this play Shakespeare was a prophet of *our* times;
when he made his young prince a philosopher, he made a bound of three
centuries into futurity. *Hamlet* was not ripe, nor could it have been
understood, in the time of Shakespeare. Of all his works it has had to
wait longest for rehabilitation. 'Yes, Hamlet is truly a man of these

present times. It is thou Werther, thou Lara, thou Obermann, it is, above all, thou immortal René, in whom we see the sons and brothers of Hamlet—the train which leads him to glory, the flowers which compose his crown. Hamlet lived in a barbarous age and in a barbarous court, but it is an anachronism: he was born yesterday. . . . It is to our own age that Hamlet belongs; it is our age that has discovered him, this age which has been heated and excited by the catastrophes of the last fifty years; and Hamlet has himself grown to maturity in the midst of the psychological literature in which we have all been nourished.'[4] The writer of this justly points to the 'psychological literature' of the age as having educated the public to see Hamlet in a new light, naming Goethe's *Die Leiden des jungen Werthers* (1774), Étienne de Senancour's *Obermann* (1804), Chateaubriand's *René* (1802), and Byron's *Lara* (1814), as the principal sources of the new characterisation. This French eloquence was only a way of giving emphasis to ideas which had become widely current and were given more sober, but equally emphatic, expression by more sober writers. It was Emerson's view that not until the nineteenth century, whose speculative genius is a sort of living Hamlet, could that tragedy have found such wondering readers ('Shakespeare' in *Representative Men*). 'I believe,' wrote James Russell Lowell, 'that Shakespeare intended to impersonate in Hamlet not a mere metaphysical entity, but a man of flesh and blood: yet it is certainly curious how prophetically typical the character is of that introversion of mind which is so constant a phenomenon of these latter days, of that over-consciousness which wastes itself in analysing the motives of action instead of acting' ('Shakespeare Once More'). The parallel between *Hamlet* and *In Memoriam* was remarked upon. In each of them the great questions of eternal interest are debated by a mind for whom profound grief has made this world a sterile promontory. Schopenhauer had analysed the pessimism that characterised modern thought. But Hamlet had invented it. 'The world has become sad because a puppet was once melancholy' was Oscar Wilde's summing-up at the end of the century ('The Decay of Lying' in *Intentions* (1891)).

The German youth love *Hamlet*, said Heine, the ironic commentator, because they, too, feel that the time is out of joint; they, too, regret that they were born to put it right; they, too, like Hamlet, feel their utter weakness and declaim 'To be or not to be . . .' (*The Romantic School* (1833), ii, 2). In Hamlet, as the Germans saw him, experience had

[4] The article was translated in *The Stage*, No. 13 (11 January, 1845), p. 98.

N

destroyed his equipoise, weakened his power to act, and morbidly stimulated his powers of thought. He thus had a striking (even if accidental) analogy with the German predicament. From the time of Tieck onwards the notion that *Deutschland ist Hamlet* had been depressingly current, and the famous revolutionary poet Ferdinand Freiligrath wrote a poem called *Hamlet* in 1844 in which he tried to arouse the German nation from their lethargy, irresolution, and weakness.

> Deutschland ist Hamlet! Ernst und stumm
> In seinen Toren jede Nacht
> Geht die begrabne Freiheit um
> Und winkt den Männern auf der Wacht.

The resistance to Hamlet had a curious result in stimulating one of the most successful works of Shakespeare criticism of the century. The *Commentaries* of Georg Gottfried Gervinus are still known by name in England; impressive in bulk and in range, they both won respect and provoked impatience in their own time. Gervinus was a patriot and a liberal, who made courageous though over-sensitive incursions into politics and political journalism. But in some respects he became a disappointed man, who saw German unification taking place in a manner of which he did not approve. This was the background to his great work on Shakespeare which he published in four volumes at Leipzig in 1849–50, and which went through several editions; the third (1862) was well translated into English by F. E. Bunnétt in 1863, and revised and sponsored by Furnivall in 1875. His Shakespeare studies were partly a refuge from his disappointments on the political scene, but they were also inspired by his patriotism. Gervinus supposed Shakespeare, of course, to be as much the intellectual property of Germany as of England, and he held up this national poet to his countrymen as a salutary object of admiration, one who is always the champion of healthy practical activity. To the Germans who had personified Shakespeare and themselves as Hamlet Gervinus offered Henry V instead— the active, energetic, resolute Shakespeare.

By other Germans the author of *Hamlet* was, too, a thinker in the foremost ranks of modern patriotic spirits, a forerunner of the struggle between popular and autocratic parties, in which England was to engage first among the nations of Europe. Hamlet, wrote one tendentious German longingly in 1870 (Bismarck was at the height of his power), is 'a Prometheus-sigh for freedom and deliverance, for honour and influence, for security and peace'. It portrays the collision between an effete society buttressing itself up against the past, and 'an idea, ever young, to which all the future belongs'.[5] The work comes like an oracle, which is only fully understood for the first time when its purpose has been fulfilled.

Hamlet, said Swinburne, is the Teutonic-Titanic evangel (*A Study of Shakespeare* (1880), p. 178), and Browning's Bishop Blougram ridiculed the aspiring literary man:

> You, Gigadibs, who, thirty years of age,
> Write stately for *Blackwood's Magazine*,
> Believe you see two points in Hamlet's soul
> Unseized by the Germans yet—which view you'll print . . .

But in 1879 Furness dedicated his New Variorum *Hamlet* to the German Shakespeare Society, 'representative of a people whose recent history has proved once for all that Germany is *not* Hamlet'.

Hamlet, in fact, did not remain static as Werther or René. He shared the characteristic intellectual development of the nineteenth century, and by the end he had become something like Matthew Arnold, or even Mrs Humphrey Ward. As the representative of the modern sensitive intellectual man, he shared the fate and metamorphoses of the modern sensitive intellectual man. All of us (it was said) feel something of ourselves in Hamlet, but we take our choice in what we feel: his subjection to the spiritual part of his nature; his communion with thoughts of another world; his scepticism; his thinking too precisely on the event; his being propelled, rather than propelling; his being driven like a leaf before the wind; his waiting for circumstances—the catalogue can be extended indefinitely.[6] It is not surprising that Hamlet can be seen behind (for example) Browning's Sordello and Arnold's Empedocles. And when the young Edward Dowden boldly declared that 'Hamlet's baffled movement, his beating to and fro in a vast and obscure world which he cannot comprehend, has in it something pathetic and something sublime' (1874), p. 352), he gave Shakspere a moving description of the valorous Victorian intellectual, bereft of his doctrinal Christianity and unable to orientate himself in the new

[5] H. A. Werner in the *Shakespeare-Jahrbuch*, 1870, 37–81; from Dowden, *Shakspere, His Mind and Art*, p. 320–1.

[6] George Dawson, *Shakespeare and Other Lectures* (1888), p. 18.

universe revealed by science and moralised by agnosticism. Mrs Humphrey Ward in one of her novels (*Robert Elsmere*) set out to draw a full
portrait of the modern highly-cultivated, intelligent, self-conscious man;
and critics were quick to see the resemblance between her Edward
Langham and Hamlet. 'The worship of intellect, the absorbing interest in
music and the theatre, the nervous excitability... taking refuge in irony
and sarcasm, these and countless other points stamp them as temperaments of kindred mould. And in both lives the tragic woof is the same;
it is the tragedy of spiritual impotence, of deadened energies and
paralysed will, the essential tragedy of modernity. Hamlet fascinates us,
just as Langham fascinates us, because we see in him ourselves; we are
all actual or potential Hamlets.' This is the language of Goethe and
Coleridge, which has matured and mellowed in the course of nearly a
century of intellectual history. Actually they are the words of the
young E. K. Chambers in 1894,[7] at the beginning of his career as a
Shakespeare scholar.

It is instructive to compare the modern English Hamlet as he appears
in Mrs Humphrey Ward's *Robert Elsmere* (1888) with the modern
French Hamlet recreated by Paul Bourget in *André Cornélis* (1887).
In 1865 Karl Elze wrote disparagingly of French criticism of Shakespeare in an article 'Hamlet in Frankreich' in the first volume of the
Shakespeare-Jahrbuch.[8] His assumption that France had made little
progress since Voltaire, and had scarcely enlarged its critical horizons,
naturally gave some offence. Yet the future of Hamlet was in France,
not in Germany. The work which Voltaire had supposed to be like the
fruit of the imagination of a drunken savage had in fact been making
a powerful impact in the course of the nineteenth century. Talma
mostly played in the old version of Ducis, with the unities and decorum
observed, though some innovations in the direction of Shakespeare
were received variously with disgust or delight. After seeing him as
Hamlet in 1809 Madame de Staël wrote to him that in this role he
seemed to her like Shakespeare's genius, but without his inequalities
and without his low jests. Those questionings about destiny, the destiny of us all, in the presence of the crowd of listeners who will one day
die and who listened as to an oracle; that profound melancholy, that
voice; that expressiveness of countenance which reveals feeling; that

[7] Introduction to the Warwick Shakespeare *Hamlet*, pp. 22–3.
[8] Translated in his *Essays on Shakespeare* (1874).

characterisation beyond human proportions; it was all admirable, thrice admirable. [9]

As authentic a Shakespeare was often to be seen in Paris as in London. Still, some of the adaptations went too far, even by the standards of the English stage. Alexandre Dumas, who was fond of repeating that, after God, Shakespeare has created most (*c'était l'homme qui avait le plus créé aprés Dieu*[10]), was less fanatical when it came to the production of the plays for the Parisian stage. In the version of *Hamlet* which Dumas prepared from young Paul Meurice's translation for performance in 1847, a new ending was provided that dooms the prince to live on like the Wandering Jew. Hamlet exclaims after the catastrophe:

> Et moi, vais-je rester, triste orphelin sur terre,
> A respirer cet air imprégné de misère ?
> Est-ce que Dieu sur moi fera peser son bras,
> Père ? Et quel châtiment m'attend donc ?

And the ghost briefly replies:

> Tu vivras.

Absurd though this may seem, it was not inconsistent with the French re-imagining of Hamlet. Théophile Gautier wanted to see a performance of the play in a setting of Piranesi's *Carceri*. Victor Hugo, in his book on Shakespeare in 1864, contradicted Goethe for attributing Hamlet's conduct to innate inadequacy for his task and to unconquerable weakness of will; rather, Hamlet's was an immedicable scepticism of the spirit and an irremediable propensity to nebulous intellectual refinement.

'I read nothing now—nothing except Shakespeare,' Flaubert wrote to George Sand in 1875, 'whom I have taken up again from one end to the other. It is invigorating, it puts air into your lungs as if you were on the top of a mountain. Everything seems flat by the side of that prodigious *bon-homme*.'[11] But this sort of opinion was by now a little old-fashioned in France. Shakespeare the *bon-homme*, the passionate Romantic, was on the decline, and other influences were at work. Disillusion,

[9] A. Augustin-Thierry, *Le Tragédien de Napoléon, François-Joseph Talma* (Paris, 1942), p. 163.

[10] 'Comment je devins auteur dramatique' in *Théâtre complet* (Paris, 1889 ff.), i, 15.

[11] Lettres de Gustave Flaubert à George Sand (Paris, 1884), p. 271 (11 December, 1875).

disappointment and vague dissatisfaction were heritable from Hamlet. The Romantics had valued Hamlet, of course, for their own sakes; but for the *fin de siècle* he was a special analogical character. George Sand's somewhat lachrymose essay of 1845[12] had perhaps shown the way ('Oui, te voilà tout entier, Hamlet, dans ce cri de l'humanité révoltée contre elle-même'). 'You were formed to taste misfortune, and you had full opportunity for exercising your taste. You were well served, Prince,' exclaimed Anatole France after seeing Mounet-Sully at the Comédie-Française. 'And how you relish the evil in which you are steeped! What subtlety of taste! Oh! you are a connoisseur, a *gourmet* in sufferings.'[13] Both Jules Laforgue and Stéphane Mallarmé made a symbol of Hamlet, each in his own way. We meet Laforgue's ironical, perhaps satirical, version of Hamlet in his *Moralités légendaires* (1887). There, *Les Suites de la piété filiale* are very different from those we are familiar with. Hamlet, abandoning the responsibility of vengeance and in the act of eloping with an actress from the troupe that came to play at Elsinore, is stabbed to the heart by Laertes (*idiot d'humanité*) at midnight on Ophelia's grave. '*Qualis . . . artifex . . . pereo!*' he manages to articulate, and then 'rend son âme hamlétique à la nature inamovible'. 'Il se promène, lisant au livre de lui-même' was Mallarmé's famous description in *Hamlet et Fortinbras*,[14] where he contrasted the lethal consequences of Hamlet's character with the no more lethal conduct of Fortinbras. 'The black presence of the doubter spreads poison, so that all the great ones die, without his taking the trouble, usually, to stab them behind the arras.'

Mallarmé's emphasis on Hamlet as a destructive force, contrary to the dominant interpretations since Goethe and Coleridge, leads straight forward to the critics of the twentieth century who have tried to convince us that we should abandon the long theatrical tradition of Hamlet as 'the Darling of the English Audience'. G. Wilson Knight asks us to contrast the sickly attitude of mind in Hamlet with the healthy and robust life of King Claudius's court. L. C. Knights persuades us that the command of the ghost has been for 'a sterile concentration on death and evil' and that 'Hamlet's intellectuality, the working of his mind, is largely at the service of attitudes of rejection and disgust that

---

[12] Reprinted in *Questions d'art et de littérature* (Paris, 1878).
[13] 'Hamlet at the Comédie-Française' in *On Life and Letters*, First Series.
[14] *Oeuvres* (Paris, 1945), p. 1557.

are indiscriminate in their working'.[15] And Miss Rebecca West in *The Court and the Castle* (1958), asserting that the play has been consistently misread for centuries, concludes that Shakespeare 'leaves his damned world damned for ever on his page'.

[15] *An Approach to 'Hamlet'*, pp. 59, 89.

A Reader's Guide to 'Hamlet'

STANLEY WELLS

*

Some men hold
That he's the sanest, far, of all sane men—
Some that he's really sane but shamming mad—
Some that he's really mad but shamming sane—
Some that he will be mad, some that he *was*—
Some that he couldn't be. But on the whole
(As far as I can make out what they mean)
The favourite theory's somewhat like this:
Hamlet is idiotically sane
With lucid intervals of lunacy.

from *Rosencrantz and Guildenstern*
by W. S. Gilbert

F. P. WILSON has said 'a man who set out to read all the books about *Hamlet* would have time to read nothing else, not even *Hamlet*'. Such a man would have helpful guides on his passage through nature to eternity. Paul S. Conklin's *A History of 'Hamlet' Criticism*, 1601-1821 (1947; re-issued 1957), draws on the play's stage-history as well as English, French and German criticism. The period up to 1877 is covered by the bibliography in the New Variorum edition, and A. A. Raven's well-annotated *A 'Hamlet' Bibliography and Reference Guide*, 1877-1935) 1936), takes up the tale from then. *Shakespeare Survey* 9 includes, among a number of other articles on *Hamlet*, Clifford Leech's 'Studies in *Hamlet*, 1901-1955'. Readers whose time is limited will value C. C. H. Williamson's anthology, *Readings on the Character of Hamlet* (1950), rather perhaps for its out-of-the-way items than for its abbreviations of better-known writings.

The Text

H. H. Furness's New Variorum edition (2 vols., 1877: paper-back edition, Dover Publications, 1963), though out-of-date in many respects, is still a useful repository; it contains, for instance, a reprint of the First Quarto and a translation of *Der bestrafte Brudermord*. Edward Dowden's Arden edition (1899, etc.) will be superseded by Harold Jenkins's New Arden edition (forthcoming). The most recent fully-annotated edition published in England is J. Dover Wilson's (1934; 2nd edition, 1936); the American one by J. Q. Adams (1929) has a valuable commentary. Albert B. Weiner has edited the First Quarto in a modernised text (Barron's Educational Series, 1962). *William Poel's Prompt-Book of 'Fratricide Punished'* (i.e. *Der bestrafte Brudermord*) is edited by J. Isaacs for The Society for Theatre Research (Pamphlet Series No. 5, 1956).

Collotype facsimiles of the First Quarto (1603) and the Second Quarto (1604–5) with introductions by W. W. Greg were published for The Shakespeare Association in 1951 and 1940, respectively. Probably the best facsimile of the First Folio is that prepared by Sidney Lee (1902); there is a more recent one edited by H. Kökeritz and C. T. Prouty (1955).

The textual problems of the play are surveyed by E. K. Chambers in *William Shakespeare: A Study of Facts and Problems* (2 vols., 1930) and by W. W. Greg in both *The Editorial Problem in Shakespeare* (1942; 2nd edition, 1951) and *The Shakespeare First Folio* (1955). More detailed studies include *The Manuscript of Shakespeare's 'Hamlet' and the Problems of its Transmission*, by J. Dover Wilson (2 vols., 1934); *The 'Bad' Quarto of 'Hamlet'*, by G. I. Duthie (1941); 'The Textual Problem of *Hamlet*: a Reconsideration', by Alice Walker (*Review of English Studies*, 1951, pp. 328–38) and several articles in *Studies in Bibliography*, VII (1955).

Sources and Date

Israel Gollancz edited *The Sources of 'Hamlet'* (1926) and Kenneth Muir considers the subject in *Shakespeare's Sources*, Vol. I (1957). Sources and analogues of *Hamlet* will be reprinted and discussed in a forthcoming volume of Geoffrey Bullough's *Narrative and Dramatic Sources of Shakespeare* (1957–). 'The Date of *Hamlet*' is investigated by E. A. J. Honigmann in *Shakespeare Survey* 9.

N*

Stage History

No comprehensive stage history of *Hamlet* has been published. J. Dover Wilson's edition includes a useful survey by Harold Child. The chapter on *Hamlet* in A. C. Sprague's *Shakespeare and the Actors* (1948) is a valuable record of stage business in productions up to the beginning of the present century. Complementary to this is '*Hamlet*' *Through the Ages* (1952, etc.), a pictorial record with notes, compiled by R. Mander and J. Mitchenson, and edited by Herbert Marshall. Hazelton Spencer's *Shakespeare Improved* (1927) includes information especially on the version attributed to Sir William Davenant. Garrick declared 'I had sworn I would not leave the stage till I had rescued that noble play from all the rubbish of the fifth act': G. W. Stone Jr. comments on Garrick's version and reprints his revision of the offending act in 'Garrick's Long Lost Alteration of *Hamlet*' (*PMLA*, 1934, pp. 890–921). Additional material on stage history may be gleaned from G. C. D. Odell's *Shakespeare from Betterton to Irving* (2 vols., 1920) and Bertram Joseph's *The Tragic Actor* (1959). Rosamund Gilder's *John Gielgud's Hamlet* (1937) is perhaps the most detailed record of a single interpretation. It includes 'The *Hamlet* Tradition', by Gielgud himself. In his anthology *Specimens of English Dramatic Criticism* (World's Classics, 1945), A. C. Ward includes Colley Cibber's account of Betterton as Hamlet, the passage from Fielding's *Tom Jones* on Garrick, Dutton Cook on Irving, Shaw on Forbes-Robertson and Hubert Griffith on Sir Barry Jackson's modern-dress production. Other notable accounts are Lichtenberg's of Garrick (in *Lichtenberg's Visits to England*, edited by M. L. Mare and W. H. Quarrell, (1938); also in the New Variorum *Hamlet*, Vol. II, pp. 269–72), Hazlitt's of Edmund Kean (in *Dramatic Essays*, Vol. II, edited by William Archer and Robert Lowe, 1895; reprinted as *Hazlitt on Theatre*, a 'Dramabook' (n.d.)), and Max Beerbohm's of Sarah Bernhardt ('Hamlet, Princess of Denmark', in *Around Theatres*, 1953).

Critical Writings

This section, though it follows a generally chronological arrangement, is not intended as an historical survey of *Hamlet* criticism. The aim has been to select from the mass of available material writings likely to be interesting and helpful to a modern reader.

Seventeenth-century allusions to *Hamlet* are collected in *The Shakespere Allusion Book* (2 vols., 1932). Dr. Johnson's comments, which

include a character sketch of Polonius and a classic exposition of 'To be
or not to be . . .' are in *Johnson on Shakespeare*, edited by Walter
Raleigh (1908). Selections from Goethe's *Wilhelm Meister* (1795)
commenting on *Hamlet* ('Here is an oak tree planted in a costly vase,
which should have received into its bosom only lovely flowers; the
roots spread out, the vase is shivered to pieces') are reprinted in the New
Variorum edition (Vol. II, pp. 272–4) which includes also many
extracts from critical writings of the eighteenth and nineteenth
centuries not easily available at the present time.

S. T. Coleridge, who saw in Hamlet 'great, enormous intellectual
activity, and a consequent proportionate aversion to real action', is
described by Conklin as 'the most influential critic of *Hamlet* that ever
lived'. His scattered writings on the play are best read in T. M. Raysor's
edition of *Coleridge's Shakespearean Criticism* (1930; Everyman Books,
1960, 2 vols.). Charles Lamb's essay 'On the Tragedies of Shakespeare,
Considered with Reference to their fitness for Stage Representation'
(first published in 1811; reprinted in e.g. *Shakespeare Criticism: A
Selection*, edited by D. Nichol Smith, World's Classics, 1916, etc.) has
rather surprisingly been referred to by Peter Alexander as 'the finest
piece of criticism ever written on *Hamlet*'. Lamb argues that Hamlet's
'profound sorrows, these light-and-noise-abhorring ruminations,
which the tongue scarce dares utter to deaf walls and chambers'
cannot be represented by 'a gesticulating actor, who comes and mouths
them out before an audience, making four hundred people his con-
fidants at once'. William Hazlitt's main statement is his essay on the play
in *Characters of Shakespeare's Plays* (1817; much reprinted, e.g. World's
Classics, 1917, etc.; the standard edition of Hazlitt is *Complete Works*,
edited by P. P. Howe, 1930–34, 21 vols.). Even this great theatre-
goer's Hamlet is of the study, not the stage. 'It is the one of Shakespeare's plays that we think of oftenest, because it abounds most in striking
reflections on human life, and because the distresses of Hamlet are
transferred, by the turn of his mind, to the general account of humanity.
Whatever happens to him, we apply to ourselves, because he applies it
so himself as a means of general reasoning. He is a great moralizer . . .
There is no play that suffers so much in being transferred to the stage.'

Perhaps the best of the Victorians is Edward Dowden; there is a
section on *Hamlet* in his early *Shakspere, His Mind and Art* (1875, etc.).
Tillyard found that the footnotes to Dowden's Arden edition, published
twenty-four years later, formed 'the best interpretation of the action

of *Hamlet'*. A. C. Bradley's critical limitations have been frequently castigated, but many later critics have taken as their starting-point his two fine lectures on the play in *Shakespearean Tragedy* (1904; St. Martin's Library, 1957). Disagreeing with critics who find that Hamlet 'at *any* time and in *any* circumstances would be unequal to the task assigned to him', he considers that it is 'the very cruelty of his [Hamlet's] fate that the crisis of his life comes on him at the one moment when he cannot meet it, and when his highest gifts, instead of helping him, conspire to paralyse him'. He finds a key to Hamlet's character in the melancholy induced by his misfortunes. Bradley's remarks include some forward-looking ones on the style of Hamlet's speeches.

J. M. Robertson's *The Problem of 'Hamlet'* (1919) elaborates the theory that *Hamlet* 'is an adaptation of an older play, which laid down the main action, embodying a counter-sense which the adaptation could not transmute'; as a result, *Hamlet* suffered 'an ultimate aesthetic miscarriage'. Robertson's views influenced T. S. Eliot, whose famous judgement that 'so far from being Shakespeare's masterpiece, the play is most certainly an artistic failure' comes from an essay first published in 1919 and collected in *The Sacred Wood* (1920), *Selected Essays* (1932), etc.

In *Shakespeare's Tragic Heroes: Slaves of Passion* (1930) Lily B. Campbell develops her thesis that in *Hamlet* Shakespeare undertook to answer 'the problem of the way men accept sorrow when it comes to them'. G. Wilson Knight writes of *Hamlet* in *The Wheel of Fire* (1930, etc.) and in *The Imperial Theme* (1931, etc.); '*Hamlet* Reconsidered (1947)', published in later editions of *The Wheel of Fire*, in which he withdraws some of the more extreme views expressed in his earlier essays, is his best study of the play. A. J. A. Waldock's '*Hamlet': A Study in Critical Method* (1931) offers a sane and lucid assessment of *Hamlet* criticism in an attempt to permit an unprejudiced view of the play. E. E. Stoll, who had published *Hamlet: An Historical and Comparative Study* in 1919, wrote again on the play in *Art and Artifice in Shakespeare* (1933), developing the view that Hamlet is 'a dramatic figure, not a psychological study'. He stressed Hamlet's heroism, and found the 'delay' part of the dramatic structure, not an expression of Hamlet's character. J. Middleton Murry, in *Shakespeare* (1936), presents a Hamlet who, deprived of his faith in life, yet triumphantly succeeds in 'conquering his fear of the unknown futurity'.

Two important works published within a comparatively short time of each other are J. Dover Wilson's *What Happens in 'Hamlet'* (1935, etc.) and H. Granville-Barker's *Prefaces to Shakespeare. Third Series: 'Hamlet'* (1937). Not all Wilson's interpretations of specific points of the action have won general acceptance, but his book retains its power to delight and surprise. Granville-Barker brought to the play all his experience and authority as a producer; his successors could have no better guide.

'Hamlet: The Prince or the Poem?' is the title of C. S. Lewis's British Academy lecture given in 1942. Lewis comes down firmly in favour of 'the poem'; he finds the play 'above all else, *interesting*'; but rather for what is said than for who says it. In *The Time is Out of Joint* (1948), Roy Walker offers a systematic scene-by-scene commentary. H. B. Charlton, in *Shakespearian Tragedy* (1948), finds that Hamlet's 'supreme gift for philosophic thought allows him to know the universe better than the little world of which he is bodily a part'. This induces a progressive paralysis ending in despair. For Charlton (as, to some extent, for Bradley) the graveyard scene marks 'the nadir of Hamlet's fall': not 'the calm attainment of a higher benignity' but 'a fatalist's surrender of his personal responsibility'. Salvador de Madariaga's *On 'Hamlet'* (1948) is a powerful astringent against over-romantic views; the author sees Ophelia as 'a fast girl' and Hamlet as a callously egocentric figure whose delay is caused fundamentally by his lack of concern for anyone outside himself; when at last he kills Claudius he is revenging not his father but himself. Another controversial study is Ernest Jones's *Hamlet and Oedipus* (1949), the final revision and expansion of material first published as early as 1910. Jones sees Hamlet as the victim of an Oedipus complex and considers too that the play reflects a similar state of mind in the author. Jones's learning was immense and he was sensitive to literary considerations: this book should not be dismissed because of prejudice against its approach. It is, however, more convincing on the play's hero than on its author.

Less controversial, but no less stimulating, is the chapter on *Hamlet* in Francis Fergusson's *The Idea of a Theater* (1949, etc.). Taking issue with Eliot's criticisms, the author attempts to demonstrate the unity of the play by means of a study of analogical relationships within and beyond it. He stresses the interplay of ritual and improvisation in the dramaturgy. E. M. W. Tillyard considers *Hamlet* in *Shakespeare's Problem Plays* (1950, etc.). He argues that as the hero does not undergo 'any definitive spiritual revolution' the play is not 'tragic in the fullest sense'. G. R. Elliott's *Scourge and Minister: A Study of 'Hamlet' as Tragedy of Revengefulness and Justice* (1951) is another scene-by-scene commentary. The author sees Hamlet as obliged to pass through a proud revengefulness to a state where vengeance becomes an expression of true justice. This is a rather laborious book with, nevertheless, some interesting ideas. More succinct is D. G. James's admirable study *The Dream of Learning: An Essay on 'The Advancement of Learning', 'Hamlet' and 'King Lear'* (1951), which essays to place *Hamlet* in the philosophical context of its time. James sees the play as a study in the failure of a man to achieve a 'just commingling' of passion and reason. In 'The World of *Hamlet*' (*The Yale Review*, Vol. 41, 1952; reprinted in *Tragic Themes in Western Literature*, edited by Cleanth Brooks, 1955, and in *Shakespeare: Modern Essays in Criticism*, edited by L. F. Dean, 1957 and 1961)Maynard Mack investigates 'the imaginative environment that the play asks us to enter'.

Bertram Joseph's *Conscience and the King* (1953) examines especially certain crucial issues and concepts of *Hamlet*, using contemporary evidence to determine how they might have struck the play's first audiences. In *Hamlet, Father and Son* (1955), Peter Alexander is concerned mainly with the concept of tragedy embodied in the play, which he examines with especial reference to Aristotle. He stresses Hamlet's noble heroism as opposed to the idea of the 'fatal flaw'. This is an attractively written book with a wide range of reference; it has as much to say on the Greeks as on *Hamlet*.

Also much concerned with Greek drama is H. D. F. Kitto, whose chapter on *Hamlet* in *Form and Meaning in Drama* (1956) concludes a book devoted otherwise to Aeschylus and Sophocles. In forthright and lively style, the author presents *Hamlet* not as an 'individual tragedy of character ... but something more like religious drama'; its 'central theme is the disastrous growth of evil'. Helen Gardner, in *The Business of Criticism* (1959), devotes part of a chapter to considering what questions can fruitfully be asked about the play. Allan Gilbert, in a chapter of *The Principles and Practice of Criticism* (1959), lays stress on Hamlet's wit and satire, and the contribution that these qualities make to the play as entertainment.

Harry Levin's *The Question of 'Hamlet'* (1959) is an acute and perceptive piece of close criticism, 'directed toward a close re-reading of the play as a whole, relating its style and structure to other aspects more frequently discussed by scholars and critics'. L. C. Knights followed his essay on *Hamlet* in *Explorations* (1946) with *An Approach to 'Hamlet'* (1960), in which he argues that Hamlet's consciousness is corrupted to a point where he is 'unable to affirm at all'. In John Lawlor's *The Tragic Sense in Shakespeare* (1960) a chapter called 'Agent or Patient?' discusses *Hamlet* in relation to other revenge plays of the period. For Lawlor, 'the centre of interest in Shakespeare's play is not in the ethic of revenge, but in the overburdened human agent'. John Holloway's chapter on *Hamlet* in *The Story of the Night* (1961) stresses Hamlet's movement 'from centrality to isolation'; his need to assume and enact a *rôle;* the spread of evil caused by Claudius's crime; and the way in which 'chance turns into a larger design, randomness becomes retribution'.

Style

Many of the critics referred to above comment on the style of the play. The pioneering study of Shakespeare's imagery is Caroline Spurgeon's *Shakespeare's Imagery, and what it Tells Us* (1935). Mikhail M. Morozov includes *Hamlet* in 'The Individualization of Shakespeare's Characters Through Imagery' (*Shakespeare Survey* 2). There are valuable stylistic studies in W. H. Clemen's *The Development of Shakespeare's Imagery* (1951) and M. M. Mahood's *Shakespeare's Wordplay* (1957).

Miscellanea

Charles Dickens' account of Hamlet as played by Mr. Wopsle, alias Waldengarver, is in Chapter XXXI of *Great Expectations;* the play figures too in James Joyce's *Ulysses*. G. B. Shaw's comments are collected in *Shaw on Shakespeare*, edited by Edwin Wilson (1962). W. S. Gilbert's clever skit *Rosencrantz and Guildenstern* is in his *Original Plays* (Third Series, 1895, etc.). *Three Tales of Hamlet* by Rayner Heppenstall and Michael Innes (1950) is a collection of entertainments written for the Third Programme of the B.B.C.. Michael Innes also has a detective novel, *Hamlet, Revenge!* (1937; Penguin Books, 1961), in which the action centres on a performance of the play. Sir John Gielgud, with an Old Vic company, has recorded his interpretation on H.M.V. ALP 1482–4; and the Marlowe Society, with professional players, performs Dover Wilson's text uncut on Argo RG 256–260. *Hamlet: The Film and the Play*, edited by Alan Dent (1948), is the book of Sir Laurence Olivier's film of the play.

Index